ADULT EDUCATION IN ENGLAND AND WALES

A Critical Survey

ADULT EDUCATION IN ENGLAND AND WALES

A Critical Survey
by
John Lowe

U of Edinburgh
11 Buccleuch Place
Edinburgh, Scotland

London
MICHAEL JOSEPH

First published in Great Britain by
MICHAEL JOSEPH LIMITED
52 Bedford Square
London, W.C.1
1970

7181 0700 4

Set and printed in Great Britain by
Unwin Brothers Limited at the Gresham Press, Woking,
in Imprint type, eleven point leaded, and bound by
James Burn at Esher, Surrey

To
MARGARET

CONTENTS

NOTES AND ABBREVIATIONS

On 1 April 1964 the functions previously carried out by the Minister of Education were transferred to the Secretary of State for Education and Science. For convenience, however, the Secretary of State is invariably described as the Minister.

The term adult educator describes any one engaged in the education of adults either as a teacher or an administrator. The term adult educationist, however, refers only to those who make a special study of the aims, organisation and problems of adult education.

The term teacher is preferred to tutor to describe those who teach adults, except when reference is made to persons specifically designated as tutors in their terms of appointment.

The following abbreviations have been used in the text:

A.E.	Adult Education
D.E.S.	Department of Education and Science
E.C.A.	Educational Centres Association
F.E.	Further Education
L.E.A.	Local Education Authority
N.C.L.C.	National Council of Labour Colleges
N.I.A.E.	National Institute of Adult Education
O.F.E.	Other Further Education
R.B.s	Responsible Bodies
T.U.C.	Trades Union Congress
T.W.G.	Townswomen's Guilds
U.C.A.E.	Universities Council for Adult Education
U.G.C.	University Grants Committee
W.E.A.	Workers' Educational Association
W.E.T.U.C.	Workers' Educational and Trades Union Council
W.I.	Women's Institutes
Y.M.C.A.	Young Men's Christian Association
Y.W.C.A.	Young Women's Christian Association

PREFACE

i

People who write about adult education usually begin by saying why it is of prime national importance. They see themselves, one suspects, engaged in defending an embattled salient on the educational front, while the public, unaware of their heroic struggle, goes about its business.

The truth is that adult education, at any rate as traditionalists understand it, interests a small percentage of the population and receives scant consideration from the public authorities. There is a widespread belief that it is inessential and that its provision can be left largely to voluntary effort. For many it still brings to mind a pre-war picture of earnest men and women plodding away at worthy but dreary subjects, designed to be either uplifting or educationally remedial. A large section of the population feels that education is one thing and real life is something else. When school is left behind, the book of learning is rudely closed and never reopened. Such people would perhaps like to think that life itself is the only true educator.

The national government and the local authorities still treat adult education as a marginal responsibility. They behave as though no kind of systematic education is required once people have passed the age range of 15 to 22. Their attitude can clearly be seen from the small amount of money they allocate to adult education. For the session 1966–67 the total grant awarded by the Department of Education and Science to the Workers' Educational Association and the University Extra-Mural Departments was no more than £1,072,711. Even if adult education is interpreted in the widest possible sense to include such ventures as, say, Centre 42, the expenditure from public funds remains trifling. One need only refer to the far more generous provision made by public authorities in other countries to become aware of Britain's failure to provide adequate facilities. Contrast, for instance, the variety and richness of the cultural and educational provision in Munich with that of any city in the United Kingdom outside London, or consider how many more facilities are provided in the United States, a country still frequently dismissed as brashly philistine.

Educationists themselves do not have much regard for adult education. In most universities departments of extra-mural studies have always occupied a fringe position institutionally as well as metaphorically. Until recently local education authorities paid little attention to adult education, though to their credit not a few are now trying to make up for lost time. In relatively few areas has appropriate accommodation been set aside exclusively for its use and many of the premises and class-rooms in service are unsuitable. If the amount of inquiry undertaken in a given field is any indication of the interest it arouses, then the position of adult education is indeed precarious, for only a handful of re-searchers have turned their minds to its needs and problems.

Is this not just as it should be? Should adult education perhaps be forced to jostle for a place in the long queue of leisure-time activities competing for public custom? After all, people are on the whole prosperous and content. Why should they not spend their time and money as they see fit? Why should the government or the local authorities pay much heed to adult education unless a majority of taxpayers positively clamour for it?

This survey of the present position in England and Wales has been written in the belief that the public authorities should regard the provision of educational facilities for adults as a major priority. At the same time, it would serve no useful purpose un-questioningly to defend the existing forms of adult education or simply to recommend that larger funds are required in order to provide more of that which is already available. Rather I would suggest that both adult educators and the public authorities must re-think their whole attitude towards the educational needs of adults.

ii

I have attempted to make the survey as comprehensive as possible by treating the field in its entirety and by considering all the ways in which adults may be educated. In other words, I have equated adult education with the education of adults for any purpose whatsoever, not excluding aspects of industrial training. If I appear to have devoted a disproportionate amount of attention to the non-vocational sector, it is partly because it is the sector with which I am most familiar, but mainly because relatively little vocational education for adults was available until the passing of the Industrial Training Act in 1964. It will also readily be seen that I have inevitably brought more experience to bear upon some topics than upon others.

Geographically, the survey is deliberately limited to England and Wales because in Scotland and Northern Ireland adult education is differently organised in several notable respects. It may be argued that Wales should also have been treated as a separate entity; in practice, the pattern of provision in Wales is essentially similar to that in England, though I have thought it prudent to comment on a few distinctive features in an Appendix.

I have tried to place the institutions and topics discussed in their historical as well as contemporary setting and to touch upon some of the philosophical and sociological themes associated with the growth of adult education. It will soon be obvious to even the most cursory reader, however, that it was not my object to discuss perennial matters of concern with any degree of profundity. That is a task for a philosopher or maybe a sociologist which badly needs to be done but which lay outside my own remit.

Mainly for the benefit of the growing number of students of adult education I have included some diagrams, statistical tables and check-lists, though realising that these may interrupt the flow of the narrative. Some readers may choose to skip these interpolations.

The survey is divided into five parts. The first part is devoted to a discussion of the changing scope of adult education. The second, and by far the longest part, describes the functions and problems, under several heads, of those agencies chiefly responsible for the provision of adult education. The third part deals with the characteristics of students attending formally organised courses and tries to estimate the extent of public participation in the various forms of adult education. The fourth part is concerned with three essential elements in any expansion of the national system: the co-ordination of activities at all levels, the development of research and, related to it, the training of professional adult educators. The survey concludes with a brief summary of recommendations for further development.

Some aspects of my account are doubtless controversial and several of my judgements may strike at least some people as unfair. I also realise that the pattern of adult education recently began to change and that the situation described may soon yield place to another—I hope it does. But I see no point in sheltering behind academic reservations at a time when important decisions ought to be taken, and taken without delay.

The facts and views presented are derived from six principal sources:

    (i) published and unpublished works on adult education;
    (ii) visits to various educational establishments;
    (iii) attendance at special conferences and seminars;
    (iv) informal discussions with colleagues;
    (v) interviews with professional teachers and administrators;
    (vi) two inquiries—one concerning student characteristics, the other concerning informal activities.

The evidence about students is based on a survey undertaken in February 1963 with the aid of a number of kind and tolerant colleagues in various sectors of the adult education field. The evidence about informal activities in Liverpool is mainly drawn from an inquiry undertaken in the same year by a working party, of which Mr Michael Argles, then of the Institute of Education, University of Liverpool, and now Deputy Librarian of the University of Lancaster, acted as convener. Apart from the data relating to the survey of student characteristics the facts and figures quoted usually refer to the situation in 1967; not a few statistics relate to 1968; in some cases, however, it was impossible to obtain recent information.

The survey was made possible thanks to the Nuffield Trust, which made available generous funds, and to the University of Liverpool, which agreed to my secondment from my normal work as a resident staff tutor in the Department of Extra-Mural Studies. It was the brain-child of the Director, Professor T. Kelly, who has himself done so much to further the cause of research in adult education, notably in the historical field. He was consistently helpful and drew my attention to several lines of enquiry. It was also thanks to his careful scrutiny of my final draft that I was able to correct several inaccurate statements and to remove some verbal infelicities.

Everyone with whom I talked or corresponded was singularly frank and informative, but to make fitting acknowledgement to all those who helped me would take unduly long. I must, however, single out the names of several people to whom I owe a special debt of gratitude. Professor S. G. Raybould, the general editor of the series to which this volume belongs, read the whole manu- script in draft and suggested a number of changes which I was pleased to adopt, particularly as he magnanimously refrained from comment upon certain views diametrically opposed to his own. Mr Barry Pashley, now a lecturer in Hull University, provided me with valuable material gleaned from studies he undertook during two years as a research assistant at Liverpool University. Miss Elizabeth Gittus of the Department of Social Science of Liverpool University, now at Newcastle University, gave tech- nical advice about administering the survey on student character- istics and was otherwise generous with her time and advice. Mr Kenneth Prandy, formerly a research assistant in the same depart- ment, assisted in processing data and made several valuable suggestions.

Professor H. A. Jones was a frequent source of advice and penetrating comment. Some of my views were formed by talking to and studying the ideas expounded at various times by Mr Edward Hutchinson, Secretary of the National Institute of Adult Education. I am in any case in his debt and that of Miss Grieves, his former librarian, for the use I made of the National Institute of Adult Education Library, which, though small, is exceptionally helpful. I also made regular use of the Library of the Department of Education and Science. Among other people who provided me with advice and indispensable evidence about their special fields were: Mr Geoffrey Stuttard, Lecturer in Industrial Relations, Department of Extra-Mural Studies, London University; Mr Jeffrey Roberts and Mr Glyn Pritchard of the Workers' Educa- tional Association; Mr K. M. Reinhold, Secretary of the National Federation of Community Associations; Mrs Marjory Gray, formerly Social Studies Adviser of the National Federation of Townswomen's Guilds; and Mr John Robinson, Further Educa- tion Liaison Officer of the B.B.C. Finally, I must particularly thank Mrs Carol Atherton and Miss Rita Heatlie for their ungrudging secretarial assistance.

Department of Adult Education
University of Edinburgh

1968

ACKNOWLEDGEMENTS

I am grateful to the following for permission to quote brief extracts from the publications mentioned in the text: The British Broadcasting Corporation; Her Majesty's Stationery Office; Kent Education Committee; The Library Association; The National Institute of Adult Education; *New Society*; The Oxford Delegacy for Extra-Mural Studies; Pergamon Press Ltd.; Reader's Digest Association Ltd.; Times Newspapers Ltd.; *Universities Quarterly;* The Workers' Educational Association.

Chapter One

FROM 'ADULT EDUCATION'
TO THE EDUCATION OF ADULTS

i

Within the last ten years there has been a flow of books, pamphlets, articles, propaganda statements and working party reports, each concerned to argue the case for or to discuss trends in adult education. Since 1957 we have had a conspectus of the field from Professor Peers, a symposium edited by Professor Raybould, an excellent Fabian pamphlet from Dr Mabel Tylecote, and a vigorous statement of ends and means on behalf of the Liberal Party by Mr R. Pahl. From the Universities Council of Adult Education, the Workers' Educational Association and several other bodies we have had working party reports and declarations of principle and intent. 1963 saw the publication by the National Institute of Adult Education of a report on staffing and accommodation which was at once an objective summary of facts and figures and an explicit challenge to the government to take action. This was followed in 1966 by a complementary report on recruitment and training. In 1966 there also appeared from an unexpected though welcome source a report by the National Union of Students which contained on its first page the ringing affirmation, 'adult education must be accepted as an integral feature of any plan for educational advance'.[1] The output in Britain has been paralleled by a spate of international publications to which British adult educators have contributed. All this is most encouraging and undoubtedly it has had some effect upon public policy and the very nature of adult education in this country.

Nevertheless, it is disquieting that the protagonists of adult education should still feel obliged to plead so hard for their cause. As long ago as that false dawn which marked the end of the First World War, adult education was accorded the status of a national priority. The case for its expansion has never been more lucidly and memorably expressed than in a report submitted to the Coalition Government that has become famous, in adult education circles at any rate, as the *1919 Report*.*

Towards the end of the First World War the government appointed several committees to recommend ways and means of reforming society. Among these was the Adult Education Committee constituted in July, 1917, 'to consider the provision for and possibilities of adult education (other than technical or vocational) in Great Britain, and to make recommendations'. Written in stately prose and imbued with a strong humanitarian purpose, the report of this committee, published in 1919,[2] embraced both a declaration of faith in the central importance of adult education in the life of the nation and a practical programme of action that is in part still relevant. Acclaimed in Britain at the time of publication as a manifesto, it came to enjoy an international reputation, especially in North America where it has since been a frequent source of inspiration.

For the Committee education was much more than a means of leading individuals into the good life; it was also the key to creating a better society. In 1919 the main obstacle to progress appeared to be the twin evils of poverty and ignorance. Neither one of these evils could be eradicated in isolation; economic, social and educational advance had to go forward side by side. Hence it was the special concern of the Committee that people should not seek education for their personal benefit alone but for the common good.

Though in the light of half a century of subsequent experience adult educators are now disinclined to express themselves with the same moral confidence and do not readily share the same sanguine view of the essential nobility of mankind, they cannot fault the Report on grounds of inconsistency or inadequate homework. Hardly an argument in favour of adult education has since been put forward which the Committee had overlooked. Never has there been such a thoroughgoing survey of the aims and organisation of adult education in Britain. Anyone who is remotely interested in the education of adults cannot avoid studying the Report, least of all anyone who sets out to write about the subject. As a point of departure for this present survey, therefore, it is worth trying to explain why the Report failed to make the impact that seemed originally destined for it and why today less distinguished

* Occasionally referred to as the Smith Report.

men than those who sat on the Committee are having to do their small best to preach the gospel.[3]

In its first interim report, entitled *Industrial and Social Conditions in Relation to Adult Education*, the Committee defined precisely what kind of social and economic conditions would be required in the better society they envisaged. The essential thing was to give people more leisure by reducing the hours spent at work, and to ensure that they could earn enough money and have enough comfort and energy to enjoy it. The public authorities had a duty to abolish overcrowding and sordid living conditions and to create an environment that would allow privacy, cleanliness and comfort. Rural housing schemes and urban slum clearance were alike essential; urban housing estates should be so designed that men could live near their place of work and their wives could care for their children in well-planned homes. Holidays with pay should become the general rule and there should be more half-holidays, especially for agricultural workers. Social security benefits should be extended in order to free workers from the evils of want, sickness, unemployment and penurious old age. Finally, the state system of compulsory education must be vastly expanded.

The cumulative effect of all these changes would be to make the worker realise that the economic system was not, as he commonly supposed, an unjust and impersonal tyrant but an essential component of existence. At the same time, since he would spend fewer hours at work and suffer less fatigue, he would enjoy his leisure and turn it to profitable use. His personality would flower and there would be plenty of opportunity to satisfy his mental wants.

These requirements have for the most part been met. If much social distress remains to be alleviated and new social problems have arisen, the working and living environment is at least as congenial as the Committee could have wished within what was for them the foreseeable future. Moreover, most people can now have ample leisure if they choose to take it. Yet the enlightened cultural and social milieu that the Committee assumed would result is not with us; economic progress has not been matched by the same degree of educational progress; the desired reforms have not produced the desired results. Some people have gained immeasurably from attending adult education classes both as persons and servants of the community but they form a tiny band—the age of an enlightened people seems as remote as ever.

Why has social reform not fulfilled the Committee's expectations? Why has adult education, as conceived in 1919, not become a national priority? Several reasons are obvious. Material progress has been accompanied by unforeseen factors: in many occupations men prefer to work overtime rather than accept an effective reduction in the length of the working week; increased leisure and spending power have become easy targets for a skilfully promoted mass entertainment industry; above all, it is the middle classes rather than the working classes who have taken most advantage of improved cultural and educational opportunities. The Committee also overestimated the human appetite for knowledge and understanding, mainly because they were inclined to believe that it is a natural instinct for men and women to reach for higher things.

Then again, it is possible, inevitably, to pin some of the blame upon successive governments, particularly those between the wars, for not responding imaginatively to the Committee's recommendations. But governments are seldom moved by other than practical considerations and to them adult education has always looked not unlike a dispensable amenity such as a sports field or an art gallery, which might perhaps qualify for Treasury support when money was plentiful but assuredly not in the economically blighted years of the twenties and thirties. Thus most of the Committee's recommendations met the same fate as the coeval recommendation to set up day continuation schools, that is, temporary enthusiasm followed by indifference.

However, there remains a more fundamental explanation. It is that the Committee adopted the circumscribed definition of adult education evolved in Britain before 1919 and in so doing missed the chance to strike the utilitarian note to which alone governments might have listened. The Committee's brief meticulously restricted them to the consideration of '. . . adult education (*other than technical and vocational*)'.* When analysed, their interpretation of that brief would seem to ascribe three principal aims to adult education: to enable at least some adults to compensate for a lack of formal education; to emancipate intellectually a select number of potential working class leaders so that they might play a responsible part in local and national politics; to civilise the masses by diffusing among them the cultural values—the élite

* My italics.

culture—which the Committee members held dear. The Board of Education so far endorsed their recommendations as to agree in 1924 that adult education, in the inherited narrow sense, should become eligible for grants so long as it was non-vocational. There-after, as Professor S. G. Raybould has pointed out, the English pattern of adult education came to mean liberal education, pre-cisely because public funds were earmarked for that purpose and for that purpose alone.[4] Noble though their intentions and impeccable their methods of inquiry, the authors of the 1919 Report were thus largely responsible for perpetuating an official and popular view of the education of adults doomed to make a relatively slight impact upon a nation which assesses all forms of education in utilitarian terms, despite pretences to the contrary, and that has hampered progress ever since 1919.

ii

The restricted use of the term adult education transmitted by the 1919 Report has caused semantic confusion and led to a deplor-able neglect of the education of adults as a whole. Let us first consider the confusion to which it has given rise.

In Britain virtually alone among nations, the term adult educa-tion is almost never used in the wide sense of all education for persons aged eighteen and over.[5] It does not denote the education of adults as distinct from the education of children and young people, but commonly refers only to *non-vocational* education voluntarily undertaken by people over eighteen. Indeed, many politicians, educationists and laymen, particularly if their ideas were formed before the Second World War, still confine its appli-cation to the traditional courses arranged by the Workers' Educa-tional Association and university extra-mural departments. What staff tutor in a department of extra-mural studies has not heard people saying something like 'Oh! You are in Adult Education. That's the W.E.A. isn't it?'

Supposing we do want to describe that branch of education which is concerned with the general needs of those who are over eighteen and not in full-time attendance at an educational institu-tion, what term can we use? If we adopt the phraseology of the Department of Education and Science, then we must invoke the term 'Further Education'.[6] Even this, however, is not in popular usage truly comprehensive, for it is usually equated with only the *vocational* education or training of those who have recently left school. In short there is no omnibus term for signifying the education of adults. How fortunate they are in the United States and Canada where no one has ever thought to question that adult education simply means 'the education of adults'.

The limited application of the term adult education leads to two further difficulties. The first is caused by the unreliability of the distinction frequently drawn between vocational and non-vocational provision, where the implication is that 'vocational' means job-betterment and 'non-vocational' means that the student is not seeking material gain. To begin with, the motives of students may be mixed; certainly they are often different from what the organisers of classes think they are, and it is well established that whereas many students in so-called vocational classes have in fact no vocational motive, a number of those attending so-called non-vocational classes do have such a motive, although sometimes they may not confess to it. It is also known to most teachers that many people can only be touched through an appeal to their material interests, and that the hope of personal advantage may hold their attention during the early stages of a course when without a strong incentive they might hastily withdraw from it.

Confusion is also caused by the changing policies of providing bodies. Both university extra-mural departments and the W.E.A. now offer factory-based courses. Are these non-vocational courses or are they not? Extra-mural departments and short-term residential colleges are also offering an increasing number of courses for professional groups. Do they cease to provide adult education when offering such courses? And when technical colleges or art schools offer courses of any kind for adults, but particularly non-vocational courses, are they *not* concerned with adult education? Then there is the widespread assumption that the liberal content of adult education is what divides it from vocational education. It is enough to look at the list of courses advertised in almost any L.E.A. prospectus for Further Education to see how impossible it is to separate the liberal content from the rest of the programme, despite the predominance of practical subjects. It goes without saying that in practice some vocational classes deal with humane studies and many more are taught in an essentially humane spirit. After all, it has been official policy for several years to liberalise the curricula of all Further Educational institutions and such institutions often provide adult education courses of the traditional kind. Perhaps the only reliable way of testing whether a course is liberal or not is to ascertain the motives of the teacher and the students.

The second difficulty is to know where to set limits. When can one say that adults are being educated? To what extent are the B.B.C. and I.T.A. engaged in adult education? How does one classify some of the more purposeful activities of the Women's Institutes and of the Social Studies Groups of the Townswomen's Guilds? One answer is to insist that 'education' can only take place when the providing body has a recognised professional status and when the aim is sustained study. According to this definition the sole activities to qualify would be classes provided by the L.E.A.s and the 'Responsible Bodies'.* But this is too exclusive a qualification since much admirable work is also done by several other organisations as well as a host of informal cultural and social agencies; indeed it is probable that a good proportion of educational facilities is provided by agencies whose purpose is not primarily educational. Furthermore, it is at least an arguable proposition that the educational effect of the output of the mass media far exceeds that of all the formally sponsored courses put together. Thus, the most recondite talks on the Third Programme still appeal to upwards of 50,000 listeners and a television lecture on a celebrated painter by Sir Kenneth Clark may be viewed by millions.

Probably no solution to the problem of terminology will be found until we discard the notion that adult education comprises only liberal studies and that recreation is not education at all. The continuing education of adults will have to be seen as a whole, of which vocational, non-vocational, general, formal, informal, liberal and recreational education are constituent parts. No doubt a large section of the public will always think of adult education in terms of a familiar stereotype such as an evening institute or the W.E.A. But there is no excuse for educators who do not adopt a holistic view.

Even then we are left with the fact that, for psychological reasons, adult education is an unhappy term. The very word 'education'

---

* The name frequently given to university extra-mural departments and the districts of the W.E.A. See below Chapter 5.

strikes an unresponsive chord in many adults, for whom it is either what goes on within the formal structure of schools or it is nothing. In his enquiries the late J. Trenaman discovered that some people who had not been to grammar schools were resentful of the educational system.[7] And when 'education' is qualified by 'adult' it is commonly regarded as dreary. It is hard to know what term to substitute. 'Continuing Education' is used in North America and conveys much the same idea as 'l'éducation permanente', the term used in France. 'Continuous learning' is perhaps even more apposite but cannot be used in every context. Most alternative terms seem to suffer from one drawback or another. 'Lifelong integrated learning', the latest term adopted by UNESCO, sounds like jargon. Perhaps the solution is for educators consciously to start using the words 'adult education' in their widest sense, that is, meaning the education of adults, and to find a way of giving them a new and acceptable popular connotation. The B.B.C. and the independent television companies could help most in getting that usage generally adopted. Certainly they are uniquely well placed to give adult education the widespread appeal it has so far lacked.

Apart from engendering problems of definition the restricted interpretation of the term adult education has had a deleterious effect upon the whole development of post-school education in Britain. Those responsible for organising courses of a liberal and non-vocational type have unwittingly assumed a hierarchical attitude, thereby erecting a barrier between the few who attend courses and the mass of the population who do not. The type of education supplied by university extra-mural departments and the W.E.A. has been rated highly, while every other type has been left to struggle for a place lower down an implied scale of esteem: it has been 'merely' vocational or remedial or frivolous. This attitude no doubt reflects our tradition of respect for the 'pure scholar', for the amateur who wears his learning lightly, for the humanities rather than the sciences, as well as a slight disdain for the applied use of knowledge and the professional worker. The consequence of this attitude is that the needs of the community at large have been neglected. For instance, by assuming their function to be the provision of formally organised non-vocational courses in the humanities, universities have been slow to ask themselves whether they do not have other social obligations to the community outside their walls. They have not gone out of their way to look for social needs or tried to anticipate them. Again, the tendency has been to wait for interested students to enrol when the dynamic aim ought to have been to make everyone in some sense a student: in other words, the programme has really selected the student. Policy-makers have been unduly concerned with liberal values and have failed to identify, let alone satisfy, practical human wants of social or economic provenance. Yet what are the grounds for assuming that in the context of her own personal development a woman attending an evening institute is not deriving as much benefit from a class on cookery or flower arrangement not provided by a university as someone else is deriving from the study of archaeology in a university extension or tutorial class? We greatly underestimate the value of group activities of any kind. There are few people who cannot learn something if given the right opportunity. Again, the nation has long been faced with the enormous problem of enabling manual workers to cope with new skills and techniques. At last the government has established Industrial Training Boards with wide powers, but it is the Ministry of Labour that is responsible for them. The courses and facilities provided by the Boards, although necessarily concerned with the education of adults, are not felt to lie within the province of the D.E.S.

Of its nature the kind of educational service provided by the Responsible Bodies can be enjoyed by no more than a severely limited number of people. This is, of course, partly because of such factors as a lack of resources and inadequate official support, but it is very largely because neither the inclinations nor the intellectual capacities of the great majority of the population fit them for the formal type of class offered by the Responsible Bodies. They prefer 'to do' rather than 'to study'. A high proportion are suspicious of academic exercises.

iii

The argument of this chapter is, then, that 'adult education' has been, and still essentially remains, a neglected segment of the national education system because of its almost exclusive historical identification with that type of liberal and non-vocational education provided by university extra-mural departments and the

W.E.A. The irony of the neglect is that a good deal of adult education in the broad sense in which other countries interpret it has always taken place. The Kent Education Committee apparently recognised this truth some time ago, to judge from the following extract from a pamphlet published at the end of the Second World War:

> It is vital that, whilst the importance of the older forms of adult education must be ever present to our minds, we shall not shrink from the implications of this broader conception of adult education, which must result in the acceptance by education authorities and organisations of responsibility for activities which once would have been deemed hardly fitting for such bodies to associate themselves with.[8]

That statement is over twenty-three years old. The nation has meanwhile gone some way towards adopting the 'broader conception' then desired, and indeed the last decade has witnessed unprecedented material growth. But, if typically pragmatic, the progress achieved has been hesitant and largely unstructured, still impeded by the narrow definition that restricted the members of the 1919 Committee. The rate of advance has not matched the urgency of the social need. If the education of adults is to cease being a marginal national concern, it is now imperative that the government, the local authorities and the general public should begin to perceive it in its vast range and diversity, recognise its untapped potential as a source of community and national development, and accord it generous and sustained support.

Perhaps the chief obstacle to rapid progress is that in England and Wales we have no taxonomy for describing the education of adults. If only we knew exactly what forms of education and what scale of provision are currently being provided, then at least we would have a firm base from which to plan development. How can we best describe adult education?

The possibilities are embarrassingly numerous. We can classify activities according to whether they are vocational or non-vocational, compulsory or voluntary, lax or rigorous. We could attempt to demarcate a series of academic levels. The subject matter might be broken down into categories. We might even define educational experiences in terms of the method of communication between teacher and learner. The International Congress of University Adult Education has recently adopted a formula for the purpose of cross-cultural comparisons that classifies educational provision according to the adult needs it is designed to meet. Five categories are differentiated:

(i) remedial education: fundamental and literacy education;
(ii) education for vocational, technical and professional competence;
(iii) education for health, welfare and family living;
(iv) education for civic, political and community competence;
(v) education for self-fulfilment.[9]

Each of these formulae for classification tends to be unsatisfactory, however, chiefly because it describes only one or two facets of the total field. At the same time, attempts to devise a conceptual framework comprehending all possible formulae seem doomed to end in hair-splitting pedantry.

The important thing is to devise a descriptive method which will present the field as nearly as possible as a whole and show the relationship between one kind of activity and another. The best way of achieving this object would seem to be to classify adult education according to the agencies or sponsors involved and to postulate a hierarchy not of esteem but of degree of involvement. There are doubtless several possible ways of designing such a classification but it is hoped that the table on p. 30 will afford both a comprehensive and relatively accurate guide.

In succeeding chapters the anatomy of adult education will be described and discussed by reference to the principal agencies listed in the Table. It will be appropriate to begin with an analysis of the role of the State and the Local Education Authorities.

TAXONOMY OF ADULT EDUCATION AGENCIES

I	II	III	IV	V
Government or Local Authority Institutions Existing Primarily or Exclusively for an Educational Purpose	Government or Local Authority Institutions Including an Educational Aim in Their Programmes	Independent Institutions Existing Primarily or Exclusively for an Educational Purpose and in Receipt of Grant-Aid from Public Funds	Independent Institutions Including an Educational Purpose among Their Aims and in Receipt of Grant-Aid from Public Funds	Wholly Independent Institutions Existing Primarily or Exclusively for an Educational Purpose
Evening Institutes	H.M. Forces	Universities (Extra-Mural Departments)	Community Associations	National Adult School Union
Most Adult Education Centres	H.M. Prisons	Workers' Educational Association (HQ and Districts)	Townswomen's Guilds	Field Studies Council
Most Short-Term Residential Colleges	Civil Service	Y.M.C.A.—Wales	Women's Institutes	The Co-operative College
Village Colleges	Mental Hospitals	Long-Term Residential Colleges	National Association of Women's Clubs	Some Residential Colleges (Short Term)
Literary Institutes	Nationalised Industries	Rural Music Schools	British Film Institute	Some Adult Education Centres
Certain Further Education Establishments		Seafarers' Education Service		Correspondence Schools and Colleges
Industrial Training Boards		Miscellaneous Bodies		

VI	VII	VIII	IX	X
Wholly Independent Institutions including an Educational Purpose among Their Aims	Wholly Independent Institutions including a specific Educational Purpose among Their Aims or using the means of achieving Their Aims	Auxiliaries of Education	The Mass Media, in so far as They Consciously Fulfil an Educational Function	Voluntary Local Associations including an Educational Aim among their Activities
The National Council of Social Service	The Churches	Libraries	Broadcasting	Festival Societies
Some Industrial and Commercial Firms	Central Health Council	Museums	Books	Societies
Professional Associations	The Hansard Society	Art Galleries	Newspapers and Periodicals	Clubs
Learned Societies	Health and Welfare Agencies	Arts Councils		Drama Groups
The Trade Unions	Miscellaneous Bodies	Musical Societies		
The Y.M.C.A.		The Theatre		
The Y.W.C.A.		Centre 42		
The Co-operative Union		Films		
Working Men's Clubs				
Miscellaneous Bodies				

REFERENCES

1. R. Peers, *Adult Education: a comparative study* (1958); S. G. Raybould (ed.), *Trends in English Adult Education* (1959); M. Tylecote, *The Future of Adult Education* (1960); R. E. Pahl, *Adult Education in a Free Society* (1962); W.E.A. Working Party Report, *Aspects of Adult Education* (1960); U.C.A.E., *The Universities and Adult Education* (1961); 'Accommodation and Staffing' in *Adult Education*, January 1963, pp. 229–312; 'Recruitment and Training' in *Adult Education*, March 1966, pp. 319–90; N.U.S., *Adult Education* (1966).
2. Ministry of Reconstruction: Adult Education Committee, *Final Report* (H.M.S.O., 1919). An abridged version with an introduction by R. D. Waller was published in 1956 with the title *A Design for Democracy*.
3. For a perceptive assessment of the Report, see Professor Waller's introduction to the abridged version of 1956, pp. 15–48.
4. Cf. *University Extra-Mural Education in England 1945–62: a Study in Finance and Policy* (1964), pp. 20–1.
5. Cf. A. J. Peters, *British Further Education* (1966), p. 192.
6. We should be indebted to Mr Peters for putting forward a precise definition: 'Education intended for persons who have left school, through provision secured either by the Minister of Education, by the Secretary of State for Education and Science acting in the capacity of the former Minister of Education—or by local education authorities in accordance with appropriate schemes or plans approved by either of these Ministers or Secretaries.' (*ibid.*, p. 3.)
7. Cf. *Communication and Comprehension* (1967), p. 191.
8. *Adult Education in Kent*, pp. 6–7.
9. A. A. Liveright and N. Haygood (eds.), *The Exeter Papers* (Boston, 1968), p. 9.

Chapter Two

THE ROLE OF THE STATE
AND THE LOCAL AUTHORITIES

i. *The Government and the Department of Education and Science*

The State acknowledged some direct responsibility for non-vocational adult education as long ago as 1907 when the Board of Education, as it was then called, made small grants towards the cost of maintaining university tutorial classes. Subsequently, in 1913, *Regulations for University Tutorial Classes in England and Wales* were issued. These offered grants for 'General Education' classes sponsored by a university or a committee containing university representatives, but prescribed stringent conditions for the sort of classes that would qualify. In the meantime, more rudimentary forms of liberal adult education haphazardly came in for support under the terms of the rules applying to the general provision of further education. However, the total amount of money contributed by the Exchequer during this period was meagre.

The prospect of a deeper concern with 'adult education' seemed assured with the appointment in 1917 of the Smith Committee to survey the whole field and to make recommendations. But although the final report of that committee inspired temporary interest among government officials and although a special adult education committee was set up in 1921 which endured until 1939, there was no hint of large-scale State intervention between the wars, though the Board of Education (Adult Education) Regulations (1924) introduced the system of awarding grants to 'Responsible Bodies'. A similar failure on the part of the government followed the end of the Second World War. The 1944 Education Act led to some expansion of the field but the initial scale of government support was not maintained.

The 1944 Act, which came into force on 1 April 1945, is rightly regarded as an imposing landmark in the history of education in England and Wales. It was imaginative and thorough, socially just and broad in scope, designed to provide educational opportunities for people throughout their lives. For Further Education in general it promised an end to piecemeal arrangements and the introduction of organised and comprehensive provision; henceforward County Colleges, Technical Schools and Colleges, Community Centres and all the other post-school establishments other than institutions of higher learning were to be administered by a single section of the newly created Ministry of Education. For adult education in particular it seemed to offer a secure and expanding function. 'Education', it was stated, 'must contribute towards the spiritual, moral, mental and physical development of the community'.[1] If it was necessary to expand technical education for the sake of economic development, it was equally necessary to ensure 'a wide development of general adult education' so that 'as individuals or as a nation' we could 'deal competently and democratically with the complex political questions of our time'.[2] Adequate educational facilities should be made available so as to enable adults to lead full lives.

The powers conferred upon the Minister of Education were virtually limitless and have remained so. There was nothing to stop him from supporting the expansion of adult education in any way he saw fit. Although in practice he would have to act largely through the L.E.A.s, he could bend the Authorities to his wishes thanks to his control over their capital investment, his power to issue Orders in Council and Regulations, and in the last resort his right to issue mandatory orders. After the passing of the Act the Minister called upon the Authorities to submit schemes for the expansion of Further Education, including Adult Education.

By 1949, ninety-five of the L.E.A.s had submitted their schemes. Among their proposals they envisaged the creation of county colleges which would also serve as community centres, and in the case of Bristol the development of an 'Educational Precinct' in which all kinds of facilities for recreation and education would be contained. The cost of their schemes over a five-year period in capital expenditure alone would have amounted to a sum of the order of £10,000,000 in the then current values.[3] It was too much for the Ministry, which released very little money. Indeed, four years later in 1953 it inflicted a cut in the grant to the R.B.s. That cut aroused a public outcry which led to the appointment of a committee under the chairmanship of Sir Eric Ashby. Some of the reforms proposed by the Ashby Committee were accepted but money continued to be doled out in driblets.

B

The fact is that a wide gap yawns between official statements and official practice. Successive governments blandly agree that they should exhort and assist people to make profitable use of their increasing leisure-time and greater affluence. So, too, do the political parties. At post-war general elections, notably in 1959, they have been careful to insert paragraphs in their campaign literature about the necessity for providing a wide range of educational, social and cultural facilities for the public good. From what governments fail to do and from what ministers say when caught off guard, however, it is only too obvious that adult education exerts a marginal claim upon their attention. In their scale of priorities they allow pride of place to producing an economically efficient society and to making people's lives materially better. To do them justice, they also seem to believe that it is not possible to advance upon more than one educational front at any given time. At one period the front may be technical training; at another it may be higher education. But never does there seem to be either time or money in any quantity to spare for the adult education front. When he was Minister of Education, Lord Eccles admitted on one occasion that while he appreciated the value of the programmes being arranged, he looked upon them as a luxury for which people should be prepared to pay the economic price. This was at least plain speaking. A more typical illustration of the disingenuous attitude adopted by ministers was given in 1953 on the occasion of the cut in the grant to the R.B.s. The T.U.C. protested to the Prime Minister. Consider the contrast between the last two paragraphs of Sir Winston Churchill's reply:

'There is, perhaps, no branch of our vast educational system which should more attract within its particular sphere the aid and encouragement of the State than adult education. How many must there be in Britain, after the disturbance of two destructive wars, who thirst in later life to learn about the humanities, the history of their country, the philosophies of the human race, and the arts and letters which sustain and are borne forward by the ever-conquering English language? This ranks in my opinion far above science and technical instruction, which are well sustained and not without their rewards in our present system. The mental and moral outlook of free men studying the past with free minds in order to discern the future demands the highest measures which our hard-pressed finances can sustain. I have no doubt myself that a man or woman earnestly seeking in grown-up life to be guided to wide and suggestive knowledge in its largest and most uplifted sphere will make the best of all the pupils in this age of clatter and buzz, of gape and gloat. The appetite of adults to be shown the foundations and processes of thought will never be denied by a British Administration cherishing the continuity of our Island life.

But these are no reasons for not looking through the accounts, and making sure that all we can give is turned to real advantage.'

The total grant awarded was in the region of £330,000. The cut to be imposed was 10% or a miserly £33,000. Presumably in juxtaposing these two contrasting paragraphs Sir Winston was guiltless of intentional irony.

It is not unusual, of course, for a gap to emerge between ministerial pronouncements and performance, between good intentions and their implementation. The essential point, however, is that expenditure upon adult education, unlike expenditure upon the schools, is permissive. There are no structures for it under the Act that must be maintained and consequently it is at the mercy of subjective judgements about what is its appropriate due.

Since 1953 the State has in fact increased its financial support, though not even remotely in proportion with its expenditure on other sectors of education or upon the Arts. In a recent statement published jointly by the U.C.A.E. and the W.E.A.[4] it was estimated that the Exchequer's total expenditure on Responsible Body and local authority work could scarcely exceed £5 million, or, more strikingly, about one half of one per cent of the State's total contribution towards educational costs. There can be no question that this scale of expenditure is petty in relation to the actual need.

Except in so far as it has to deal, like any employer, with the educational needs of public servants in government departments or government controlled services, the government avoids direct involvement in the education of adults. Acting on the assumption that the autonomy of local authorities and the enterprise of voluntary bodies must be preserved, it restricts its role to supplying grants, advice and stimulation, laying down instructions in matters of organisation and trying to harmonise the activities of the various adult educational agencies. To its credit it recognises the importance of sustaining independent bodies so that they may inject vitality and provide a variety of services; sometimes, however, its support for the voluntary principle looks uncomfortably like an excuse for inaction.

FURTHER EDUCATION IN ENGLAND AND WALES—THE OFFICIAL STRUCTURE

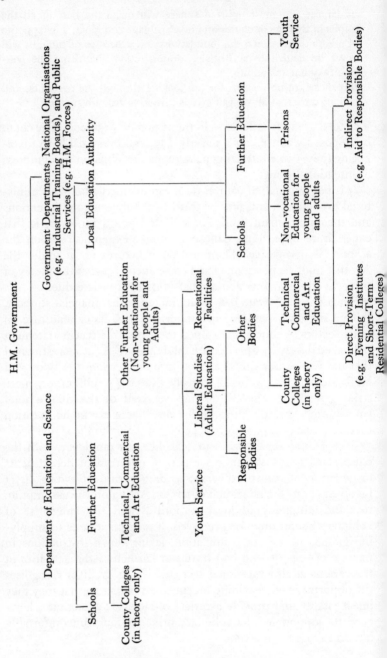

ADULT EDUCATION IN ENGLAND AND WALES—THE OFFICIAL STRUCTURE

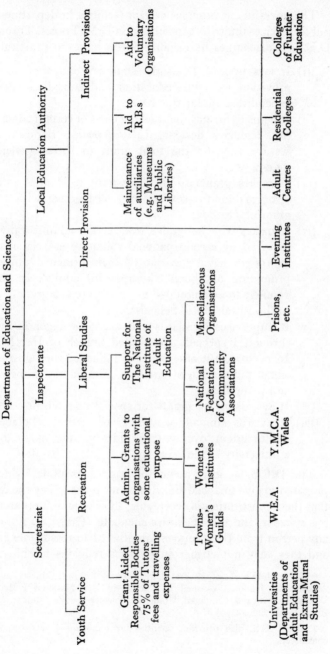

The government provides certain facilities in departments and public services under its control, e.g. in H.M. Forces. Through the D.E.S. it discharges its responsibilities in seven practical ways:

(i) It lays upon L.E.A.s the statutory obligation to ensure provision for adult education and subsidises their own expenditure under this head.

(ii) It helps to finance the teaching costs of certain adult education agencies designated 'Responsible Bodies'. In the session 1966–67 the total grant to these agencies was £1,072,711.

(iii) It makes grants to the long-term residential colleges— £109,771 for the session 1967–68 together with a capital grant of £84,892.

(iv) It makes triennial grants towards the administrative costs incurred by certain national voluntary associations (eight in 1967)* having as one of their principal objects 'the promotion of liberal education for adults'. In the year 1966–67 these amounted to £30,940 (e.g. a grant of £5,000 to the Rural Music Schools).

(v) It supervises standards and exercises a gentle influence through a specially constituted branch of Her Majesty's Inspectorate: it also exercises influence through the occasional publication of circulars, administrative memoranda and pamphlets.

(vi) It awards *ad hoc* grants for special research projects.

(vii) It awards annually a number of mature scholarships to adult students over 25 years old who were unable to attend a university at the usual age.†

The D.E.S. is strict about the conditions under which it is prepared to give financial aid. Recipients must satisfy the Minister that their constitution is acceptable, their organisation and teaching efficient, and their facilities adequate. They may not exclude any person from their courses 'on other than reasonable grounds' and they may not engage in *ex parte* religious teaching. Their

* These eight associations are: British Drama League; Educational Centres Association; National Council of the Y.M.C.A.; National Federation of Women's Institutes; National Union of Townswomen's Guilds; N.I.A.E.; Rural Music Schools; W.E.A.

† The D.E.S. also provides facilities for recreational activities not here considered.

programmes must be submitted for approval in advance and may not be changed without prior consultation.

At the D.E.S. itself a distinction was drawn until 1968 between 'Further Education' and what was described as 'Other Further Education', or, as it was more commonly called, 'O.F.E.'. Further Education comprehended all vocationally oriented work; thus technical establishments and colleges of art and commerce came within its purview. O.F.E., on the other hand, was broadly equated with all non-vocational education. For the inspectorate it consisted of the inspection of Youth Work, Adult Education (the R.B.s), Evening Institutes, Community Centres, and a few other sectors such as the Youth Employment Service, Education in Prisons, Borstals and H.M. Forces, and General Studies in Technical Colleges. No one at the D.E.S. claimed that the separation of F.E. and O.F.E. was other than an administrative expedient. Equally there was no pretence that it reflected a valid antithesis between liberal and vocational education. How could it when a determined effort is well under way to extend the teaching of liberal studies to all full-time vocational institutions? Furthermore, the separation was not absolute, for some administrative overlapping did occur, especially where the duties of the Inspectorate were concerned.

However, apart from questioning the uninspired nomenclature —Other Further Education had a symbolically dismissive ring— critics should not be too anxious to condemn this functional division. No doubt in an exemplary society all further or post-school education would be both broadly based and liberally conceived. Given the prevailing utilitarian climate, however, it is likely that if there had been a unified administrative structure since the last war, the claims of liberal adult education would have been squeezed out altogether; to have had a few officials at the Ministry deeply committed to adult education and hence impelled to fight its battles was preferable to having nothing done at all.

The officials in O.F.E. also occupied a unique vantage point from which to view adult education as a whole. It has been because of their breadth of vision that public support is given to community associations and several other voluntary bodies whose connection with adult education escapes the notice of most professional workers. There is also much to be said for treating the Youth Service and provision for recreational facilities within the same context as adult education in its traditional forms, since officials are thereby made aware of two urgent needs: the first, to build a bridge between the Youth Service and the established adult education organisations; and the second, to widen people's horizons not alone by attracting them to formal courses but also by furnishing them with opportunities for recreational and social activities.

Now that O.F.E. has lost its separate identity by being merged with F.E. it is to be hoped that adult education as such does not suffer from lack of attention. The danger is real especially since those inspectors who used to be solely responsible for O.F.E. matters will now also have assignments in Technical, Commercial and Art work, an area which is in some respects more satisfying to deal with since it is well organised and in receipt of generous financial support. The fact, however, that one part of F.E. continues to be described as Adult and Youth may perhaps be regarded as reassuring.

At the personal level there are excellent relations between officials at the D.E.S. and the adult education organisations. Nevertheless, resentment is occasionally expressed at ministerial supervision. The familiar jibe that inspectors are more ornamental than useful is palpably unwarranted, but some of the regulations they are expected to uphold are both rigid and irrational. Take the example of foreign languages: whereas evening institutes may hold classes in foreign languages, the Responsible Bodies can normally only deal with the literature of foreign countries. Sometimes this leads to an anomalous situation in which differential fees are paid to teachers lecturing in language and literature courses organised jointly by an L.E.A. and a Responsible Body. Again, the art of drama may be discussed by R.B.s but not practised. Other criticisms stem from alleged evidence of bias or omissions too insubstantial to deserve mention. Perhaps the one justifiable criticism is that the D.E.S. furnishes remarkably little information and publicity; its annual statistics about Adult Education have been modified to advantage in recent years but remain sketchy. There are, of course, difficulties in collecting statistics: the L.E.A.s and the R.B.s are quick to complain about supposedly needless form-filling; in its wider connotation adult education is so amorphous as to render fact-finding an expensive operation.

On the other hand, because the field of adult education is so fragmented, H.M.I.s in the Adult Education section of the Inspectorate play a vital part in conveying information from one area to another and in fostering collaboration between agencies and co-ordination of activities. The annual course organised at Salisbury by the Inspectorate for teachers and administrators engaged in all aspects of non-vocational education is exceptionally valuable since it enables tutors, leaders and administrators working in disparate sections of the field to come together and realise, very often for the first time, that others labour in the vineyard as well as themselves. Again, although the agencies of adult education are legion, the organisations providing formal courses are few. As a consequence, H.M.I.s come to know intimately both their staffs and their sphere of operations and can thereby dispense much excellent advice.

Praise for the efficiency and enlightened outlook of officials in the O.F.E. branch is not to be confused with praise for the D.E.S. as a whole. Adult education has so far counted for little in its counsels, its expenditure, and its provisions. Yet, as we have shown, the powers of the Minister could scarcely be greater. What is lacking is the impulse to use them. He has never indicated even roughly how much provision there ought to be and seldom specifies what particular developments L.E.A.s should support. Though official statements since 1964 have been promising, the time to cheer will be when words are sustained by deeds.

As for the government, in one respect it clearly could do more. This is in regard to the vast number of people, perhaps 20% of the working population, employed in the public services. If the government really had a deep concern for adult education, it could give an inspiring lead by affording many more educational opportunities for civil servants and employees in the nationalised industries.

ii Local Education Authorities

Local authorities everywhere will accept the view that they cannot be disinterested in the intellectual, moral and physical quality of their citizens. Just as there is civic pride in the physical aspect of a city, its public buildings and gardens, so civic pride must grow from awareness that the citizenry are able, knowledgeable and alive to cultural influences. This being so, local authorities will presumably be at

least sympathetic to all those activities, whether sponsored by themselves or not, which aim to develop a greater sense of civic responsibility and to increase the reputation of the city as a cultural centre.
It is only therefore a further step for all local authorities to recognise
the importance of the quality and quantity of adult education
available for their citizens and to use to the utmost such powers as
they possess to stimulate the provision of more and better work.[5]

The local authorities have only slowly, haphazardly and under the
promptings of the central government developed their provision
for the education of adults. Their first formal, if token, involvement in the field dates from 1889 and the passing of the Technical
Instruction Act, which empowered County and Borough Councils
to appoint Boards for the provision of technical instruction. A
second act, the Local Taxation Act of 1890, authorised them to
devote part of a new tax on spirits to educational purposes within
the framework of technical instruction. In practice, this meant
arranging some evening classes for those who had left school.

It was, however, under the terms of the famous Education Act
of 1902 that the government first squarely laid the responsibility
for adult education upon local administrations. The old School
Boards, set up in 1870, were abolished and replaced by Local
Education Authorities, the L.E.A.s, with powers in relation to
post-school education as well as to elementary and technical
instruction. In practice, the L.E.A.s paid almost no heed to the
education of adults until after the first world war. Nevertheless,
as the Ashby Committee would long after point out, the sphere
of Further Education, which was thought to embrace adult
education, was already defined by statute as an L.E.A. responsibility at a time when the W.E.A. was not yet even a lusty infant.
Moreover, had certain Draft Regulations prepared in 1917 been
enforced, they would have made that responsibility explicit by
obliging the voluntary bodies to seek such financial aid as they
required not from the Board of Education but from the L.E.A.s.

Although strongly opposed to voluntary bodies having to obtain
grants from the L.E.A.s, the Committee that prepared the *1919
Report* clearly indicated that the L.E.A.s should treat adult education 'as an integral part of their activities'. The Report recommended that L.E.A.s should:

1. develop non-vocational institutes as evening centres for

humane studies but concentrate upon social and recreational activities;

2. give financial aid to universities and voluntary bodies;
3. help to set up area Adult Education Committees for the provision of non-university and non-vocational adult classes.

Few L.E.A.s adopted these recommendations and in the event, with notable exceptions such as the London County Council and the West Riding, the L.E.A.s did not, between the wars, make a direct contribution of any substance to adult education. A majority gave very limited financial support to the Responsible Bodies; some assisted such voluntary bodies as the Women's Institutes and the Rural Community Councils, whose work did not fall within the terms of the Board of Education's Regulations. Almost none made full-time staff appointments or thought to provide special accommodation. The one praiseworthy trend was in the provision of recreational facilities and classes in physical education and handicrafts.[6]

The passing of the 1944 Education Act, however, appeared to make it difficult for any L.E.A. to shirk full responsibility for the education of adults. Whereas previously L.E.A.s had been given only enabling powers, they now found themselves statutorily obliged to ensure that facilities for adult education were made available. Section 41 of the Act contained this injunction:

> ... it shall be the duty of every local authority to secure the provision for their area of adequate facilities for further education, that is to say: (a) full-time and part-time education for persons over compulsory school age; and (b) leisure-time occupation, in such organised cultural training and recreational activities as are suited to their requirements, for any persons over compulsory school age who are able and willing to profit by the facilities provided for that purpose.

Section 42 required Local Authorities to draw up a scheme for further education. And the famous Pamphlet No. 8, *Further Education* (1947)[7], indicated what the first priority was to be: 'The immediate task of the authorities in regard to further education is to assume leadership in the co-operative enterprises of community education'. Moreover, in 1945 the Adult Education Regulations were incorporated in the Further Education Regulations, thereby making it difficult for L.E.A.s to separate the provision of adult education from their traditional sphere of operations or liberal studies from non-liberal studies.[8] At the same time, care was taken to ensure that the L.E.A.s would build upon existing foundations by consulting with and extending assistance to the Responsible Bodies and voluntary agencies rather than seeking to assimilate their type of work. Indeed, it is frequently stressed that L.E.A.s can discharge their duties by ensuring that adequate facilities are made available; they are not required to make direct provision.

The L.E.A.s carry out their duties in accordance with ministerial policy but with a large measure of latitude. They act through education committees, which in turn usually appoint sub-committees, and have three major sources of income: first, they receive from the D.E.S. a block grant representing slightly more than 60% of their total expenditure on education, a sum which they may apportion as they wish; secondly, they may borrow; thirdly, they may determine the allocation for education to be levied from the rates. In addition, they can also recover some parts of their expenditure as, for example, their outlay on education in prisons. The L.E.A.s also recoup a small percentage of their costs by charging fees to students, though these are normally low. What proportion of its income an L.E.A. effectively spends on Adult Education is a matter for its own discretion.

In 1953 the Ashby Report affirmed: 'It is clear from the evidence that the main burden for providing liberal adult education in England and Wales has been assumed by the universities and university colleges'.[9] That statement is scarcely tenable fourteen years later, for the 163 local education authorities have meanwhile outstripped the universities in terms of the sheer amount of liberal adult education which they directly provide, chiefly in their own establishments. Moreover, if they do no more than maintain their expansion at the same rate as during the past five years, they will soon surpass all other agencies put together in the volume, if not the quality, of their activities in liberal adult education. On 1 November 1967, 1,419,765 people were attending evening institutes alone apart from other establishments in which non-vocational classes were held.[10] A substantial number of these students were engaged in vocational work or classes in recreational activities or crafts but at least 200,000 were studying subjects traditionally associated with liberal adult education. This is discounting the extra-mural work carried out by the various F.E. establishments.

Yet these high attendance figures must not be allowed to obscure the fact that progress since the 1944 Act has been sporadic. By and large L.E.A.s are still not doing nearly enough for adult education. Too many of them continue to regard it as a dispensable tail of the educational system and are content to make do with expedients. If Further Education sub-committees are common, Adult Education sub-committees are few and far between. The percentage of the total adult population attending L.E.A. sponsored classes is still comparatively small, much of the work is of low quality, the accommodation is often squalid, and both administrative and teaching duties are often undertaken by people devoid of skill or enthusiasm. Any complacency is quickly dispelled by comparing the quality and amount of the present provision with that which may be found in the Austrian Volkshochschule or the programmes arranged by some of the public school systems in the United States.

There are so many local authorities and such a maze of different traditions. Hence the confusion about aims and the paucity of evidence about what is going on. So much depends upon personalities, the social philosophies of local councillors, the composition of education committees, and the predilections of chief education officers. Even the most sympathetic officials have found themselves hard put since the War to ignore the insistent demands of full-time education. Nor is it easy to blame elected councillors for concentrating upon the needs of children when besieged by worried parents who want more and better schools. Problems also vary with the size of the Authority. Still, when all such allowances have been made, it is remarkable that during the last four or five years, mainly in response to an administrative memorandum issued by the D.E.S. in 1963, some authorities should have been able to do a great deal for adult education whereas the majority have failed to conform with the spirit of the 1944 Act. Is the difference explained by the fact that some authorities are willing to lead public opinion while others fear to advance too far ahead of it? In the planning of the new town at Dawley in Shropshire, for example, provision for adult education was made from the outset.

To assess the concern for adult education of a given local education authority it is sufficient to apply four tests: How much do they spend per head of the population? Are they trying to provide suitable accommodation? Have they appointed a special administrative department? To what extent do they subsidise the work of the Responsible Bodies?

Little factual evidence is available about the expenditure of local education authorities on adult education and, indeed, the only serious attempt to work out a national estimate was made many years ago by Mr Edward Hutchinson, Secretary of the National Institute of Adult Education. In any case, since the L.E.A.s do not have a uniform method for estimating their expenditure on adult education it is difficult to make valid comparisons. Nevertheless, administrators in the adult education field have a fairly shrewd idea of what the position is. Broadly speaking, L.E.A.s may be divided into three kinds: those which allocate a substantial sum of money; others which make a small regular allocation; thirdly, those which evidently consider expenditure on adult education a waste of their ratepayers' money and therefore allocate no more than a nominal sum. Most authorities fall into the middle group, the other two groups being more or less equal minorities.

Some idea of the difficulty of ascertaining how much the local authorities annually expend on all forms of adult education is revealed by the following misleading statistics for annual expenditure per inhabitant furnished in 1957 by four of the most progressive authorities to a European inquiry:

London County Council ..		5s.	5d.
Glamorgan County Council		3s.	6d.
Borough of Chesterfield ..	£1	11s.	5d.
Borough of Leicester ..		2s.	0d.

Glamorgan County Council added some additional information:

The income in the year 1956–57 amounted to about £14,960,000 (£11,820,000 in Government Grants and £3,140,000 contribution from the municipalities), or £20 5s. per person of the population. Expenditure for adult educational purposes is £83,400 in which amount are included: courses and lectures provided by the Glamorgan County Council, the Glamorgan Summer School, Extra-Mural Classes, libraries and assistance to voluntary adult organisations. This is approximately 2s. per person of the population.[11]

It is hard to believe that Chesterfield spent fifteen times more per head of the population than Leicester. Additional information supplied by Glamorgan County Council would seem to show that their calculations left out expenditure on courses and lectures in evening institutes.

Up-to-date information about expenditure on adult education is available from two authorities which are widely regarded as being among the most progressive in the country, namely, the Inner London Education Authority and the City of Leicester. The Education Officer for the Inner London Education Authority provides the following figures:

(a) Approximate expenditure on adult education per head of population:
   (i) 1957–58 = 7s. 10d.
   (ii) 1967–68 = 16s. 6d.

(b) Expenditure on adult education as a portion of expenditure on education as a whole:
   (i) 1957–58 = 2·9%
   (ii) 1967–68 = 2·7%

This represents a percentage fall in adult education's share of the total education budget, but more than one hundred per cent increase in actual expenditure per head of population over the last ten years.

For the City of Leicester two statements are included in order to show the remarkable advance made between 1963 and 1966 in terms not only of the total expenditure but also of the percentage expenditure per head of population.

Fairly reliable information about whether or not L.E.A.s have furnished special accommodation for adult education can be derived from the Annual Directory published by the National Institute of Adult Education. From the figures recorded in the 1968 edition it would appear that 70 out of 163 authorities have now done so (1966–44). However, an aggregate of 288 separate institutions for the whole country, excluding Inner London, is hardly impressive. Furthermore, the accommodation provided may range from independent purpose-built centres and wings of new schools to old school premises perfunctorily adapted for adult use.

Population 1962–63 = 272,500

	Expd. £	Per head Pop. £	Income £	Per head Pop. £	Net £	Per head Pop. £
Evening Institutes	56,078	0·2058	21,946	0·0805	34,132	0·1253
Adult Education Centre	11,053	0·0406	6,415	0·0235	4,638	0·0170
Central Institute	35,707	0·1310	22,624	0·0830	13,083	0·0480
Other forms of further education:						
Grants to Educational bodies and institutions	4,331	0·0159	—	—	4,331	0·0159
Payments to other authorities	4,737	0·0174	—	—	4,737	0·0174
Facilities for recreation and social and physical training:						
Youth centres	33,903	0·1244	1,930	0·0071	31,973	0·1173
Assistance to youth organisations	43,123	0·0338	—	—	9,220	0·0338
Community Centres	23,678	0·0869	5,455	0·0200	18,223	0·0669

Excluding grants to the Youth Service, this gives a net expenditure of £79,184 or approximately 7s. 3d. per head of population, denoting a very substantial increase over previous years.

Population 1965–66 = 270,000

	Expd. £	Per head Pop. £	Income £	Per head Pop. £	Net £	Per head Pop. £
Further Education Centres (Evening Institutes)	85,950	0·3219	33,702	0·1262	52,248	0·1957
Adult Education Centre	28,050	0·1050	10,946	0·0410	17,104	0·0640
General Institute	49,346	0·1848	35,342	0·1324	14,004	0·0524
Other forms of further education:						
Grants to educational bodies and institutions	5,122	0·0192	—	—	5,122	0·0192
Payments to other authorities	30,541	0·1144	—	—	30,541	0·1144
Facilities for recreation and social and physical training:						
Youth Centres and assistance to youth organisations	78,652	0·1945	5,921	0·0222	72,731	0·2723
Community Centres	26,817	0·1004	5,823	0·0218	20,994	0·0786

This gives a net expenditure of £140,713 or approximately 10s. 6d. per head of population, an increase of 45% in three years.

From the 1968 edition of the Directory it can also be seen that out of 62 county councils, 82 county boroughs, and 19 London boroughs, 92 authorities (1966–65) have appointed one or two officers with special responsibility for adult education, and 76 authorities (1966–57) have appointed full-time teaching and organising staff. It is not at all clear, however, what are the precise duties of these officers and how many of them are concerned exclusively with Further Education in the formal sense. Nevertheless, it is encouraging that on a national reckoning the number of full-time appointments involving at least some responsibility for adult education had reached 1,163* by 1968, a striking improvement within a few years. A number of L.E.A.s are also seconding staff to long- as well as to short-term training courses and meanwhile paying their full salaries.

In subsidising the work of Responsible Bodies there is a wide variety of practice. A few authorities make grants towards both teaching and administrative costs, sometimes on the basis of class enrolments; the great majority contribute modest sums; and several authorities contribute not one penny. It may be, of course, that a few of the niggardly L.E.A.s consider that they make all the necessary provision out of their own resources.

Local Education Authorities can serve the interests of adult education in many different ways. Some ways are plainly more appropriate in some areas than in others—there is no need for uniformity. Their participation can be both direct and indirect. The following is an attempt to devise a form of classification:

(*a*) *Direct Provision*

    (i) All authorities   Evening Institutes
                                 Non-vocational and vocational Education in Technical Colleges, Colleges of Art and other establishments.
    (ii) Some authorities   Short-term Residential Colleges
                                 Colleges of Further or Adult Education (some of which

---

* This total is surprisingly high in view of the fact that the total for 1966 was only 306. It is very doubtful that the improvement has been so spectacular unless L.E.A.s are now using new criteria for describing full-time appointments.

have now set up 'extra-mural departments'.)
Adult Education Centres
Educational facilities in Mental Homes, Hospitals and Prisons
Special courses, e.g. the Glamorgan County Council's Summer School.

(iii) Inner London Education
Authority   Literary Institutes

(iv) Cambridge, Cumberland, Derbyshire and Leicestershire County Councils Community Colleges
Village Colleges or similar institutions.

(b) *Indirect Provision*

L.E.A.s may assist adult education in these ways:

(i) through grants to the Responsible Bodies;

(ii) through grants to such voluntary agencies as the Co-operative Guilds and Women's Institutes;

(iii) through grants to students for payment of fees or full maintenance;

(iv) through grants to such auxiliaries as Museums, Art Galleries and Libraries;

(v) through special purpose grants, e.g. to Arts Festivals;

(vi) by maintaining or helping to maintain community centres and village halls;

(vii) by maintaining or helping to maintain short-term residential colleges;

(viii) by providing teachers for voluntary bodies;

(ix) by appointing organisers to assist voluntary bodies;

(x) by subsidising the publicity arrangements of various bodies;

(xi) by providing accommodation to organisations free of charge or for a modest hiring fee;

(xii) by publicising the programmes of voluntary associations and the Responsible Bodies;

(xiii) 'by ensuring close working arrangements with the universities and other responsible bodies in regard to the provision of what are here described as courses in liberal studies';

(xiv) 'by exercising general initiative within the community through conferences, training courses, and publicity, for educational progress; and in other ways focusing attention on particular problems or new developments, and providing a forum at which local interests in these problems and support for these developments can be enlisted and directed'.[12]

Some of these functions, maintaining a residential college, for example, may be carried out by a consortium of L.E.A.s. They may also agree to take in one another's students.

The essential point, however, is that most L.E.A.s continue to sell adult education short. Elected councillors and full-time officials should cease regarding it as unimportant and fulfilling their obligations by makeshift arrangements. Rather they should treat it as essential a part of the educational services as vocational training, the need for which they can easily appreciate, and take a positive lead in subsidising and co-ordinating all the adult educational activities within their areas. Above all, they should provide many more full-time staff and appropriate accommodation. Far too much adult education is carried on in unsuitable premises or as a negligible part of the programmes of further education establishments such as technical colleges. Local authorities are not obliged to build or to set aside separate premises, although this may often be desirable. On the contrary, there is much to be said for ending the divorce between liberal and technical education by housing all forms of education designed for adults in a single multi-purpose establishment. But one way or another the accommodation ought to be provided.

Whatever the present shortcomings of the L.E.A.s the fact remains that they are bound to dominate the field of adult education. It is they who command large resources, they who hold nearly all the purse strings, they who can perceive the educational needs of communities as a whole. There can be no significant progress on a broad front unless they take the initiative, appoint the necessary staff and furnish the necessary accommodation, equipment and finance. It is encouraging to note that a growing number of L.E.A.s are beginning to assume the leadership in adult education that was several times vainly conferred upon them in the past, not only by aiding voluntary bodies but also by providing ever more facilities on their own account. From being indifferent spectators or negligent patrons they have changed into being the main direct providers of adult education. What is required now is that the great majority still offering an inadequate service should follow the lead of those few enlightened L.E.A.s which treat the education of adults as a priority and apply energy and imagination to its development.

The purpose of this section has been to present a theoretical framework for describing the role of the L.E.A.s in adult education. What facilities they directly provide are discussed in the next chapter.

REFERENCES

1. *Education Act*, 1944.
2. Further Education: the scope and content of its opportunities under the Education Act, 1944. *Pamphlet No. 8* (H.M.S.O., 1947).
3. Cf. Ministry of Education, *Annual Report* (1949).
4. *Crisis in Adult Education* (1964).
5. Cf. W. G. Stone, *Local Authorities and Adult Education: report prepared for the Rome Congress, September 26–October 1, 1955* (The Hague, 1955), p. 15.
6. Cf. Paper No. 9 (1929) and Paper No. 11 of the Adult Education Committee of the Board of Education.
7. See Ministry of Education Circular No. 133, Schemes of Further Education and Plans for County Colleges, 19 March 1947.
8. Cf. Ministry of Education Circular 61, Revised Regulations for Further Education, 9 August 1945.
9. *The Organisation and Finance of Adult Education in England and Wales* (H.M.S.O., 1954), p. 37.
10. *Education in 1966*, p. 78.
11. *The Concern of Local Authorities with Adult Education and Sport* (International Union of Local Authorities, The Hague, 1960), p. 19. The figures were actually recorded in dollars.
12. Cf. *Pamphlet No. 8—Further Education*, paragraph 93.

Chapter Three

EVENING INSTITUTES AND
ADULT CENTRES

In the past adult classes rarely had a home of their own. They were held in any kind of borrowed premises that chanced to be available and there was, no doubt, some virtue in conquering physical discomfort and ignoring ugly surroundings. Nowadays, however, when people go out from their homes they expect to feel comfortable and to like what they see around them. At the same time there is also a strong desire on the part of many administrators and educators to encourage and foster more than mere attendance at classes by involving people in a communal enterprise and relating education to community needs. The trend is, therefore, to provide for the education of adults in recognisable centres built especially for their use or adapted to meet their needs. These centres are of various kinds and bear many different titles. In a single city nearly all types may be represented.

i. *Evening Institutes*

[the evening institute] appears in various forms in different parts of the country, and, lacking a clear aim and pattern of organisation, it presents no clear image to the public.

So, sadly but accurately, commented the author[1] of the first comprehensive historical account of evening institutes. The very name is misleading since it refers not to a building but to a programme of classes. It has been the fate of evening institutes to serve as depositories for any branch of post-school education not being provided by a special agency. At intervals their functions have been modified arbitrarily in the light of new demands. Concerned at first only with remedial education for illiterate adults, they soon became responsible for the vocational training of young people after leaving school and for domestic subjects for girls. During the last war, however, there was a striking expansion in their range of work as they began to offer facilities for recreational activities and craft subjects as well as a few courses in liberal studies, always for a nominal student's fee. Education officials also began to have new ideas about their potential uses.

Since the war the D.E.S. has adopted a policy of gradually transferring all vocational work from the evening institutes to such special institutions as commercial and technical colleges. Its long-term plan is to turn the institutes into exclusively non-vocational centres offering a mixed programme of liberal studies, arts and crafts, and physical recreation. The transformation is taking place far more rapidly in some areas than in others, the rate depending not only upon the individual policies of local authorities but also upon the availability of buildings and staff. The present position is that evening institutes* fall into one of three types: a diminishing number given over largely or exclusively to vocational classes; those offering a mixture of vocational and non-vocational classes; those offering non-vocational classes only. The cardinal point is that at least two-thirds of all the non-vocational classes in England and Wales now meet in evening institutes. In other words, whatever their undoubted shortcomings, they are by far the most important providers and are bound to account for any marked rise in student numbers.

A lack of adequate, let alone special, accommodation is ultimately to blame for the unprepossessing public image of evening institutes. The use of the term 'institute' is unintentionally symbolic. Many of them continue to operate in old-fashioned schools where adults are obliged to sit in chairs and at desks designed for children. Others are housed in schools with too few classrooms and amenities to permit experiment and development.[2] There is doubtless no optimum size for an evening institute but it must be big enough to offer a variety of courses and facilities.

Principals often have no proper office and make do in cloakrooms or teachers' common rooms; some have not even the use of a telephone. In some local authority areas the low status of the institutes is demonstrated by the fact that they are never housed in grammar schools. No wonder that many people, particularly those who went to grammar schools, still regard them as places where tough and unintelligent teenagers are struggling to master vocational skills.

A minority of institutes are located in schools built since the last war, very often in newly developed housing estates. Here and there,

* In 1967–68 there were approximately 7,500 evening institutes.

a local authority may also have taken advantage of the D.E.S.'s building allowance for separate adult premises either to attach to new schools a principal's office, a common room, a storage room, a kitchen and so on, or to adapt a block in an old school. Conspicuous in this development are the authorities in Derbyshire, Oxfordshire, Lancashire, Kent, East Yorkshire, Leicestershire, Suffolk, Somerset and Sussex; in September 1968 two new schools with adult wings were opened in Oxfordshire, and all new schools built in Lancashire have an adult wing. One thing is clear: whenever an evening institute is given good accommodation it will flourish—the first enrolment night in a new school in one of the new housing estates always attracts a large and enthusiastic crowd. By the same token wherever accommodation is bad, evening institutes will continue to languish in disrepute.[3]

The staffing arrangements in most evening institutes are unsatisfactory. Though a number of full-time appointments at the Principal level have now been made in London and elsewhere, it is still common practice for the headmaster of a day school or a schoolteacher to take on the secondary task of being an evening institute principal. Indeed, some headmasters like to act as evening institute principals for fear of losing full control of their own schools. Principals apart, very few full-time organising or teaching staff have been appointed anywhere in England and Wales. This is unfortunate since running a large evening institute—that is, an institute dealing with more than 500 students—ought to be an exacting full-time job. What is more, it is a job that calls for enthusiasm and skills not necessarily possessed by day-school headmasters and school teachers; far too many evening institutes are still treated as though they were day schools. If he is to be anything more than a part-time functionary picking up a useful supplement to his regular salary, a principal must care about adult education and know how to appeal to and help adults.

Virtually all classes in evening institutes are conducted by part-time teachers. Some of these hold teacher training certificates; others have had no teacher training of any kind. Very few in either category have attended a special course on teaching adults. As a result much of the teaching in evening institutes is perfunctory and some of it is downright incompetent. Short-term training courses, now being arranged by a number of authorities and by several university extra-mural departments, will make a dent in the problem but scarcely reduce it to manageable proportions. One difficulty about providing more courses is that teaching fees are relatively low. As it is, they discourage good recruits from coming forward; if part-time teachers were required to attend training courses, many would doubtless prefer to give up evening classes altogether. The solution is to raise fees all round or to pay additional fees to those who undergo special training—or, better still, to do both.

Moved by a report on accommodation and staffing prepared by the N.I.A.E.[4] and a subsequent Administrative Memorandum from the D.E.S.[5] arising from it, a number of local authorities have appointed full-time principals, usually having responsibility for a number of evening institutes in a given area. But the criteria on which these appointments are based vary from authority to authority and there is nowhere to turn to for a study of the considerations that should apply in selecting staff. Tentatively, it is suggested that the following experience and qualities should be looked for:

  (i) previous experience of dealing with adults;
  (ii) a genuine interest in people;
  (iii) proven administrative ability;
  (iv) knowledge of the various forms of provision in the adult education field;
  (v) knowledge of the techniques that can be used in teaching adults.

Perhaps even more serious than the handicap of poor accommodation and lack of organising and teaching staff is the frequent absence of any clear purpose. Too many principals would be hard put to explain what they are doing. Very rarely is there any indication that an institute enjoys an existence distinct from the school in which it happens to be housed. Those who wish to attend classes are seldom given advice about what is best for them. Enrolment procedures are often needlessly cumbersome and impersonal. Timetables tend to be rigidly fixed; students arrive at 7.00 p.m. and leave promptly at 9.00 p.m. Classes may be discontinued abruptly when numbers fall below a certain minimum. In short, there is a general failure to design the institutes for students or to relate them to a recognizable adult education movement. This is all the more deplorable since they are better placed than all other agencies to attract adult students in vast numbers. They are so numerous; they do not frighten away those who are conscious of being non-academic; and they need not be hampered by hidebound ideas or traditional practices.

In the eyes of many traditionalists the content of the programmes of evening institutes is superficial and even frivolous. What can be the justification, they ask, for arranging at public expense classes in golf instruction, riding or car maintenance? This sort of question betrays a high-minded and unhelpful attitude, usually deriving from a conviction that only liberal studies justify public expenditure. The fact is that the content of an evening institute programme is usually determined by the economic structure of the neighbourhood in which it is situated. Thus in a low income area the emphasis will be firmly placed upon cookery and dressmaking for women and woodwork for men. In a high income area, on the other hand, art, pottery and foreign language classes may predominate and the percentage of courses in liberal studies may be significant. This response to local demand is surely justified since it is presumably not the function of evening institutes to attract the same constituency as university extra-mural departments and the Workers' Educational Association but to draw in a more popular audience. All the evidence indicates that the level of education attained by evening institute students is much lower than that of students attending Responsible Body classes. In other words, evening institutes introduce to adult education a body of students who would otherwise be lost to it, students who seek 'culture' through social, recreational and practical activities provided for a fee that may be as low as 10s. and is seldom above £2 for twenty meetings or so.

Leaving aside physical recreation and handicrafts, the courses provided by evening institutes, and indeed L.E.A. establishments generally, still seem to differ in three respects from those of the R.B.s:

(1) Their aim tends to be to offer information that is immediately applicable to life, for example, psychology for parenthood or marriage, rather than a study which, almost regardless of subject, is essentially undertaken for its own sake.

(2) There is much greater use of audio-visual teaching aids.

(3) There is usually no expectation that the students will do any private work whereas the R.B.s lay stress upon study by the student.

A frequent criticism of evening institute programmes is that they are uninspired and monotonous. Year after year the same old subjects are advertised in the prospectuses. In some institutes the same group of people may have been attending the same class in dressmaking as long as they can remember. Unless institutes are prepared to offer a variety of subjects and to risk innovations, they will not attract a more socially diversified audience.

A recent detailed study of evening institutes under the control of the Leeds Education Committee permits several useful general-isations.[6] First, they are the most popular form of adult education in the county borough. Secondly, their appeal is predominantly to females, in both juvenile (under 20 years) and the adult age range. Thirdly, among the juveniles the boys are attending predominantly (4 out of 5 of them) for vocational reasons, while the girls, in approximately inverse ratio, are enrolled for recreational activities. As the policy of the Authority to transfer the vocational functions to branch colleges is implemented, the juvenile attendance will tend to decrease in these proportions. Fourthly, the higher socio-economic sections, who are broadly speaking the better educated, are especially interested in the visual arts and studies involving some mental effort. Finally, while the institutes meet a demand for systematic learning to the extent required for mastering a language, they are making little direct provision for liberal studies.

All the signs are that evening institutes are slowly becoming more suitable as adult centres. They are at least beginning to present lively and flexible programmes. Day-time classes are increasing in number, particularly for women, and in some areas experiments are being made with lunch-time classes. As a conse-quence of their improving public image, the institutes are evidently attracting a large and more socially representative clientele. The report of the D.E.S. for 1966–67 revealed that one million four hundred thousand people had attended evening institutes, an increase of over 45,000 from the previous year. Of these, at least three-fifths were in non-vocational classes. This marked an advance in attendance figures of well over 50% from the session 1955–56.

Evening institutes have changed for the better rather more than is commonly supposed. Not only have the facilities been greatly enlarged, there has also been a marked qualitative improvement in some of the courses provided. Nevertheless, if further progress is to be reasonably rapid, certain developments must take place as soon as possible. The very name 'Evening Institute' should be dropped; why not 'Community College', the designation used by Leicestershire County Council? Programmes need to offer more variety and they should be administered more flexibly. Standards of teaching must be raised through an increase in fees to teachers and the widespread introduction of training courses. Full-time principals should be appointed wherever possible and given more autonomy and status. Greater efforts must be made to secure the cooperation and sympathy of school managers and governors as well as school teachers. Daytime classes should be arranged whenever there is a demand for them. Publicity methods must be revolutionised. Attention must be given to social as well as educational services. Students should be given advice about their educational problems and encouraged to feel that they belong to a centre devoted to their interests. Student societies should be encouraged. Particular efforts should be made to interest young people.* The aim, in brief, should be to transform the evening institutes into identifiable adult education and community centres. In two subsequent sections it will be possible to spell out in more detail the situation towards which they should be moving by reference to the achievements of the Educational Centres Association and the City Literary Institute in London.

ii. *Colleges of Further Education*

Since the Second World War the number and variety of further education establishments financed and controlled by the L.E.A.s has multiplied. These establishments go by many names and fulfil many purposes. Some of them exist to train people in one craft or profession only, such as mining or art. A great number, however, are former technical colleges or new establishments that carry out similar functions to the old technical colleges together with a variety of new functions. In short, Colleges of Further Education are commonly treated as maids-of-all-work, that is, centres where all forms of post-school education other than university education may take place. For a time there was a danger that they would

* A point well taken by Leicestershire County Council. See below pp. 282–3.

neglect non-vocational courses altogether, but this danger seems to have been averted following the issue of a government directive enjoining Principals to make proper provision for 'other further education'.

Collectively the Colleges now provide a significant proportion of the L.E.A. contribution to adult education and it may well be that they are the main L.E.A. providers of courses in liberal studies. Besides offering programmes on their own premises, about 10% of the Colleges in the counties also arrange 'extra-mural' courses in schools in their areas.

Several colleges have appointed full-time staff to deal with adult education classes and, indeed, some of them have taken the step of creating what they call departments of extra-mural studies or adult education. But whether full-time staff have been appointed or not, it is usually found on inquiry that a substantial part of a college programme is devoted to non-vocational classes. It is also noteworthy that some Principals take so much for granted their duty to provide such classes that they see no point in distinguishing between their vocational and non-vocational provision. In small towns it seems that Colleges of Further Education will become multi-purpose institutions catering for all forms of post-school education.

iii. *Educational Centres*

We do not refer to Educational Centres[7] *tout court* but to the Educational Centres Movement. The point of this distinction is that those who work in the Centres have never regarded themselves simply as complementing the work of other adult education agencies, but rather as making their own unique contribution.* For some indeed the Centres are by far the most effective of all the institutions concerned with the education of adults.

The first Centres were founded in 1909 and most of the remainder in the 1920's; originally they were known as Educational Settlements. They are not evenly distributed over the country but

* There are a number of institutions outside the Association, however, which are essentially adult education centres, e.g. The Royal Institution, Liverpool; Leeds University has two centres at Bradford and Middlesbrough. See below, pp. 113–114.

have appeared in response to local stimuli: Kent and South Wales, for instance, have been fruitful nurseries. They vary in size and in the nature of their provision. At the present time there are fifty-one Centres belonging to the Educational Centres Association (the E.C.A.) which 'exists to link centres of adult education . . . and to promote the formation of new ones'.[8] Of these, twelve are independent, twenty-nine are controlled by local authorities and four by universities; in addition, there are six residential Centres. In these days of high costs, however, it has become very difficult for Centres to maintain themselves without the support of either an L.E.A. or a university, though they use varied methods of raising funds. Whether financially independent or not, all the Centres lay great store by the right to control their own affairs.

Up to the session 1960–61 the Educational Centres Association was treated officially as a Responsible Body, receiving a grant towards three-quarters of the teaching costs of five of the independent Centres which provided classes on their own initiative. From the session 1961–62, however, although the Department of Education and Science ceased to regard the Association as a Responsible Body, it arranged to pay an annual grant (£2,555 in 1967–68). With this the Association hoped to develop broader educational activities, give more financial help to needy member-centres and continue to provide classes where required. In practice, it gives grants to some of the independent centres towards their general upkeep and for the rest subsidises only those Centres that arrange experimental classes. The Association also organises annual conferences and publishes occasional papers in place of its former News Sheet.

A comprehensive study of the Centres and their work was recently prepared by K. T. Elsdon, H.M.I., himself formerly a warden, in a pamphlet entitled *Centres for Adult Education*.[9] It is not necessary wholly to share his conviction that the Centres are miniature city states to agree with his high assessment of their worth. They are a means of education in community organisation; they can ensure continuity and allow for the presentation of a well-balanced educational programme designed to satisfy a variety of interests. Moreover, by providing a common room and concentrating upon informal group activities they can build up the idea of a centre community, so that attending classes becomes only one of the several attractions to students. But perhaps more than anything else a Centre can identify itself with and operate through the community in whose midst it is located. Mr. Elsdon is emphatic on this point: '. . . the guiding principle must be service to the community, for without this the centre will, sooner or later, cease to exist'.[10] The success of Centres in arousing and holding the enthusiasm of students is borne out by the fact that there is a steady rise in the annual attendance figures. It has also frequently been observed that the volume of work within a given district greatly increases soon after a Centre has been established. At Swarthmore, a Centre in Leeds, for example, the post-war increase has been as follows:

$$
\begin{aligned}
1946\text{--}47 &= 707 \\
1947\text{--}48 &= 1,156 \\
1961\text{--}62 &= 1,756 \\
1966\text{--}67 &= 2,158
\end{aligned}
$$

The normal administrative structure of a Centre is straightforward. In day to day control there is a warden, who may or may not be assisted by a full-time teaching staff. He is advised by and is ultimately responsible to a council, representing the members themselves and local organisations—the L.E.A.s, university extramural departments, the W.E.A. and other bodies. Implicit in the conduct of a Centre is the conviction that in the last resort members should have a large say in the way it is organised and in the planning of its programmes. In practice, it is the warden, needless to say, who usually bears the main responsibility for shaping the programme.

Anyone can belong to a centre by paying a nominal subscription fee. Payment for a particular course of study is fixed at the standard rate set by the providing body; thus, a University tutorial class might cost £1 or £1 5s. As a general rule, however, there is a reduction in the membership fee when students also join a class.

Most courses are provided by the L.E.A.s or the universities, but the Centres also arrange a few lectures and courses on their own account and several of them take W.E.A. classes under their wing. Details of the courses held during the Session 1965–66 are shown on page 63.

In view of their merits there are far too few education centres and those we have suffer from too many handicaps. Accommodation tends to be cramped and not very comfortable and more often

Enrolments and Classes in Centres 1965-66

(The figures in brackets indicate the statistics for the session 1961–62)

Centre	Centre Membership		Class Enrolments		No. of Classes	
Ashby-de-la-Zouch, Ivanhoe Community College	1,323	(1,076)	1,296	(1,265)	89	(83)
Ashford, Associate House	1,150	(339)	975	(419)	57	(24)
Atherton & Tyldesley Adult Education Centre	2,495	(—)	3,518	(—)	189	(—)
Bexley, Adult Education Centre	1,198	(1,150)	1,439	(1,420)	51	(60)
Boston, Pilgrim College	295	(306)	387	(306)	41	(29)
Brighton, Friends Centre	404	(338)	1,430	(1,618)	91	(88)
Bristol, Folk House	1,703	(1,290)	2,236	(1,436)	110	(63)
Twyford House	613	(816)	312	(171)	21	(9)
Broadstairs, Hilderstone House	1,350	(125)	2,128	(1,650)	117	(64)
Bury, Municipal School of Arts and Crafts	2,343	(—)	2,807	(—)	143	(—)
Crayford, Manor House Centre	1,432	(1,160)	2,427	(1,794)	123	(81)
Dartington, Adult Education Centre	440	(339)	553	(412)	27	(20)
Leeds, Swarthmore Education Centre	2,042	(1,756)	2,158	(1,937)	117	(101)
Leicester, Vaughan College	1,383	(1,453)	3,355	(2,695)	151	(121)
Letchworth	255	(290)	440	(86)	22	(6)
London, City Literary Institute	10,692	(—)	25,250	(—)	914	(—)
Loughborough, Quest House	516	(350)	375	(242)	26	(23)
Maryport Educational Settlement	380	(250)	300	(294)	20	(17)
Melbourn Village College	900	(579)	810	(532)	38	(33)
Plymouth, Swarthmore	1,359	(834)	1,871	(1,237)	116	(87)
Pontypool	399	(518)	331	(667)	30	(36)
Richmond Institute of Further Education	5,500	(—)	7,800	(—)	327	(—)
Risca, Educational Settlement	409	(418)	528	(541)	29	(28)
Rugby, Percival Guildhouse	1,627	(230)	604	(536)	34	(30)
Shepshed, Hind Leys Community College	547	(—)	448	(—)	57	(—)
Sidcup	1,110	(715)	1,446	(954)	72	(45)

Centre	Centre Membership		Class Enrolments		No. of Classes	
Swavesey, Village College	854	(760)	500	(650)	38	(34)
Trealaw	1,068	(305)	320	(250)	46	(23)
Trevethin, Community College	627	(—)	723	(—)	42	(—)
Tunbridge Wells	1,527	(709)	1,527	(605)	98	(37)
Walthamstow	864	(723)	1,023	(808)	57	(42)
Whitefield Centre, Lancs.	1,526	(—)	2,708	(—)	120	(—)
Wolverhampton	1,700	(1,500)	2,000	(1,750)	126	(100)
York	1,331	(1,387)	1,655	(1,694)	78	(77)
TOTALS	51,362	(19,716)	75,680	(25,969)	3,617	(1,361)

than not there is a shortage of permanent staff. In their long-term planning every local authority should have it in mind to build a modern Centre and to furnish it with adequate facilities, for there is little question that the surest way of promoting a rapid expansion in adult education is to establish a recognisable focal point in every community.

The key to a flourishing Centre rests with the personality, intellectual interests and business efficiency of its warden. What strikes the observer is that the Centres seem to have been blessed with wardens who had strong ideas and much energy. There is a militancy about the statements and actions of the Educational Centres Association which is no doubt a legacy of the social and religious fervour actuating the founders of the early settlements; some of the Centres in Wales still carry out social work in the community. Evidently the Association feels that whereas so many other agencies are merely lukewarm towards adult education, its own centres are deeply committed. Statements like 'it is not right that an education centre should always remain on the defensive against cinemas and mass amusements' have been commonplace in its annual reports since the last war. It is refreshing to encounter such a vigorous approach.

Today the Centres have reached a critical stage in their evolution. Having lost their religious impulse, they are losing some of their social dynamic as well. Moreover, their claim to a unique position in the adult education field is becoming less valid, for, thanks paradoxically to their own success, their achievements are widely recognised and their methods have been adopted by many other institutions. It is all the more to the credit of wardens that they should have applied some of their energies during recent years to ensuring that the L.E.A.s profit from their experience when planning to expand or improve facilities for adult education. The Educational Centres Association is now engaged in a determined effort to extend its membership to the many other centres that have been instituted within recent years. It deserves to succeed.[11]

iv. *The City Literary Institute*

The Inner London Education Authority (formerly London County Council) has traditionally provided a variety of facilities for adult students. As they claim in their annual prospectus : 'There is something for everyone and everyone over the age of 15 is welcome'. For young people under 21 there are recreational institutes and youth centres. Adults can choose between adult education institutes—for those 'who wish to use their leisure in a pleasant yet purposeful way'—and literary institutes. Literary institutes, as their name implies, are specially designed to satisfy the demand for cultural and intellectual activities. This section is concerned with the best known of them.

In the United Kingdom there is no adult education institution quite like the City Literary Institute. It is unique because of the size of its programme, the great number of its students, the level of its work, the appropriateness of its amenities and the variety of its courses. In the session 1967–68 it attracted no fewer than 10,874 students, a total that becomes even more remarkable when it is noted that the attendance of many students at more than one class raised the figure of enrolments to over 25,000, and that several thousand prospective students had to be turned away, in spite of the fact that there is a large number of daytime, as opposed to evening, classes and that the evening is split up into two sessions. During the same session it provided 996 classes ranging from university tutorials to day-release courses on retirement and courses on stage make-up.

Great care is taken to maintain academic standards. First, six departmental heads play a role very similar to that of a staff tutor in a university extra-mural department, interviewing and guiding part-time staff, vetting syllabuses and book-lists, seeing students and visiting classes. Secondly, applicants for nearly half the classes must be interviewed before enrolment. The purpose of this inter-

c

Statistics for the session 1967-68 were as follows:

Classes	I.L.E.A. Classes		University Extra-Mural Classes			Total
	Open Entry	Selective Entry	Tutorial	Extension	Diploma	
Study Techniques	3	1				4
Fresh Horizons		12				12
English Language and Literature	77	11	2	1	4	95
Drama	23	67				90
Speech and Communication	21	63				84
Archaeology, History, Social Studies	39	3	2		3	47
Retirement	9					9
The Study of London	24					24
Art and Architecture	114	43	2	1	1	161
Music	31	91	1			123
Geology, Geography and Travel	23			1		24
Modern Languages	38	177		4		219
Classical Languages	8	2				10
Philosophy, Psychology and Religion	20	1	2			23
Science	10			8	1	19
Further Education for the Deaf		52				52
	440	523	9	15	9	996

view is not primarily to select students but to clarify the process of self-selection. The interview, sometimes conducted by the Principal, sometimes by a departmental head and sometimes by the class tutor, aims chiefly at explaining carefully to the prospective student just what the class involves and especially what demands it will make upon him. This does not ensure homogeneity, but it does help to identify personal needs and to reduce the variation in student effort.

Providing classes is not the only function of the City Literary Institute. It also serves as an autonomous social and cultural centre where, besides attending classes, students can pursue their special interests in societies, take substantial meals, read, study and meet others socially. It is a place, too, where students are encouraged to express their wishes and run many activities on their own account.

The Principals of the Institute have wisely recognised that a programme of adult education does not touch people and hold their permanent attention if it is merely confined to offering classroom work. In addition, it must enable students to feel personally engaged in a corporate social and intellectual effort. This aim has nothing to do with using adult education as a radical arm of social progress. Nor is it to be confused with the social philosophy of the W.E.A.

Seven factors account for the remarkable success of the City Literary Institute. Some of them apply equally to other adult centres but nowhere else is it possible to find them all interacting simultaneously. They are worth examining, however briefly, because they indicate the kind of ambience in which adult education will prosper.

In the first place, the Inner London Education Authority deserves much credit. Demographic and other circumstances are manifestly in its favour, but this should not be allowed to conceal the fact that it has nearly always keenly supported adult education. After all, it pioneered the Literary Institutes and provided purpose-built premises in 1939, that is, before the post-war boom in adult education began. Now it treats the City Literary Institute with unusual generosity, giving the governing body and the Principal a free hand within wide limits and the means to experiment and innovate boldly.

The second factor, which is fundamental, lies in the spirit of the place. This is based on a recognition that students are individuals and must be made to feel that their individual presence in the Institute is noted and is thought important. There is no other reason, for instance, for writing to absentees than to let them know that someone has noticed that they were not there. In their report on the session 1961-62, the governing body wrote: '. . . however big and crowded the Institute becomes, it loses its purpose if it cannot treat each student as an individual person.' It follows from this aim that the staff should be at all times completely approachable, that everything should be done to make students aware of nearly all the activities going on within the Institute, and that the programme of classes must be flexible enough to respond to changing social conditions and emergent student needs.

The third factor is the tactful use of class secretaries. Every class has a secretary who is expected to be more than the customary cipher. Class secretaries not only look after the register but, assisted by the permanent office staff, keep a close watch on attendance and as diplomatically as possible try to ensure that there is a high level of attendance. The class secretary, usually a woman, also represents the views of her class members to the directing staff. For their part, the directing staff acknowledge her services by being easily and always accessible, by encouraging her to express suggestions and complaints and by assembling all the class secretaries together three times a year in order to discuss common problems, sum up recent progress and outline future developments. The main object is to make the class secretaries, and through them the students, feel that they have a personal stake in the present and future welfare of the City Literary Institute.

The fourth factor is the advisory service to students. This service was established in October 1961 and has been highly successful. Every evening an experienced and well-known member of the staff sits at a conspicuously situated table and deals with student problems. The guidance of these advisers has been particularly valuable in making students aware of the value of linked or related studies.

One of the most striking features of the City Literary Institute is the number and variety of its clubs and societies. For practically every social and cultural activity a society can be found. One society of long standing, L'Amicale, has a membership of 250: the newest societies to be founded are the Russian Club, the medieval section of the Archaeological Society, the Writers' Circle and the Garden Club. The societies are, of course, able to exploit the presence in London of so many distinguished scholars, authors and critics by inviting them to address their meetings.

The sixth factor helping to account for the success of the City Literary Institute is its very size for, paradoxically, the larger an institution, the more it can pay attention to individual needs, the more easily it can provide courses at different levels, and the more successfully it can satisfy abstruse tastes. A large programme also makes possible the employment of advisers and the creation of a more flexible administrative machinery than can be permitted to a small institution.

The seventh and final factor is that the City Literary Institute exists for the sole purpose of dealing with adults. It is designed for adults and suffers from none of the handicaps of the adapted buildings commonly used for adult education.

No one concerned with the City Literary Institute would claim that it is perfect. Obviously it has its shortcomings; for some of the students its function is therapeutic rather than academic. Nevertheless, it is a splendid model and the national range, volume and quality of adult education would soon be extended if every town were to build a similar centre of its own and encourage a similar zest for experiment.

v. *Village Colleges*

The creator of the Village Colleges was Henry Morris, Director of Education for Cambridgeshire (1922-54), who did much during his lifetime for rural education in Britain. The first college was founded in Cambridgeshire at Sawston in 1930 and there are now ten of them. They represent one of the most successful experiments in the recent history of adult education.

Two objects inspired Morris: to arrest the drift from the countryside to the towns and to prevent the decay of rural life. His solution to the problem was to establish colleges designed to serve the needs of children, young people and adults in a dispersed population of about 10,000. He considered it a mistake to try to deal with villages individually and thought that the wisest plan was to bring clusters of them together. 'As the community centre of the neighbourhood the village college would provide for the whole man, and abolish the duality of education and ordinary life.'[12]

The colleges are at once aesthetically pleasing and highly functional. Impington, for example, was designed by Gropius and Fry. The buildings are so organised as to be complete community centres. Every college is intended to serve simultaneously as a secondary school, a social centre, a meeting place for local societies and an adult education centre. Coherence and order are ensured by the appointment of a warden-headmaster, who is ultimately responsible for all the activities that take place inside a college. Apart from the normal school staff, he is assisted by two tutors responsible for further education and for youth work, respectively. The colleges are administered by the L.E.A. and run by boards of governors consisting of parents, adult students, nominees of Cambridge University Extra-Mural Department and representatives of the Cambridge Colleges. At the same time, students are given maximum freedom to conduct their affairs in their own way.

The Village Colleges possess two remarkable virtues. They overcome the problem of how to achieve educational continuity from school to grown-up life and they transcend the barrier normally dividing vocational from non-vocational adult education. A conscious effort is made to bridge the gap between school-leaving and entry into adult courses and activities. Children are taught to regard adult activities as an integral part of the function of the Colleges and in their final year, that is to say at the age of fourteen, they are encouraged to attend adult classes. Their 'out of school' activities take place in the same premises and at the same time as adult activities. The task of a full-time youth tutor is to concentrate upon their special needs and to help ease the transition from school to the adult world.

Vocational and non-vocational classes proceed side by side and there is no feeling that they constitute separate entities. The fact that both vocational and non-vocational students engage in the same recreational and social pursuits and that, both as parents and students, they are accustomed to making regular use of the buildings and amenities no doubt largely explains why there is no sense of conflict. Not the least valuable function of the Village Colleges is to provide a meeting place for societies and clubs, since in small villages facilities for societies and clubs are often difficult to come by or extremely crude. Moreover, through being able to attract members from a fairly wide area, societies are able to exist which could not recruit the necessary numbers or raise adequate funds in a single village.

It would serve no purpose to exaggerate the quality of work undertaken at the Village Colleges. Sustained courses in liberal studies, for example, are exceptional. Nevertheless, to succeed as at Impington in recruiting to classes of any kind about 800 students in a given year out of an adult population of 10,000 is a notable achievement and represents a rate of attendance far above the national average. It is also significant that one-third of the students are under the age of twenty.

A few authorities have followed Cambridge's example by setting up more or less similar colleges of their own. A good example of such a development is the Ivanhoe community centre in Ashby-de-la-Zouch. The counties of Oxford, Cumberland and Monmouth, and the County of Devon from 1967, have also established comparable colleges.[13] But in view of the remarkable success of Cambridgeshire in solving the problem of community education in rural areas, it is disappointing that most of the other rural authorities have not been inspired to adapt the methods used to their own environments.

vi. *The Working Men's College*

Since its foundation in 1854 The Working Men's College in London has enjoyed an honourable history.[14] The conviction of those who founded it was 'that the working man should have the opportunity of acquiring wisdom through education', and this remains the guiding principle. To this day most of the teachers are unpaid, and besides providing courses in liberal studies the College deliberately aims at building character.

The College is independent, occupies spacious premises, and owns its own six-acre playing fields with facilities for bowls, cricket, football, tennis and badminton. There are several common rooms and a library containing over 30,000 volumes. Although the College has substantial capital reserves and can count upon limited support from several private trusts, it nevertheless requires financial support for its annual programme of courses. In the past it used to rely upon a small annual grant from the D.E.S. but this was recently withdrawn. Fortunately, the Inner London Education Authority came to its rescue by giving an annual grant (1967–68— £3,000) without laying down any conditions.

The College runs upward of 100 courses a year, ranging from university diploma courses to G.C.E. Ordinary and Advanced level classes—a recent innovation. The subjects taught include music, film appreciation and practical drama, painting, modelling and calligraphy, practical courses designed for car owners and radio enthusiasts, and modern languages, for which a language laboratory was recently installed. Classes are restricted in size, the usual maximum enrolment being twenty. Recently the amount of 'A' level work has been increased and more students are now seeking admission to a university or to Teacher Training Colleges. Some students proceed to the long-term residential colleges. In addition to its class programme, the College provides meals and a variety of recreational facilities, and houses a number of societies. Students' fees are extremely low.

A decline in the student population since the war seems to have been successfully arrested. The attendance figures for 1961–62 rose to 787, the highest point attained since the end of the war, and then moved upwards again in 1962–63 to 918. There was a temporary fall during the sessions 1964–65 and 1965–66 of G.C.E. classes but this was arrested during the session 1966–67 by the advent of women on equal terms for the first time. During the session 1967–68 the College enrolled a total of 1,677 students, of whom 36% were women. In the session 1965–66 57·4% of the students were under thirty, by contrast with 43·6% in the session 1960. To judge from the statistics about students published by the College itself it would seem that less than half are manual workers. Indeed, if instead of simply classifying students according to their trades, the College classified them according to their job skills, it might well emerge that the proportion of unskilled workers is comparatively negligible.

Until a few years ago the College was an exclusively male preserve. However, women are now admitted as full and equal members. The influx of women has had a remarkable effect upon enrolments: not only have they nearly doubled but more men are also attending. This may be, of course, because there is now a greater range of subjects to choose from. Perhaps, among other things, because of its former attitude towards women, The Working Men's College is still often assumed to be an anachronism. This impression needs to be dispelled. Its programme is an interesting one and in tune with the times.

vii. *Community Associations*

Community Associations are the poor relations of adult education.[15] Educationists, not to speak of local members themselves, rarely ascribe to them an educational purpose, seeing them as exclusively committed to serving a social need. Yet many Associations contrive to offer something more than a focus or a home for social activities, and potentially they can play a dominant role in the education of adults in a given neighbourhood. Certainly the executive of the National Federation of Community Associations and the chief supporters of the movement are firmly convinced that in the widest sense their primary aim is indeed educational. This conviction is shared by sympathetic officials at the Department of Education and Science and in a number of local authorities, for they consider that an Association can educate people in a highly practical way by uniting them in a co-operative social enterprise that is as much concerned with the needs of the community at large as with the needs of its individual members. Thus one of the functions of an Association is to conduct surveys with a view to ascertaining how the life of the community which it serves can be enriched. It is mainly in recognition of such practical exercises in social studies that local authorities usually give financial support to the Associations and very often meet the greater part or all of wardens' salaries. For the same reason, the Department of Education and Science makes an annual grant of around £11,000 to the National Federation of Community Associations.

The first Associations date from 1928. They were developed by a combined effort on the part of the National Council of Social Service, the Educational Centres Association and the British Association of Residential Settlements, and were specially designed to help lessen the adverse effects of unemployment during the depression period. Their founders envisaged them as organisations through which people could learn trades, use their skills in various ways, and gain personal fulfilment from participation in communal activities. Very soon, however, local authorities and other bodies became aware of their potentiality as instruments of community education and furnished support. As a consequence, the movement took a firm hold in some parts of the country and continues to expand. Today its size is impressive. In the United Kingdom approximately 400,000 members belong to approximately 1,750 Associations.[16] Of these Associations 1,000 have their own Centres while the remainder use premises which are either rented or obtained from the Local Education Authorities. School premises are used a great deal.

The National Federation of Community Associations came into being in 1945 as an associated body of the National Council of Social Service. Only 484 of the associations actually belong to it and pay dues, but it serves the needs of all. Its chief functions are to call conferences, to give advice, especially in legal matters, to any association in need of help, and to arrange training courses for voluntary workers wherever they may be required;* refresher courses are also provided for its own professional workers. Three travelling officers are employed to promote new Associations. Other functions are to supply publicity material such as leaflets and booklets, from time to time to publish relevant monographs, and regularly to distribute information sheets. The National Federation is particularly valuable in giving the movement a central focus and in raising the level of work of individual Associations. Like nearly all the voluntary organisations, however, it exists on a shoe-string, its total budget being about £35,000, of which roughly one-third comes from the D.E.S. (Hq. administrative grant for 1967–68=£11,500) and the rest from a combination of grants from the National Council of Social Service and members' subscriptions. It pays such extremely low salaries that, if some devoted workers were not prepared to serve their fellow citizens for a token reward, it would be impossible to recruit suitably qualified staff. As it is, the National Federation is powerless to influence the movement to the extent that it knows to be desirable.

When an Association has control of a centre, it is vital to appoint an efficient and public-spirited warden. At the present time 250 wardens are engaged on a full-time basis, their salaries ranging from £825 to £1,290 if qualified and from £620 to £825 if unqualified; additional payments for longer training or higher qualifications may be paid to wardens undertaking special responsibilities. Wardens are very largely untrained. A specially designed two year training course was introduced in 1963 at Westhill Training College, Birmingham. To begin with the College is training only five wardens a year, but it is hoped, not too optimistically, that the number may be gradually increased.

No figures are available for the exact amount of organised education taking place under the sponsorship of the Associations. There seems no doubt that a minority make little or no provision. These are mainly the older Associations where the outlook is parochial and there is a certain hostility towards *education*. However, the majority do run systematic courses, usually in collaboration with one of the Responsible Bodies but sometimes independently, and all qualify as educational charities. Several wardens consider that to hold classes is essential if an association is to

* Substantial financial assistance for these courses has been provided by the Carnegie United Kingdom Trust.

maintain a sense of purpose. A few, notably the famous centre at Lymington in Hampshire, arrange broadly based and academically advanced programmes. At the same time, to measure the value of an Association in terms of the number of classes it offers would be to fall into the error of assuming that the only valid kind of education is that which is formally organised. In the words of the secretary of the National Federation: 'A Centre is, after all, just a pile of bricks and mortar, which is given a "soul" by the association of human beings who manage and use the buildings.' Too many classes and too much formal organisation could well detract from the communal effort of the Associations. Their educational merit should be assessed in sociological terms.[17]

The chief reason why adult educators ought to be interested in Community Associations is that they are largely dealing with those people who are unlikely to be drawn into the traditional type of classes, that is, with people who are allergic to organised educational programmes. In other words, Community Associations can provide an opportunity for experimenting with new methods of communication and for vastly extending the scope of provision within the adult population. Close links ought to be formed between the established adult education agencies and the Associations.

Every Community Centre ought to have a warden, preferably employed full-time, and every warden ought to be given some training, especially in educational aims and methods. The staff of the National Federation should be immediately increased and much better paid. Where are the funds to come from? Both the D.E.S. and the L.E.A.s ought to give more financial help, for here is a movement with an enormous potential that has scarcely been tapped. It would represent a sound social investment.

Independent centres provide a physical base and a recognisable focus for adult education activities. The country requires more of them. Ultimately we should perhaps aim at having one centre in every area in which there is an adult population of 500 or more. Centres need not always be organised in the same way or be independent of other forms of education. In small towns, Colleges of Further Education or Community Colleges could house all forms of further education; in rural areas, the village college could meet all demands; in large cities, there could be a variety of centres, including university centres. Wherever possible *all* forms of education should be housed under the same roof so as to ensure not only continuity in the educational process but also the most economic use of resources. These features should characterise every type of centre: a full-time staff headed by a warden or principal; independent facilities for social and recreational as well as educational activities; an element of student participation not restricted to the appointment of class secretaries but involving the formation of societies and committees and student representation on the governing body. It goes without saying that centres should also be attractively decorated and well equipped. The days of achievement through gloom are long since past.

REFERENCES

1. H. J. Edwards, *The Evening Institute* (N.I.A.E., 1961).
2. Cf. 'Accommodation and Staffing for Adult Education' in *Adult Education*, Vol. 35, No. 5, January, 1963, pp. 229–312.
3. Cf. Department of Education and Science's own report for 1962 (p. 65): 'The use of even the best school premises, which seldom extended to social and cultural facilities, involved inevitable compromises. The absence of any administrator or organiser with a special responsibility for non-vocational classes also appeared to lead sometimes to poor arrangements for accommodation.'
4. 'Accommodation and Staffing for Adult Education' in *Adult Education* Vol. 35, No. 5, January 1963, pp. 229–312.
5. 6/63 (1963).
6. I. Hanna, 'Adult Education Students' in *Rewley House Papers*, 1965–66, pp. 14–43; see also Mr Hanna's unpublished M.A. thesis (Leeds University Library).
7. Cf. *Annual Report* of the E.C.A. (1956): 'It is claimed that these centres are in fact doing work which is not being done in precisely the same way by any other body'.
8. Cf. the rubric to the report of the Association for the session 1961–62.
9. Published in 1963 jointly by the N.I.A.E. and the Educational Centres Association. See also A. J. Allaway, *The Educational Centres Movement* (1961).
10. *Centres for Adult Education*, p. 9.
11. See H. A. Jones, 'The Centre Idea—Student Participation' in *Adult Education*, Vol. 39, No. 4, pp. 198–208. See also the pamphlet published by the Educational Centres Association in 1967—*The Centre of Adult Education*.

12. H. Morris, *A Memorandum on the Provision of Educational and Social Facilities for the Countryside with special reference to Cambridgeshire* (1929).

13. Cf. for example, J. A. Nettleton and D. J. Moore, *School and Community: Adult Centres in Cumberland Schools* (1967).

14. J. F. C. Harrison, *A History of the Working Men's College 1854–1954* (1954).

15. The object here is to deal with the Community Associations from an educational point of view. For a penetrating assessment of their aims, organisation and problems by a sociologist, see two articles by P. Collison: 'The Community Association Movement in England—Some Statistical Perspectives' in *International Review of Community Development* (No. 10, 1962, pp. 113–18); 'The Community Movement—An Overall View' in *Case Conference* (Vol. 9, No. 10, April 1963, pp. 281–4).

16. Figures supplied by the Secretary of the National Federation.

17. In 1949 the National Council of Social Service published an admirable pamphlet by Harold Marks on the educational value of Community Centres—*Community Associations and Adult Education*.

Chapter Four

RESIDENTIAL COLLEGES

Residential Colleges are of two kinds: long-term and short-term. The long-term colleges are independent and well-established; the short-term colleges are mostly controlled by the L.E.A.s and have been opened since the last war. They are often lumped together in the same context, but their functions are sharply differentiated and it is essential to consider them as two distinct categories.[1]

i. *Long-Term Residential Colleges*

The first long-term residential college, Ruskin, was founded in 1899 and the second, Fircroft, in 1909. The object of their founders was to provide an opportunity for serious-minded working men, whose full-time education had been cut short at an early age, to enjoy the experience and privilege of a sustained period of study and reflection under residential and collegiate conditions.[2] Four more colleges with similar aims were founded after the First World War and there are now altogether six colleges in England and Wales.* Apart from Ruskin and Fircroft these are: Plater College, formerly called the Catholic Workers' College (1921), Coleg Harlech (1927), the Co-operative College (1919), and Hillcroft College (1920).† Fircroft is exclusively for men and Hillcroft for women. The colleges discuss common problems and co-ordinate their policies as necessary through The Residential Colleges Committee.

Though independent voluntary bodies, all except the Co-operative College receive grants from the D.E.S., under the terms of the Further Education (Grant) Regulations, 1959, amounting to 40–50% of their total expenditure. For the session 1966–67 these grants came to £109,771. They also obtain indirect aid from both the L.E.A.s and the trade unions in the form of scholarships

---

* Scotland has one residential college—Newbattle Abbey.

† Excluding such primarily religious establishments as William Temple College and Woodbrooke College.

granted to students for the payment of fees. Fees, currently about £300 a year for British students, are more or less standardised. In order to reduce expenditure and to keep the administrative and domestic staff employed throughout the year, some of the colleges augment their incomes by providing conference facilities and arranging short residential courses during vacations. The colleges are chronically short of funds and would welcome larger grants.

Under the terms of the D.E.S. regulations rendering them eligible for grants, the colleges are expected to offer: 'facilities designed for the liberal education of persons of at least 18 years of age and suitable to be accepted as part of the public provision for further education'. Each of them eschews any intention of providing vocational training. On the contrary, they are concerned to provide a broadly based education for people who feel a strong sense of obligation towards the community. Ruskin College states that one of its aims 'has always been that its students should return to their former occupations and provide voluntary leadership in their local communities'. Again, a clause in its articles of association sums up the aims of Coleg Harlech as: 'to enlarge the vision of its students, to develop their latent capacities for leadership and service, and to stimulate their mental and spiritual growth'. These aspirations are common to all the colleges. At the same time, the dominant motive of the majority of students may well be vocational. Certainly a substantial number of them—perhaps as many as one half—proceed to a university or a training college or an institution offering a social science diploma. Moreover, one needs only to talk to tutors to find that they are not at all discomfited by the increasing strength of this vocational impulse.

Early in 1964 there was a television programme about Coleg Harlech which included interviews with a number of students and staff. A point repeatedly stressed was that industrial workers found their year at the college a most uprooting experience. One after another they said that when they went home during the vacations, they could no longer talk to their 'mates' as equals nor be accepted by them without embarrassment. This may be one reason why so many of the students seek professional outlets at the end of their course.

Each college offers courses of one year's duration; Ruskin,

Coleg Harlech and Plater College also offer courses for two academic years. Students at Ruskin and Plater College may prepare for the Oxford University Diploma in Economics and Political Science; a few are also permitted to prepare for the University Diploma in Public and Social Administration. By acquiring one of these diplomas they can then obtain senior status or exemption from the first public examination if subsequently accepted as students by a college of Oxford University. Students at Ruskin are allowed to attend university lectures and to make use of certain university facilities. Some of the students at the Co-operative College in Loughborough enjoy similar privileges at Nottingham University. Elsewhere, there is the problem of deciding whether or not students should take examinations at all and, if so, what form the examination should take. At Coleg Harlech, where formerly one of the cardinal principles was *not* to prepare students for examinations, students used to be admitted to University Colleges in Wales on the recommendation of the Warden and without any qualifying examination, but the regulations are now being more strictly enforced and many students find it necessary to submit themselves for 'A' level examinations if they wish to enter a university. The tradition at Fircroft is firmly opposed to the whole idea of preparing adult students for an examination, in the belief that this would thwart the essential purpose for which the college exists.

College wardens all feel that the mere fact of living in residence is of enormous benefit to their students, and at least one college discourages students from going home at the weekends in order that they may appreciate to the full the benefits of social and intellectual intercourse. In its prospectus, Fircroft summarises the main advantages of residential study: 'students gain a great deal from a year of residential study. Living together in a close community of widely differing individuals united in a common purpose of learning, they develop a strong sense of fellowship and habits of intelligent co-operation. Freedom from the anxieties of everyday life gives them time to study deeply and to discuss life's basic problems'. The value of residence is further enhanced by the fact that a minority of students in each college come from overseas. Getting to know them personally and learning about customs in their countries is part of the educational experience gained by the British students.

During the session 1967–68, the student numbers ranged from 167 at Ruskin to 40 at Plater College. Coleg Harlech had 101, Hillcroft 53, the Co-operative College 15 (on a one-year course), and Fircroft 50. This gave a total of 426 (men and women) students, the highest figure yet achieved. A small number of these came from overseas, mainly from the Commonwealth. Wardens seem to agree that there is an optimum size for a residential college though they differ as to what that size should be. Ruskin feels it could deal efficiently with 200 students and by 1968 had overshot its intermediate target of 160. The former Warden of Coleg Harlech considered that 120 is the maximum number that can be supervised without sacrificing care and attention for each student. He defined the ideal number of students as that number which the warden can know individually. The Warden of Fircroft College prefers his college to be small and sees the optimum size at about 60. Clearly a college cannot afford to be too small; otherwise overheads per student may become uneconomically high, it will become impossible to provide a full range of subjects, and it may be difficult to supply appropriate recreational and social amenities for the students. Fircroft itself is able to make use of the general services provided by the Selly Oak group of colleges.

The colleges insist that they should have sufficiently large teaching staffs to guarantee close attention to the needs and problems of individual students. As things are, they are finding it difficult to achieve this end. At Coleg Harlech, for instance, the recent increase in student numbers has been so steep as to reduce the staff-student ratio, and more members of staff are undoubtedly required to deal with over 100 students. The present staff is as follows: warden, seven full-time tutors and two part-time tutors. The salary scale for full-time tutors is wisely geared to that of university extra-mural departments in order to ensure the recruitment of men of high ability. Unfortunately, however, several colleges also have an assistant-tutor scale with no machinery for automatic promotion. This makes for insecurity. There is moreover no satisfactory equivalent of the senior staff tutor scale in extra-mural departments and though some wardens themselves receive material emoluments, their salaries are less than generous when weighed against their responsibilities. It is also apparent that, while tutors have long vacations, they may be overworked during term time. In at least one college the basic teaching load is 25 hours per week, excluding private sessions with individual students and miscellaneous duties.

The demand for places in most of the colleges* now exceeds the supply available. At Coleg Harlech a sudden expansion has taken place during recent years—from 50 sessional students eight years ago to more than twice that number today—and there, for the session 1967–68, many applications had to be turned down. For the session 1967–68 Ruskin received 402 *bona fide* applications for 80 places. All this pressure means that the selection process occupies an increasing amount of time and has become a heavy burden.

Students come from a wide variety of occupations and as a rule have left school at either 15 or 16. Their ages range between 20 and 40, with the average at about 28–9 and a few students aged over 40 (one of the Fircroft students in 1966–67 was in fact 65). No formal educational qualifications are required for admission, but the colleges reduce the field by giving preference to candidates who have already attended adult classes and shown evidence of having a social conscience. Fircroft expresses clear preference for those who have already assumed some community responsibilities. The choice of students is further controlled by an interview, an essay and a report on the student's work. Gaining acceptance is still no guarantee that a student will be able to take his place, for he has still to obtain a grant to cover his fees and personal expenditure. And here a difficulty arises, for, as the Warden of Coleg Harlech pointed out in his report for 1962, 'many good students whom we interviewed and accepted were in the event unable to obtain grants and were not in a position to pay for themselves'. The trouble is that while nearly all the L.E.A.s are now generous, a declining number are niggardly and others apply conflicting criteria. Thus whereas some will give grants only to those who wish to prepare for university entrance, others will assist only those who disclaim any interest in obtaining university entrance. The result is that a number of students attend the colleges at great personal sacrifice, and a minority have to pay for themselves;

* Except for Plater College, however. Here there is a lively demand from overseas, but as the Principal complained in his report for 1961–62 (p. 5), 'there is a "paucity" of applications from Catholics in Britain who could make the grade'.

during the session 1966–67 six students at Coleg Harlech were paying for themselves. It is perhaps time for all L.E.A.s automatically to give adequate grants to students who have been awarded places.

Students' motives for attending the colleges are mixed. Many are acutely conscious of the gaps in their education and wish to fill them; others find their lives frustrated and their jobs dull and are seeking an outlet for self-expression. A good number have been stimulated to undertake intensive studies as a result of attending part-time classes, especially classes provided by the Workers' Educational Association. As has been said, some are primarily concerned to get a more satisfying job. But however strong the vocational motive, the colleges take some comfort in the fact that a proportion of students go back to their former walks of life resolved to place their experience at the disposal of the community. In any case, the students who turn to entirely new jobs mostly choose the social services or become teachers.[3] And, until recently at any rate, the adult education movement itself, especially the W.E.A., recruited many of its staff from graduates who had started their recent academic work at the Colleges.

How high are the standards and what is the value of the long-term residential colleges? That the students are expected to work hard is obvious from the most cursory glance through the syllabus and time-table of any one of the colleges. That their grounding is good is equally obvious from the roll-call of their subsequent academic achievements. Many of them reach the level of a student at the end of his first year in a university. Dr J. Blumler, a former Ruskin tutor in social and political theory, has analysed the subsequent careers of students who had attended the colleges between the years 1945 and 1954.* He found that a quarter had obtained good university degrees although the great majority had previously experienced only an elementary education.

The content of syllabuses used to be rooted in social studies. At Ruskin and at Plater College this is still the case. Elsewhere the range has been considerably extended. Fircroft finds time for

---

* Dr Blumler analysed questionnaires supplied by 180 former students of Ruskin who had entered the College during the period 1945–53. Questionnaires were also completed by 199 students from Fircroft, Hillcroft, Coleg Harlech and Plater College (1945–54 entrants).

painting and drama. At Coleg Harlech where they 'feel that the greater the diversity of subjects taken, the greater will be the value of the college', there is an obligatory basic course for all students entitled 'The Twentieth Century', in which a team of tutors conduct a comprehensive survey course on aspects of the twentieth century including ideas, literature, history, economic thought and Welsh Affairs. All the colleges rely a good deal upon tutorials, seminars and frequent essay writing. But however wide the syllabus content may be or whatever the methods adopted, the essential aim of the colleges always remains the same—to turn out informed and socially responsible citizens.

In addition to their normal residential courses, some of the colleges hold summer schools. Ruskin used to run correspondence courses but has now relinquished them to the T.U.C. Coleg Harlech has recently begun to provide correspondence courses in connection with B.B.C. programmes for the teaching of the Welsh language. There were 238 student enrolments during the session 1966–67.

Two criticisms are made of the value of long-term Residential Colleges, the one minor and the other major. The minor criticism is that their students tend to be political activists. This is plainly the view of certain members of the Conservative Party. It is to the credit of these critics, however, that they have not given positive expression to their opposition and, indeed, it was Sir Edward Boyle when Minister of Education who first approved capital grants to the colleges. In any event, there is no evidence that courses in the colleges are not conducted with the strictest regard for objectivity. The author of *The Story of Ruskin* justly observed: 'Its history, and especially that of its former students, affords some support for the idea that it is possible for education to be informed by a strong sense of social purpose while holding firmly to the idea of a disinterested search for truth.' It is also worth adding that the colleges are subject to the same amount of supervision by the Inspectorate as any of the other government-subsidised adult education agencies.

The second and major criticism of the colleges is that with expanding educational opportunities the need for them has diminished and eventually they should disappear altogether. It is almost a platitude to demonstrate the falsity of this suggestion even on statistical grounds. The swelling application figures speak for themselves. No one has more dramatically exposed the fallacy than the Warden of Fircroft, Mr Philip Hopkins. One of his most telling points is that the residential colleges can offer only 400 places in a country where the adult population between the ages of 20 and 45 is 17,000,000; in a given year 'only one in every 42,500 of this total age-group can be granted a place. If we can assume that the past selection-error-rate for these 17 million people was as low as 1% (it was certainly much higher), there is a potential recruitment reserve of 170,000 'under-educated' adults— enough to fill our colleges for well over 400 years.'[4]

The value of the long-term residential colleges is indisputable. They provide a unique opportunity for a second educational chance for those adults who are conscious of a desire to learn, an opportunity which is almost universal in North America. This function is all the more vital in that the public demand for full-time study has been increasing apace since the last war—the more educational opportunities there are, the greater the demand for them. The colleges also help to overcome the problem of what to do with the late developer and how to tap the deep reservoir of underdeveloped talent that still remains in this country despite the expanded provision of full-time education. Knowledge of their existence can also act as a spur to many students in part-time education. In short, we should seriously be considering whether to enlarge the present colleges if they wish to be enlarged and whether to establish a number of new colleges. The existence of many such institutions would go some way towards satisfying the pent-up demand for higher education that has become so grave a national problem.

The future of the colleges has been under discussion of late. All of them submitted evidence to the Robbins Committee on Higher Education, Ruskin preparing a particularly forceful memorandum. The Robbins Committee itself took the point and commented: 'The submissions the colleges have made to us show beyond doubt that there is great demand for their courses. We recommend that consideration should be given to assisting them in the immediate future by capital grants, and also by enabling suitable entrants to obtain adequate financial support during their studies.'[5] Following this recommendation capital grants for extension and development of the order of £400,000 were approved from 1965 on.

SHORT-TERM RESIDENTIAL COLLEGES

AH Alston Hall, Lancs.
AP Attingham Park, Shropshire
AC Avoncroft Coll., Worcs.
BB Battle of Britain Ho., Middx.
BH Belstead House, Suffolk
BM Burton Manor, Cheshire
DE Debden House, Essex
DF Devon Centre for FE, Totnes
DH Dillington House, Somerset
GH Grantley Hall, Yorks.
HR Holly Royde College, Manchester
KC Kingsgate College, Kent
KH Knutson Hall, Northants.

LC Lampton Castle, Durham
MA Missenden Abbey, Bucks.
MP Moorpark College, Surrey
NA Newbattle Abbey, Dalkeith
PM Pendley Manor, Herts.
PH Pendrell Hall, Staffs.
RP Roffey Park Inst., Sussex
UM Urchfont Manor, Wilts.
WA Wansfell Adult College, Essex
WM Wedgwood Memorial Coll., Staffs.
WH Westham House, Warwicks.
WR Wrea Head College

NA

Newcastle
LC
Durham
WR
Scarborough
Ripon
GH
Leeds
AH Manchester
Liverpool
HR
BM Chester
WH
Stoke
Shrewsbury
AP
PH Birmingham
KC
AC Warwick Northampton
WH
Ipswich
BH
PM St. Albans
Oxford HA
DE WA
BB
Devizes
UM Guildford LONDON
MP
KC
Taunton DH
RP
DF

ii. *Short-Term Residential Colleges*

The emergence of short-term residential colleges is a remarkable feature of post-war developments in England and Wales. In 1945 they scarcely existed. Now there are at least 40 of them and they are flourishing. In those colleges sponsored directly or indirectly by the L.E.A.s alone 58,956 students attended 1,774 short courses during the session 1966–67.[6] With the advent of the Industrial Training Act the colleges may well multiply. Public attention was first drawn to their potential value by the advocacy of Sir Richard Livingstone and reports of the outstanding success of the Danish Folk High Schools. Organisers of summer schools and weekend courses had long appreciated their worth. Practical encouragement was then given by the 1944 Act which empowered local authorities to allocate funds for the establishment of colleges. Their subsequent growth has been haphazard and bears no relation to any national pattern. In fact, some local authorities took over country houses which their owners could no longer afford to maintain and then, having considered several possible uses for them, decided to turn them into colleges. It is partly for this reason and partly, too, because the colleges tend to reflect the special interests of their respective governing bodies and wardens that they differ from one another considerably in terms both of organisation and programming.* Some are wholly maintained by L.E.A.s; others are run jointly by L.E.A.s and bodies such as the universities; three are run by university extra-mural departments;[8] and a minority are run by private trusts. Ultimately, however, nearly all of them are dependent upon public funds or the teaching resources of publicly supported bodies. The Department of Education and Science is unwilling to give them direct grants, principally on the ground that they do not provide a nation-wide coverage. Some co-ordination of the work of the colleges is assured through The Conference of Wardens of Short-Term Residential Colleges.

The basic function of a short-term residential college is to provide study courses varying in length from one day up to three

---

* This section is concerned only with those residential colleges which are open to all comers; the Field Studies Centres, religious colleges and managerial training colleges are referred to elsewhere. Neither are those institutions discussed that have mushroomed all over the country where board and lodging are offered for study groups or conferences.

or even five weeks. These courses are concerned with liberal studies and usually have no vocational purpose. They may be designed for specialist groups or for the general public and fall into the following four categories:

(i) *Open Courses:* These are open to the general public at a standard fee.

(ii) *Closed Courses:* These courses are arranged for specialist groups.

(iii) *Outside Courses:* These are courses arranged by external agencies for their own personnel. The college may or may not play a part in planning and conducting the programme.

(iv) *Local Courses:* Some colleges arrange courses for non-residents living in the neighbourhood.

The most popular period for courses is the week-end. This is the time when most people are free and two days is usually the maximum period during which people are prepared to stay away from home. Nevertheless, there is a demand for one-day as well as for longer courses. The five-day (mid-week) course is now quite common and a good number of courses extend over a fortnight. A few colleges also arrange courses lasting up to four or five weeks. More colleges are making a virtue of the weekend habit by arranging a series of linked courses; at Wedgwood full-scale tutorial classes are presented by this means. In nearly all the colleges there are seasonal variations in the pattern of attendance.

The staffing of the colleges is fairly standard. In charge there is a warden assisted by one or more tutors and a bursar on the administrative side; there are very few deputy wardens. The salaries and conditions of wardens are good but those of deputy wardens and tutors compare unfavourably with those of staff tutors in extra-mural departments. Wardens normally have a rent-free house and the staff usually receive material emoluments. In many colleges the permanent staff themselves carry out a good deal of the teaching, some being called upon to do far too much of it. But by and large the bulk of the teaching is done by visiting lecturers; Wedgwood, for example, relies entirely upon visiting staff.

One problem facing the colleges is that wardens and their staffs find difficulty in escaping from the routine of supervision, since they are constantly in contact with students even when they are not actually teaching. There can also be so striking a repetitiveness about their teaching programme that it may require conscious effort to avoid staleness. At least one experienced warden has stated that he regards four years as the maximum period during which a warden or tutor can continue to be effective.

The colleges, which can usually accommodate about 40 students, are costly to run and represent a substantial capital investment. One admits privately to an annual deficit of £17,000, and all of them require greater or lesser subsidies. Since most of them are largely financed out of public funds, there has necessarily to be a good case for justifying their existence. As providers of education, that is, they must be seen to have unique features.

From the need to justify their relatively high expenditure and because, too, they are relatively new and have their critics, the protagonists of residential colleges have been vocal in hailing their special virtues. They like to think they afford the ideal adult education setting, and, echoing Sir Richard Livingstone, that atmosphere is as important as what is taught. Thus, the fact that the colleges are nearly all attractively located and that most of them are architecturally pleasing is an essential part of their function. One warden has observed, '. . . the real contribution of Knuston Hall to adult education lies as much in the quality of residence as in the content of the programme'. Informality is also important. Wardens believe that the colleges enable people with different interests and from different jobs to come together and to get to know each other socially. Hence some colleges attempt to arrange as many long courses as possible, for the longer the course the more participants can shed their inhibitions and profit from an exchange of ideas with other people. There is a feeling, however, that if courses last too long the forces that initially operated favourably on the group may begin to have the opposite effect. The residential college is also seen as a place which because of its amenities and its aesthetic charm can favourably influence newcomers towards adult education as a whole. Moreover some, if not all, of the colleges would claim that they are successful in persuading their students to follow up their week-long or weekend courses by attendance at other adult classes.

One of the strong points in favour of residential colleges is that they can go far towards bridging the classic division between vocational and non-vocational provision. Sometimes through force of circumstances, but more often voluntarily, they have devoted a good part of their programmes to courses designed for those engaged in industry and commerce or have allowed outside organisations to make use of college facilities for conferences or staff training. From such enforced provision, two good results have followed. In the first place, they have been extremely successful in using technical and semi-vocational classes as a launching-pad for the discussion of human and social problems. In any case, they are able to combine a more or less vocationally oriented programme with leisure time activities designed to humanise and liberalise the attitudes of their students. Nor does it follow that industrial firms insist upon technical courses. This may be inferred from the statement of one warden: 'In our approach to employers we stress the fact that we are not concerned with nor feel any responsibility for technical training and it is possible they receive this information *with relief*.' In the second place, they have learnt the value of running courses designed for industry and liberal studies side by side, especially at weekends. This practice has been remarkably effective in bringing together groups of people who would rarely or never otherwise meet or begin to comprehend each other's point of view. The contribution of some residential colleges towards the study of social problems and the human aspects of management for industry, trade unions and the professions, has been considerable and seems bound to increase as a result of collaboration with the Industrial Training Boards.

In practice, some colleges take their aims much more seriously than others. One reason for this is that a great deal hinges upon the policies and expectations of governing bodies. Another more important reason is that a college inevitably mirrors the energy and enthusiasm of its warden. Wardens shoulder many responsibilities: they must plan the year's programme; they must shape each course; they must administer the whole establishment; they must lecture and be good at public relations; they must be always on call. Thus, what a college achieves and the character it assumes is bound to be determined by them. But beyond this personal factor there are fundamental differences in policy between the colleges. Whereas one group believes in proselytising, another does not. Wedgwood College, for example, on the one hand, sees its provision as 'designed to meet the needs of the area and where possible *to stimulate* new demand both with different groups of people and also in different subjects'. According to Avoncroft, on the other hand, '. . . college staff will promote courses, *if requested*, or co-operate with other bodies in obtaining teaching staff or material for study'. Again whereas some colleges are adult education centres in the widest sense—e.g. Attingham Park, Knuston Hall, Dillington Hall—consciously serving the educational and cultural needs of the whole neighbourhood, others simply concentrate upon their residential function. One further difference is that the subject emphasis changes from place to place. A few colleges offer a high proportion of courses for industrial firms and the trade unions; at Pendrell Hall, for example, they arrange a programme of study groups for industry 'as part of our provision for Adult Education in the Midlands'; at Avoncroft, most weekends are devoted to trade union studies. Other colleges see to it that their programme is centred on liberal subjects whether it is largely designed to meet technical needs or not. Some colleges throw the emphasis very heavily on the side of general studies.*

The colleges usually place no bar upon attendance. According to the Attingham Park prospectus: 'No qualification is needed other than the enthusiasm to take part. The atmosphere is informal and no one need feel discouraged through lack of scholarship.' In practice, it may be that many would-be students are kept away by the comparatively high fees. These are not excessive—usually much less than the realistic economic cost of £3 per student per day—but they are probably prohibitive for some people. The fee for one weekend, for example, is equivalent to one quarter of a manual worker's average weekly wage.

Nevertheless, whereas initially the main problem of the residential colleges was how to attract students, particularly during the middle of the week and during the harsh winter months, there is nowadays usually a surplus of applications, especially when a college is situated fairly near an urban centre.

The striking popularity of the colleges at the weekend is intriguing in view of the fact that administrators in most branches of adult education are constantly told by both staff and students that there is little point in arranging classes on Friday evenings or at any time on Saturdays and Sundays. Evidently there are

* The N.I.A.E. publishes a bi-annual calendar giving details of the courses about to be offered in nearly all the short-time residential courses.

many people who find attending classes during that period a pleasurable and rewarding experience, provided they live in residence.

The demand for places comes from two sources—the general public and special groups. Both sources raise problems. The first problem is concerned with the general public. The colleges can do even less about ensuring minimum standards than most providing bodies. As has been seen, the students are self-selecting except in so far as they are put off by the fees. Moreover, as long as local authorities are giving financial support, they are likely to insist that all rate-payers should be entitled to attend. Unless, therefore, colleges deliberately arrange a programme of high-level or abstruse courses, they are bound to be faced with a wide range of intelligence and interest. One really wants to know how far recruitment (apart from industrial courses) overlaps with recruitment to R.B. classes and how far each college has built up its own stage army that marches round and round.

The second problem is concerned with the necessity of striking a reasonable balance between 'outside bookings' on the one side and non-vocational courses on the other. The colleges are especially in demand by industrial and commercial firms wanting in-service training, and by professional associations anxious to elevate the status and further the specialist skills of their members. Some practitioners consider that each college should concentrate upon a particular demand, whereas others feel that they should offer as wide a range of subjects as possible and cater primarily for the general public. The important thing is that the fundamental aims of the colleges should not be abandoned through falling into the trap of offering what is profitable—and specialist courses usually are—or easily organised. A few colleges undoubtedly concentrate too much upon professional and technical training. Out of 68 courses offered by one L.E.A. college during the session 1961–62, only 21 were open to the general public. To their credit other colleges offer experimental courses at the risk of losing students and firm bookings.

A few other problems are worthy of mention. One is how to ensure that local authorities do not try to use the colleges primarily as training centres for their own employees at the expense of traditional adult education courses. Another problem is not directly within the power of the colleges to solve. It is—in some areas at any rate—how to attract more students sponsored by the trade unions and the W.E.A. so that the clientele will not be drawn exclusively from one socio-economic group. A further problem stems from the fact that plans have to be drawn up on a very long-term basis; major programmes are planned twelve to eighteen months ahead of time. This tends to preclude flexibility, for wardens cannot seize upon a sudden public interest in a topic without disrupting their programmes. The solution is, of course, to free them from the curse of trying to make their colleges pay, so that gaps can be left in the programme to be filled in as late as possible.

But of all the problems confronting the colleges the most serious concerns the value of the type of courses that are offered. The central question is, can short *ad hoc* courses ever serve a deep purpose? Almost inevitably they are bound to be in the nature of introductions to subjects and to skirt gently around difficulties. If one reads through the syllabuses or prospectuses of the colleges, it is apparent that they are largely trying to purvey popular culture. The impression is of the evening institute type of provision rather than of the relatively intensive courses presented by university extra-mural departments and the W.E.A. In an article in the *Times Educational Supplement*, a correspondent suggested one solution to this problem:

> The old idea of the general student must give way to the concept of the student who has recently completed a course of organised study by which he has found his way to the next stage in the journey. . . . There will always be a place for the general discussion of cultural topics, at the level of intelligent conversation but that place may not always be the Adult College.[7]

The colleges might also consider providing longer courses and more linked courses. There is, too, perhaps a case for paying closer attention to the needs and abilities of individual students. When the Open University is launched in 1971, it may be that the colleges will have to face up to this matter. The problem of providing more intensive and sustained study will never be entirely solved, however, unless we are prepared to establish institutions similar to the Danish Folk High Schools—that is to say, institutions able to provide courses of three months' duration or longer.

REFERENCES

1. For a detailed study of both types of Colleges see the unpublished M.A. thesis of L. Speak, Residential Adult Education in Great Britain (Leeds, 1949); see also G. Hunter, *Residential Colleges: Some New Developments in British Adult Education* (1952).
2. Cf. *The Story of Ruskin College* (O.U.P., 1955); *Fircroft, 1905–59,* (1959).
3. Cf. the summary of appointments taken up by Fircroft students in Ministry of Education, *Education Report,* 1962, p. 71.
4. Fircroft College, *Annual Report* (1961–62).
5. *Higher Education: Report of the Robbins Committee* (H.M.S.O., 1963), p. 169.
6. According to a recent report 28 colleges are wholly or partly maintained by L.E.A.s (cf. *Education in Britain,* H.M.S.O., 1966, p. 33).
7. *Times Educational Supplement,* 7 September 1962. Reproduced by permission.

Chapter Five

THE RESPONSIBLE BODIES

The temptation to extol the work of the universities and the Workers' Educational Association, familiarly known as the W.E.A., at the expense of other organisations is a strong one that is not always resisted. By comparison their programmes are much better organised and more purposeful; they employ in the main first-class teachers and provide easily the largest number of serious courses; there is a coherence and sophistication about their work which is not found in that of the majority of local authority institutions; they have been associated with adult education for a long time and have given more thought to devising efficient methods for its provision than any other agencies; they are able to deal boldly and objectively with controversial subjects in the areas of politics, economics and social studies which the L.E.A.s, for example, are inclined to leave severely alone, and in this respect they are quite indispensable; apart from the National Institute of Adult Education, they are incomparably the most reliable spokesmen for the aims and problems of adult education. It is precisely because the universities and the W.E.A. possess these attributes that it is important to emphasise their uniqueness: necessarily they can deal only with small numbers, and their kind of provision is unsuitable for that great section of the population upon which it is hoped adult education will make an increasing impact in the years to come.

Together with the Welsh National Council of Y.M.C.A.s, the university extra-mural departments and the seventeen W.E.A. districts are known as *Responsible Bodies*, a characteristically banal designation first used in the Grant Regulations of 1924. A *Responsible Body* can be either a university or a voluntary body or a joint body consisting of representatives of L.E.A.s, universities and voluntary bodies, which is recognised by the D.E.S. as providing liberal adult education and which is eligible to receive grant-aid for its teaching work. In practice, nearly all the R.B.s are universities or university colleges or W.E.A. districts.

Grants to the *Responsible Bodies* are made under the terms of specific regulations concerning the kinds of courses that may be arranged. The kinds of courses are:

(*a*) tutorial classes, comprising courses provided by a university lasting, unless the Minister otherwise approves, for a period of three educational years, and comprising in each session not less than twenty-four meetings of at least two hours duration;

(*b*) sessional courses, that is courses lasting for one educational year and comprising not less than twenty meetings of at least one-and-a-half hours duration;

(*c*) terminal courses, that is courses comprising not less than ten meetings of at least one-and-a-half hours duration;

(*d*) other courses, comprising meetings other than the above;

(*e*) training courses, that is courses for the training of teachers and lecturers in adult education;

(*f*) residential courses, that is courses involving a period of residence, whether in vacation or at other times.[1]

Following consultation with the appropriate L.E.A.s and other bodies the R.B.s are required to submit their proposals for each session's work along with an estimate of costs; individual courses do not require approval. The grant awarded is restricted to the payment of teaching costs, which may be supported up to 75% of the total outlay;* administrative costs, grants towards which may be obtained from L.E.A.s, must be borne by the R.B.s themselves. Full-time lecturers and tutor-organisers may only be appointed with the consent of the D.E.S., though it is to be noted that the salaries of a number of full-time lecturers in extra-mural departments are now wholly met out of university funds.

During the sessions 1965–66 and 1966–67 attendance at the various courses arranged by the R.B.s under the terms of the regulations was:

			1965–66	1966–67
Tutorial classes	..	..	12,315	12,750
Sessional	..	..	47,200	50,437
Terminal	..	..	17,797	50,180
Residential	..	..	48,970	18,374
Training	..	..	564	721
Other ..	..	..	96,682	103,868
Total ..	..	..	223,528	236,330[2]

* In practice, the grant is rarely paid at the full rate of 75% of teaching costs.

i. *The Universities*

The wider purpose of the university should be to make university learning available to all who seek it and are able to profit by it, wherever they may be and whatever purpose they desire to serve in their own lives and in the larger society. The aim must be to enhance the quality of living and promote social leadership.[3]

Every university and university college in England and Wales, except Reading, which conducts classes only in the town of Reading, and those universities founded since 1963, has a special department to deal with adult education, usually designated the Department of Extra-Mural Studies.* Where there has been a positive orientation towards research in adult education the department may be called simply the Department of Adult Education. Manchester now has both a department of extra-mural studies and a department of adult education under a single head. Cambridge, London and Oxford established committees with full-time officers to organise extra-mural classes before the First World War and most of the other departments were founded between 1920 and 1939; the last to be established was at Keele in 1962. At the present time there are 21 departments, each of which is recognised as a Responsible Body by the Department of Education and Science. In addition, it must be stressed that all universities engage to a greater or lesser extent in extra-mural activities whether or not they choose to formalise them by creating a special extra-mural department. The University of Sussex, for instance, announced in 1968 that it proposed to appoint a Professor of Education, who would also act as Director of the Continuing Education Programme, but not to establish a distinctive adult education or extra-mural department.

The whole of England and Wales is served by one or other of the extra-mural departments, which have agreed among themselves to avoid overlapping. Until recently, Oxford and Cambridge had enclaves scattered throughout the country. Nearly all of these have now been taken over by other universities, but Oxford retains control of Kent and East Sussex. Apart from London, where the University serves the population of the Metropolis and a good part of the Home Counties, the average population served

* Scotland has five departments of extra-mural studies and Northern Ireland has one.

D

is about $2\frac{1}{4}$ millions. The areas of the departments usually correspond approximately with the W.E.A. districts but have little relevance to local government boundaries. In spite of its clumsiness, the system seems to work, but adjustments will certainly be needed as departments increase in number.

Departments differ in size and complexity as well as in the nature of their work. At the same time there is a large degree of institutional conformity. The most common practice is for an Extra-Mural Board to exercise overall control and for sub-committees to deal with specific areas of responsibility. As a rule these will include at least a joint committee for tutorial classes and an extension committee. The Board and its committees normally include representatives of the university staff, the W.E.A., and the local education authorities, the Tutors' Association and other local organisations. Some departments now have a single committee, a practice which may become more common if the decline in tutorial classes should continue.

Departments receive their income from the Department of Education and Science, the local authorities, university funds, and other sources. It is difficult to obtain exact figures for the percentages received from each of these sources, but, as a rough guide, it can be assumed that departments receive approximately half of their total income from the D.E.S., one third from general university funds and one sixth from the L.E.A.s and miscellaneous sources. The D.E.S. contributes about three-quarters of the expenditure upon tutors' salaries, fees and travelling expenses and in return requires that departments should submit programmes of work for approval. For 1967–68 the total grant to all departments from this source was approximately £894,110 as compared with £265,000 in 1951–52 and £71,000 in 1938–39. The trebling of expenditure between 1952 and 1966 has been largely due to straight increases in university salaries and does not reflect a proportionate expansion in the volume of work. The income from L.E.A.s is a variable factor since it depends upon the quirks of local policy. The greater part of the universities' own contributions ultimately comes from the Treasury by way of the University Grants Committee and usually pays for office and some teaching accommodation, administrative charges, including the salaries of administrative and clerical staff, library provision and sometimes computer facilities, printing and publishing as well as other miscellaneous items. The bulk of the income from other sources derives from students' fees, though in fact no serious reliance is placed upon fees, which are economically realistic only in the case of courses that are not grant-aided. The scale of students' fees varies from place to place and from course to course; shorter courses cost relatively more than longer courses; and W.E.A. tutorial and sessional courses tend to cost less than any other courses.[4]

Two representatives of each university are members of the Universities Council for Adult Education, an advisory body set up in 1947 in place of the Universities Extra-Mural Consultative Committee (1926–47). Its functions are to facilitate the exchange of ideas and to co-ordinate policy. The Council has been active during recent years, forming a number of sub-committees and publishing the results of several enquiries, notably a working party report entitled *The Universities and Adult Education* (1961). The Council also holds an annual conference, which may be attended by observers, and publishes an annual report. It has organised a number of national and international conferences and encourages occasional refresher courses for tutors. There is, however, a feeling among tutors that the Council has become insufficiently representative of those who regularly meet students face to face.

In theory, at any rate, the universities regard the provision of a liberal education for adult students 'as a normal and necessary part of their functions'. They recognise, that is, that beyond their obligation to train undergraduates and to prosecute research they have a larger duty to the community. In the event, however, they seem unable to decide whether to embrace adult education wholeheartedly or to reject it, and it would be idle to deny that a considerable number of university teachers have little interest in extra-mural work. Professor Waller once wrote:

> The position has probably long been much as it is now—a few important people in every university fully recognise the significance of extra-mural work; they practically always include the Vice-Chancellor, who is more aware than most people of the public relations aspect of the matter; a large number accept extra-mural departments with mild benevolence; many accept them but rarely give them a thought; while in every university there are probably a few professors who object to them . . .[5]

At the same time, there are administrators employed by the local education authorities who feel that the universities play an arbitrary and increasingly superfluous role in the field of adult education. There is also a surprising amount of resentment in some quarters at what is regarded as their patronising attitude and their failure to adapt their aims and methods to changing social demands. In other words, despite having achieved parity of university status and tenure for their staffs, extra-mural departments have by no means yet achieved parity of esteem within the universities or an unassailable position outside them.

There is no set of canons applying to the conduct of every extra-mural department. However, the following extract from a statement issued jointly by the Association of Chief Education Officers and the Universities Council for Adult Education succinctly summarises the characteristics and functions that are shared in common:

> We are agreed that the universities are in a position to make a distinctive contribution to adult education in virtue of their specialised knowledge, their engagement in original research, their long experience in the adult educational field, and their traditional concern for the humane studies. The manner in which this contribution is made varies according to the local circumstances, and is bound to change with changing social and educational conditions, but from the very beginning of extra-mural teaching it has always included (a) provision for the general cultural education of adults and (b) provision for the special needs of particular professional groups.[6]

To this one may add these common characteristics: high-level teaching; academic detachment; a special concern about maintaining intellectual standards.

The total number of full-time teaching staff employed in extra-mural departments in 1966–67 was 304 including 18 specifically employed to work with H.M. Forces. Some departments have large staffs—Leeds had 33; others are quite small—Leicester had 6. The D.E.S. authorised an increase of 12 in the total of full-time tutors for 1963–64 and there have since been a few more additions, but this has made only a small impression in relation to the actual need. The following table illustrates the changes since 1939–40:

Year	1939–40	1944–45	1946–47	1961–62	1966–67
Full-time tutors	130	119	159	271	304(18)*
Part-time tutors	629	865	1015	2162	5103

* (18) = for Forces work.

In the case of eight departments the head is a Professor, but the remainder are controlled by heads described as 'directors' or, in the case of Oxford and Cambridge, 'secretaries'. In most but not all universities the head of the extra-mural department sits on senate, the academic governing body. The practice of appointing full professors shows some signs of spreading. All the same, the status of a number of directors remains lower than that of heads of internal departments.

In three respects extra-mural departments are at some disadvantage within the universities. First, they are often short of senior administrative staff. Only five departments have deputy directors; for the rest, the normal procedure is for someone designated a senior staff tutor to act in effect as deputy director; a few departments also employ administrative officers. This usually means that directors are so preoccupied with programme planning and routine administration that they have little time for reflection and for initiating, leave alone supervising, research. Several ill effects ensue. For one thing, a director may often be slow to adapt the policies of his department to changing social expectations. For another, it is hard for directors to spare time to ensure that high standards of academic work are being properly maintained. Above all, directors are prevented from pursuing their own private research and from teaching, with the result that they acquire within the universities the reputation of being administrators rather than academics. The second disadvantage is that, in a happily diminishing number of universities, there are fewer opportunities for staff tutors to become senior lecturers and readers than for internal staff. Thirdly, the staff of extra-mural departments sometimes find themselves confined to the periphery of university life; the use of the nomenclature 'staff tutor' rather than 'lecturer' is itself tendentious, and it is not without significance that several departments have recently adopted the style of 'lecturer'.

There is a functional distinction between staff tutors (lecturers) and organising tutors (lecturers). The precise duties of staff tutors vary from department to department but they are commonly required to teach four or more tutorial courses* or their equivalent each year and generally to advise the department in matters pertaining to their special subjects. Organising tutors usually have a

† See below, pp. 105–6.

lighter teaching load than staff tutors, but are required to organise the extra-mural programme in a particular area. Most organising tutors are described as 'Resident Staff Tutors' but some of them do no more than confine their teaching to or arrange their *own* classes within a particular region. The precise duties of an organising staff tutor are predicated by the policy of his department as well as by his own personality and interests. As a rule, however, outside large urban centres the resident tutor is the key person in the extra-mural, if not in the whole adult education, field. For he not only organises classes, he also acts as a university ambassador to the community and often fills the role of intellectual father-figure in the area in which he lives. With the appointment of more organisers by the L.E.A.s his influence may now decline.

Several problems arise from the employment of full-time extra-mural staff. One is the difficulty of appointing suitably qualified staff in such disciplines as sociology and the natural and physical sciences. A second and most important problem is whether a department should carry a small or a large staff. A large staff assures the optimum amount of coverage in terms of subjects and geographical area; staff tutors can be sent where other lecturers will refuse to go; they also guarantee continuity and departmental stability. On the other hand, the demand for a subject is not always consistent and a time may come when it is difficult to find employment for tutors in certain subjects. Moreover, there is much to be said for relying heavily upon the teaching services of internal lecturers, and this presupposes having a small permanent staff. Whatever the policy adopted by a particular department, it must take into account the traditional attitudes of internal staff to extra-mural work as well as long-term trends in the public demand for subjects. It is too risky to appoint a subject specialist just because a demand for his subject has made itself felt. An appointment should be made only when there is convincing evidence that the demand for the subject in question will endure for a long period.

Another problem concerns the duties of staff tutors. Should their work be restricted exclusively to teaching or should they also have administrative and organisational duties? The advantage of sticking to teaching is that the tutor can devote all his time to preparing classes and keeping up with his subject and his research. The disadvantage is that he may well turn into a thoroughgoing subject specialist and either never become or cease to be in any practical sense an adult educationist. Certainly, unlike many of their predecessors, a majority of present-day tutors are not concerned about the aims and problems of adult education as such. There is no conclusive evidence that staff tutors are less engaged than organising tutors but it would seem that the nature of the latter's work is bound to induce a certain sense of commitment. Another point in favour of employing tutors who organise as well as teach is that they provide a pool from which to select suitably qualified recruits for the higher administrative posts. As it is, there is a tendency for directors to be the only members of some departments with a grasp of developments in the broad adult educational field. Whether he organises or not, a staff tutor has to find a way both of giving time to adult education for its own sake and demonstrating that he is a scholar worthy of a university post.

A further problem, which is also a frequent source of controversy, concerns the employment of part-time tutors, who, over the whole country, outnumber full-time tutors by a ratio of seventeen to one. Of the part-time tutors substantially more than half are not members of a university department. Now whereas some extra-mural departments insist that it is essential to employ none but university lecturers for that large part of their programme which cannot be covered by their own full-time staff, other departments consider that the personal qualities and skills in communication called for in teaching adults are sometimes lacking in university lecturers and that sixth form masters, for instance, are often more effective as communicators besides being academically sound. They also point out that there are subjects, such as the Theatre and Fine Arts, that are fitting for extra-mural departments to offer but for which no university lecturers may be available. If the current demand for extra-mural courses is to be met, most departments have no choice but to employ non-university staff.

Obviously, however, the more intimately internal university staff are connected with extra-mural work, the more extra-mural work will receive the moral encouragement and the material support of the universities. Departments should try to ensure, therefore, that a large proportion of their part-time staff are drawn from internal departments. For this reason it is essential to pay realistic fees to part-time lecturers. One curious sidelight on social evolution is that the great teachers associated with the early and virtuous days of the tutorial class movement were paid three or four times as much as lecturers today when the change in value of the pound has been allowed for. At the same time, in fixing the scale of fees the inadequacy as adult tutors of a great many internal lecturers must be squarely recognised.

A. *Courses*

Regulations laid down by the D.E.S. largely dictate the types of courses provided by all the extra-mural departments. Beyond this, it is unsafe to generalise, for departmental policies differ, some laying emphasis upon one activity, some upon another. But, broadly speaking, the kinds of provision may be summarised as follows:

(1) *In collaboration with the W.E.A.*

Tutorial Classes	(two or three sessions of 24 meetings)
Sessional Classes	(one session of 20/24 meetings)
Summer Schools	

(2) *Extension Courses*
   (*a*) Non-Vocational

Tutorial Classes	(two or three sessions of 24 meetings)
Sessional Classes	(one session of 20/24 meetings)
Terminal Classes	(one session of 10/19 meetings)
Short Courses—including week-end schools (2/9 meetings)	
Single Lectures	
Summer Schools	
Residential Courses	
Study Courses	(one to four annual sessions)
Diploma or Certificate Courses	
International Exchanges	

   (*b*) Specialist or Vocational
     Refresher and Postgraduate Courses
     Certificate Courses
     Day Release Courses.

(1) *Courses in Collaboration with the W.E.A.*

For a period of almost forty years up to the end of the Second World War, adult education in England and Wales was dominated by what was in effect a coalition of the W.E.A. and the Universities. Their main aim was social reform, which they sought to achieve by educating working class leaders and by concentrating upon the study of politics, economics and social studies. Virtually all the provision of the extra-mural departments was made through the W.E.A. In 1968, the links between the universities and the W.E.A. are in general palpably weaker than they once were. Although relations in a few districts remain as close as ever, in many collaboration is perfunctory and in one or two districts barely veiled hostility prevails. The fact is that many university extra-mural departments no longer believe it is their main function to promote social emancipation. Nor do they view the W.E.A. as their chief source for the recruitment of students. The joint national body which used to cement the universities and the W.E.A. is now no more. In its place there is a small Standing Joint Consultative Committee.

Tutorial Classes, arranged in conjunction with the W.E.A., which undertakes to recruit students, have traditionally been regarded as the hard core of work in adult education. Before the War they constituted overwhelmingly the greater part of most extra-mural programmes, a principal reason being that the Board of Education provided financial support for that type of class alone. The War led to a recession in numbers from which there was a remarkable recovery which reached a climax in 1951. Since 1954–55 there has been a gradual decline. Yet the tutorial class is likely to remain of central importance so long as the D.E.S. cares to regard it as the staple form of provision.

A tutorial class is confined to liberal studies and normally extends over three sessions, each containing 24 meetings of two hours. In each period the time is usually divided more or less evenly between lecture and discussion, but it is evident that other methods of class work are being increasingly used. No entrance qualifications are required other than an assumed willingness to undertake a long period of sustained and serious study. Nor does the D.E.S. any longer insist upon maximum or minimum enrolments, although in practice departments tend to stay within the range formerly laid down, namely a minimum of 18 students and a maximum of 32 students at starting. Small numbers are essential so as to ensure a close rapport between tutors and students and participation by the students. The classes are entirely non-vocational in intention and there are no examinations. At the same time students are expected to produce written work and to engage in private study.

In theory, the students themselves choose the subjects for tutorial classes. In reality, though a good deal of democracy genuinely informs the planning and conduct of tutorial classes, they are usually laid on by departments in the light of what they think desirable and of the availability of academic staff.

There is no cause to treat the tutorial class as a sacred cow. Even in its vintage years it never quite merited the claims made by its champions and its appeal was always severely limited to a tiny segment of the population. Since the Second World War there has been a relative drop in the level of attendances. It is difficult, too, to avoid the impression that classes are sometimes maintained only by depressing standards and refraining from insistence upon that written work and private reading so often lauded in annual reports. Again, it is questionable whether a course spread over three years is still universally viable in view of the increasing mobility of our society. This fact is obscured by the convention in some districts of allowing additional students to join tutorial classes in the second and third years, and so creating a situation in which it would be possible for a class to proceed apparently satisfactorily to its conclusion with very few of the first year students still attending in the third year. For example, since one third of the original enrolment may be added in the second year, subject to an overall maximum of 32, a class might run as follows and still not infringe the regulations:

	Enrolments			
	Original	Added		
1st year:	21	—	=	21
2nd year:	14	7	=	21
3rd year:	2	7	=	9

The truth is that tutorial classes are splendid at their best but unsatisfactory when kept artificially alive. Moreover, by concentrating their resources upon them extra-mural departments may hamper developments in other directions. The only valid test of the degree of public demand for tutorial classes is for an extra-mural department to offer a programme of mixed courses and not automatically to allocate staff tutors to conduct tutorial classes when a demand is made for their services by W.E.A. branches. Of course, a good tutor will keep a tutorial group together, but he can just as easily and successfully deal with other groups in other types of courses. Tutorial classes ought to be made to compete with other forms of provision. By propping them up universities may neglect other ways of serving both community and individual needs. Nevertheless in certain areas such as London, where the old tradition has remained unbroken, the tutorial classes continue to multiply and to provide adult education of a very high order, even if the students are more 'middle class' than they used to be.

As its name implies, a sessional class is a course of 20 or 24 meetings completed within one academic year. Though sometimes a fourth year continuation of a tutorial class, or a try-out for a full-fledged tutorial course, a sessional is usually an *ad hoc* course. The advantage of sessionals, or the disadvantage as a traditionalist might consider, is that they do not commit either tutors or students for an unduly long period, and their popularity is borne out by the increase in their numbers since the War.

(2) *Extension Courses*

The term extension, as used since the War, appears to mean extra-mural courses provided by university extra-mural departments independently of the W.E.A. In most departments extension courses are now as numerous as W.E.A. tutorial classes or greatly outnumber them. Contrary to widespread belief, extension courses were already rapidly expanding by 1939;[7] it is only the rapidity of their increase since the War which is remarkable. Their main purpose is either to bring adults up to date with the latest developments in subjects taught in the universities or simply to enable students to pursue a liberal interest. Very often they serve in practice as refresher courses for such professional workers as school teachers. Frequently, too, the very choice of a highly specialised subject limits the size of the potential audience. At least one department makes no pretence of serving other than well-educated members of the public and several departments are becoming less and less concerned with students who have little education.

Extension courses may be of any length but the commonest units are as follows:

4–6 weeks; 8–12 weeks; 20 weeks; 3 years or more.

A course of 10–19 weeks is commonly described as a terminal, one of 20 weeks may be variously described as a sessional, a study course, or a certificate course, and a three-year course may be described as a tutorial, study or certificate course.

Opposition to extension courses comes mainly from traditionalists. But there are others who also object to them because they feel that short courses addressed to the general public are too disjointed and superficial to evoke serious thought or study. In fact, there is no evidence that longer courses appeal more strongly to serious students than do shorter ones, and many tutors consider that students attending extension courses are by and large more able academically than those in tutorial classes and just as determined. In any case, the fact must be faced that many members of the public interested in attending extra-mural courses are increasingly unwilling to commit themselves for a prolonged period. There would seem to be an optimum period of attendance for each group of students, and it is the job of the administrators, relying on a combination of hunch and observation, to identify the length of that period and plan courses accordingly.

University tutorials are virtually the same as W.E.A. tutorials except for the obvious difference that they are conducted exclusively by a university. In general, a higher standard of attainment is demanded than in the normal run of tutorial classes.

Study courses may be of two, three or four years' duration and normally consist of about 20 meetings per session. Each year is designed to be self-sufficient and adequately qualified newcomers may join in any year. Private reading, written work, and practical work, if necessary, are obligatory.

Most departments are reluctant to issue diplomas and certificates because they do not wish to be associated with overtly vocational forms of provision. It is doubtful if, in any case, their universities would approve of such awards. One objection is that adult classes ought to be aimed at socially and intellectually heterogeneous groups. With the introduction of awards discrimination would enter in and soon all the less able students would be driven away. Another objection often urged, but not necessarily valid, is that preparation for examinations will put an end to the traditional freedom of adult classes to adjust the syllabus and the progress and pace of the work to the personal needs of the student. In very recent years, however, the opinion has been gaining ground that it is unnecessary to draw a rigid line between certificate courses and non-certificate courses since it is the spirit in which a subject is treated that matters and not the end product.

Several universities have been providing non-vocational certificate courses for some time, particularly London, which has a special administrative section to deal with courses leading up to diplomas and certificates of proficiency. Leeds and Leicester also offer certificates. These certificate courses usually consist of 24 meetings per session, extend over three or four years and include examinations.

In spite of the loud clamour for more places in higher education it is curious that no university outside London has yet offered facilities of any significance for part-time study towards a first degree.* Maybe such courses are alien to the British University tradition and otherwise undesirable, but at least there should be more discussion about them. There is no reason why safeguards could not be introduced to preserve standards.† The universities in general could also afford to be generous by modifying their entrance regulations in order to admit a bigger quota of mature students.

Summer schools are a feature of the adult education tradition and deserve special mention. During recent years they have been undergoing important changes. In the first place they are attracting greater numbers; secondly, they are offering more varied and experimental programmes; and thirdly, they are venturing far afield—large parties of students are now going abroad and at least one department of extra-mural studies organises an annual school in the United States; conversely, the practice is spreading of providing courses in Britain for groups of foreigners.

Perhaps the most significant direction in which extra-mural work has expanded during the last decade has been in the provision of courses either for established professional groups or to meet

* It is doubtful if facilities for part-time study for degrees are offered in more than ten universities, though it is now possible for students to prepare for degrees in numerous Further Education Establishments.

† See below, pp. 226–9, where the plan to launch an Open University is considered.

individual demands for professional qualifications*. Extra-mural departments have been moving in to fill the gaps created in Britain by the absence of sufficient schools of applied sciences, particularly in social studies and public administration. Criminology, for example, has been a subject especially in demand; so also has Child Care. Courses are now arranged for such groups as mental health workers, magistrates, hospital administrators, prison officers, local government officers, and the clergy. Some of this work is pitched at the postgraduate level. Since only a few professional courses are grant-aided by the D.E.S. the great majority are run on realistically economic terms.

Another function of extra-mural departments continues to be the provision of courses in liberal studies for industry and even for technical colleges. Some departments are also arranging courses in the humanities for scientists.

B. *Subjects*

It is often supposed that public interest in subjects is in a permanent state of flux. Statistical evidence does not entirely support this notion. The U.C.A.E. Report for 1959–60 commented as follows upon students' attitudes towards subjects: 'Indeed, the consistency of students' interests year after year, as revealed by the table of subjects studied, suggests either that there exists a peculiarly proper balance of subjects in extra-mural work and that it has been attained, or that students are notably conservative in their concerns, or that the pattern is largely shaped by the availability of tutors.'

There is a wide spectrum of subjects. Since 1945 the weakest section has been that of the Physical, Biological and other Sciences, though there has been a spectacular increase in the number of courses in these subjects. The weakness probably goes even deeper than it appears, for many science classes are addressed to highly specialised groups. Two obstacles hinder expansion of science classes. The first is a shortage of suitably qualified lecturers. Departments find it difficult to secure full-time tutors with adequate academic standing, while internal lecturers often fail to present a subject in an arresting and digestible form. The second obstacle is the lack of public interest. Perhaps this will be remedied

* See below, p. 114.

only when the right topics are dealt with in sufficient quantity. What the right topics are is a matter that departments are now anxiously trying to discover. One university that may well have identified the answer is Bristol, for there during the session 1966–67 the extra-mural department arranged no fewer than 125 science-based courses, 22% of the total number of courses.

Some people merely regret whereas others deplore the relative decline in Social Studies. It is easy to sympathise with their belief that adult education ought to continue to be the instrument of civic and social education that it so clearly was between the wars, but departments must go at least half way towards meeting the demands of their students, and students nowadays are on the whole much more concerned to enrich their own experience or to improve their qualifications than to study for the sake of serving the community. In any case, it is probable that in many fields of social study professional courses such as the London Extra-Mural Diploma in Sociology have superseded the general courses formerly arranged by the R.B.s.

In the session 1966–67 the total number of courses organised in a sample of subjects was as follows: Archaeology and History (1,060); Social Studies (671); English Language and Literature (549); Visual Arts (583); Music (357); Economics including Industrial Relations (407); Physical Sciences (233); Biological Sciences (344); Modern Languages, Literature and Culture (203); International and Commonwealth Affairs (194).

C. *Students*

During the session 1966–67, 126,433 students attended 5,858 courses arranged by university extra-mural departments in England and Wales. These courses broke down into the following categories:

Tutorials	—	694
Sessionals	—	1,828
Residential	—	701
Other Courses	—	2,457
Day Release	—	178

The work of the extra-mural departments has been steadily expanding since the last war and there is no indication of any slackening. Indeed, it can reasonably be claimed that the size of the student population served is determined by the number of academic staff available. The appointment of more staff, particularly of organising tutors, in virtually any department would almost certainly result in an increase in the amount of provision. The steady rate of expansion can be illustrated by the following table:

Number of Courses provided at 5 year intervals from 1939–40*

	Tutorial Classes	Sessional Classes	Terminal Classes 10–19 mtgs.	Classes 3–9 mtgs.	Residential	Total
1939–40	680	349	96	58	–	1,183
1944–45	576	795	130	204	–	1,705
1946–47†	740	938	182	221	–	2,081
1951–52	998	1,270	304	272	–	2,844
1956–57	950	1,479	1,045	821	335	4,630
1961–62	803	1,836	1,258	957	653	5,507
1966–67	694	2,141	1,495	1,406	796	6,532

Though the number of tutorial classes is now on the decline, there are still almost as many as there were in 1939. For the rest, the tendency is towards a gradual or steep increase according to the type of course. If the first and the last years of the War are taken as exceptional and 1946–47 is used as the point of departure, it can be seen that within 20 years the total number of courses has increased by considerably more than 200%. It is to be noted however, that some departments have outdistanced others.

Detailed characteristics of students attending extra-mural classes are discussed in Chapter 15. It will be sufficient at this stage, therefore, to indicate current views about the kinds of students universities ought to deal with. There is no doubt that the chief concern in the past was to aid the educationally underprivileged, and some people both inside and outside the universities are convinced that this primary purpose should remain unaltered. Hence the significance of the arguments for and against the three-year tutorial class. A recent working party report of the

---

* These statistics are for all university extra-mural departments including those in Scotland and Northern Ireland.

† This has been chosen as the first normal year after the war.

U.C.A.E. described this attitude as 'a hangover from 50 years ago when the universities had a guilty conscience about the working class',[9] and in truth the trend towards dealing with the comparatively highly educated seems to be irreversible. As far as actual teaching is entailed, extra-mural departments are surely right to insist that students should aspire to university standards, for it is their task to provide courses at the highest academic level especially now that the L.E.A.'s have enormously increased the number and variety of their programmes. However, to do this at the expense of studying the needs of the whole of society would be tragic, for besides teaching it is the responsibility of extra-mural departments to throw out creative ideas and to give leadership. The education of adults in all its branches would be much the poorer if the universities were to stick religiously to providing high-level courses. It is encouraging, therefore, that several extra-mural departments are playing a crucial part in the provision of day-release courses for industrial workers.*

D. *Other Features*

A remarkable feature of the traditional conduct of adult education has been the conscientious attempt to ensure an adequate book supply for students. Each university extra-mural department usually has a library containing not merely large stocks of books but also collections of audio-visual aids, including tapes and gramophone records. Many departments employ a full-time librarian. Hull University's adult education library contains no fewer than 55,000 volumes, looked after by two librarians. The practice of issuing book-boxes to classes of fairly long duration is widespread and of incalculable educational value. In addition, students sometimes have permission to use the main university library. The contribution made by universities towards supplying books and teaching materials for *bona fide* adult students is seldom given the notice it deserves.

A few departments have controlled their own teaching centres for some time: Nottingham and Leicester have had centres since before 1939; Birmingham and Leeds acquired some after the War. Now Liverpool and Southampton also have their own centres. The conviction that independent and appropriately designed pre-

* See below, pp. 164-5.

mises are essential to the efficient conduct of adult education is taking as firm a hold among universities as it is elsewhere.

The value of residence is equally recognised. Manchester, Cambridge, and Leeds now have their own colleges. With the aid of a large grant from the Kellogg Foundation, Oxford has adapted premises in the centre of the city which enable it to offer a continuous series of high-level courses and conferences. Many departments also share with other bodies control of certain residential colleges in which they arrange regular week-end courses.

Much space has been devoted to the role of the universities in adult education. Necessarily so, since, like it or not, they have tended historically to dominate the field. Despite the rising influence of the L.E.A.s they must surely continue to play a leading part, In the sphere of professional training they are likely to move closer to the American university extension model by arranging ever increasing numbers of specialised courses, conferences and seminars. Not a few will no doubt begin to offer opportunities for part-time degree students. However, perhaps the most important role for university extra-mural departments in the future will be to act as research centres for the study of community problems and the ways in which education may help to solve them, and generally to stimulate the development of adult education as a serious field of knowledge.*

The Universities Council for Adult Education is alive to the need for changing functions. In 1961 it published a detailed and imaginative conspectus of the functions of university extra-mural departments and future trends, the tone of which may be summed up from a brief quotation: 'extra-mural departments must be prepared to experiment boldly with new approaches and techniques.'[10] It is salutary to be reminded, however, that an extra-mural department may well produce admirable development plans and yet fail to implement them for lack of funds. Departments still operate on limited budgets and with a shortage of full-time staff.†

---

* See below chapters 18 and 19.

† In this chapter there has been no attempt to discuss the implications for university extra-mural work of the emergence of a number of new universities. It is clear that if all the new universities elect to have an extra-mural department, a few well-established departments will find their areas drastically reduced and one or two may cease to be viable. There may also be the problem of what to do with surplus staff. Recognising this contingency the U.C.A.E. has taken

ii. *The Workers' Educational Association*

By far the most powerful of the voluntary agencies in the United Kingdom is the Workers' Educational Association, founded in 1903. It both stimulates a demand for and administers classes. Non-sectarian and non-political—despite its tendency to incline leftwards over most political issues—it is fortified by a proud 60-year-old tradition and the firm conviction that it is performing an indispensable service. Its senior officials automatically take their place on adult education committees at the national and the local level. To judge from its annual returns since 1961 a decrease in branch membership during recent years (1966-67—40,000 members) seems to have been temporarily arrested. In any case, the loss in formal membership has been amply offset by an increase in the total number of students attending classes—94,392 in 1959-60, 98,236 in 1960-61, 105,189 in 1961-62, 114,898 in 1963-64, 119,417 in 1964-65 and 124,058* in 1965-66. But in spite of the expansion in its student population the W.E.A. is no longer as robust a force as it was before the Second World War.

Taken at its own pardonably high estimation the W.E.A. is much more than an agency for providing classes. It is a democratic national movement dedicated to improving the condition of society. Its constitution proclaims two objects: '(i) to stimulate and to satisfy the demand of workers for education, and, (ii) generally to further the advancement of education to the end that all children, adolescents and adults may have full opportunities for education, indeed for their complete individual and social development.' It also defines one of its tasks as ensuring that the public is well-informed about all educational matters.

Over the years, the structure of the W.E.A. has undergone little change, but in the wake of a recent report† it appears to be on the verge of a major reformation. At the centre there is a general council consisting of 150 members—three representatives from each district as well as representatives of the trade unions and other bodies. This council elects the national executive. A small permanent secretariat is responsible for general administration.

steps to consult with representatives of the new universities and it now seems unlikely that there will be any friction or need to disrupt the existing pattern.

* These figures include enrolments in Scotland and Northern Ireland.

† See below, pp. 121-2.

England and Wales are parcelled out into seventeen virtually autonomous districts, each of which is governed by a hierarchy of an
annual general meeting, an elected district council and an executive committee. Day-to-day control rests in the hands of a *district
secretary* (17) assisted by one or more *organisers* (14) and—in
most but not all districts—several *tutor organisers* (85).* District
secretaries and organisers are either mainly or exclusively administrators, whereas tutor organisers are called upon to conduct
classes in addition to arranging classes for other tutors. The
districts are divided into branches which enjoy a large measure
of autonomy and which are run entirely on a voluntary basis.
There are about 2,000 branches in England and Wales. Over
2,500 societies and associations are affiliated to the Association at
the national, district and branch level.

The districts are the strong-points of the movement, for in practice the Association is confederal rather than federal in structure.
Indeed, each district is a *Responsible Body* in its own right. It is
this fact which explains why it is treacherous to generalise about
the W.E.A., why a statement founded on observations in one part
of the country is likely to be controverted by evidence adduced
from elsewhere, and why friends and critics of the Association
sometimes appear to be debating at cross-purposes. One example
of the prevailing diversity is the variable status accorded to the
tutorial class from region to region: for example, in the North-East
the tutorial class remains the keystone of the programme whereas
in the North-West it has become relatively unimportant.

The centrifugal tendency of the Association may not be innate,
since the degree of initiative displayed by the national executive
may well determine the degree of independence shown by the
districts. Certainly some members complain that the movement
has lost its erstwhile capacity to make a positive impact on national
affairs and others say they would welcome more guidance and
dynamic leadership from the centre. Outside the W.E.A. there is a
prevalent impression that it is outmoded. It may be, of course, that
it is the critics who are misreading the times and that the national
council and the administrative H.Q. have come to the wise conclusion that the exuberant public activities of its founder, Albert
Mansbridge, and his contemporaries would be out of place today.

---

* The figures in brackets indicate the number of officials employed in each
category in England and Wales.

Not all the districts are vigorous, and ineffective branches may be found everywhere. The picture presented by the W.E.A. is something like this: a national executive and headquarters apparently exercising less drive and authority than in the past; a few energetic and markedly successful districts; some districts holding their own; other districts showing signs of decay; and striking disparities in achievement from branch to branch within the same district.

In recent years the headquarters has been receiving an *ad hoc* annual grant from the D.E.S. towards administrative costs (£3,550 for 1968–69) but it is largely maintained by dues received from the districts. As Responsible Bodies the districts receive a grant of approximately 75% of teaching costs from the D.E.S. and variable subventions from the local authorities towards administrative costs. For the rest, their income is derived from individual membership fees, affiliation fees and miscellaneous grants. The financial position of some districts is healthy but several of them, particularly in the north, are chronically insolvent and hard pressed to meet their share of teaching costs. In 1961 a deputation from the national council asked the then Minister of Education if he would increase their grant. He replied that he could not do so and recommended that they raise their fees. A further vain representation was made in 1963. During the session 1967–68 the total expenditure of the districts was £485,700 (1965–66—£382,419) of which about £230,000 came from the D.E.S. (1965–66—£191,000).

The Association suffers from its inability to pay salaries and provide facilities commensurate with the duties its salaried officers are called upon to perform. A district secretary, for example, receives at his maximum no more than an extra-mural staff tutor at about the middle of the scale. Tutor organisers also receive substantially lower salaries than university staff tutors, and all organisers are badly paid. Comparisons are becoming even more odious as local authorities appoint full-time adult education staff in greater numbers. Although extra-mural staffs and D.E.S. officials may feel that the work of the W.E.A. is at a lower level than extra-mural work, it cannot be denied that outstanding qualities are required in any district secretary who is to do a good job. The paragon of district secretaries must be a good administrator, an accountant, a skilful organiser, a competent speaker, and a personable colleague. He sits on the same committees as directors of education and heads of extra-mural departments and must keep his end up. Men with such many-sided attributes are not easily found nowadays for the same reason that able trade union officials are in short supply, and when found they should not be expected to stay forever in their posts out of a sheer sense of service to the community. If a high level of efficiency is to be attained, much better salaries will have to be paid. The position of the W.E.A. tutor organisers is particularly anomalous because direct comparisons can be made between their salaries and those of university staff tutors. So long as the wide differential is maintained, so long will tutor organisers feel restless and frustrated. And unless quixotically disinterested, they are likely to apply for staff tutorships or L.E.A. posts at the first available opportunity. It is no wonder that the turn-over of teaching staff is rapid.

Apart from organising classes for the general public either in collaboration with the universities or on its own account, the W.E.A. also arranges classes at the specific request of trade union branches, the Co-operative Guilds, Townswomen's Guilds, and other bodies. Twelve types of educational provision made by the W.E.A. may be distinguished:

(1) *With University Extra-Mural Departments*
   (i) Tutorial Courses
   (ii) Sessional Courses
   (iii) Day-Release Courses
   (iv) Other Courses

(2) *Independent W.E.A. Courses*
   (v) One-Year Courses
   (vi) Terminal Courses (10 to 20 meetings)
   (vii) Short Courses (3 to 9 meetings)
   (viii) Summer Schools (occasionally with extra-mural departments)
   (ix) Week-end Schools
   (x) Day Schools (Conferences)
   (xi) Special Schools
   (xii) In-Service Training Courses

The main difference between courses organised in collaboration with the universities and courses organised by the W.E.A. itself is that the former tend to be longer, more intensive and more limited in the range of subjects. In other words, the W.E.A.'s own courses are intended to have a more popular appeal and to be less exacting than those arranged jointly with the universities.

Social Studies still remains the most popular subject, but it is to be borne in mind that it covers virtually five distinct subjects, viz., Political Science and Government, Economics and Economic Problems, Industrial Organisation, Sociology and 'Other Social Studies'. Other popular courses are History, especially Local History, English Language and Literature, Music and the Visual Arts. Science courses account for less than 12% of the total attendance.

As well as maintaining a reasonable quota of Social Studies classes the W.E.A. has steadily extended its range of subjects. Indeed, it is probably true to say that most districts are inclined to provide courses which are known to be fashionable rather than to concentrate upon such traditional topics as economics and political science. In this respect, at any rate, the Association is making a determined effort to act as a consumer organisation.

Only a minority of students attending W.E.A. classes are drawn from the ranks of manual workers and those with little education, a fact that is demonstrated by the W.E.A.'s own annual statistics and borne out by local inquiries.* Undoubtedly, the gravest cause for alarm is the relative failure to serve the interests of the 'educationally under-privileged'. Individual districts and branches try to tackle the problem by sponsoring factory-based and pre-retirement courses, some of which are highly successful, but such efforts are hampered by a lack of funds and a consequent shortage of full-time organisers. A desire to experiment, to depart from a staid, unadventurous programme, is often killed by the knowledge that when an experiment succeeds it may be impossible to capitalise on it for lack of resources. A more serious impediment, however, is the cautious policy of most branches. By and large they are reluctant to try out new courses and have not the time or personnel with which to venture into the factories. Pioneering work in industrial plants has got to be initiated for the most part by the district secretaries themselves, aided by the few organisers or tutor organisers under their control. In this crucial area of provision the W.E.A. is restricted by its tradition of relying upon

* See below p. 243.

voluntary service. Full-time officials cannot dictate to branches; if branches are apathetic or unwilling to experiment there is little district secretaries can do about it.

The W.E.A. is proud of having survived many vicissitudes and of having adapted its programmes to the revolutionary social changes that have occurred since its foundation. And no one is likely to deny that it has served Britain well, particularly in preparing many able men and women for influential roles in public life. Notwithstanding, it has plainly lost its old confidence and it is exposed to fire from many quarters. The criticisms commonly levelled against it are as follows:

(i) It is failing to cope with the needs of the educationally under-privileged while denying itself the opportunity of effectively serving other social groups by clinging to an out-moded title and presenting a public image which is associated with the Labour movement and with dreary 'improving' classes that, as one journalist has put it, 'went out with hunger marches'.

(ii) It is serving the interests of no more than 0·2% of the adult population. Though numbers alone should not be regarded as the measure of an educational movement's success, this is a low percentage for an organisation that claims 'to satisfy the demand of workers for education', especially as, in any case, most of its students can scarcely be described as 'workers'.

(iii) Standards in non-university classes are often low or at least seem to be low.

(iv) Too many branches are inept when it comes to planning programmes and organising committee affairs.

(v) Its public relations and publicity methods are often ineffective.

(vi) A large number of its so-called students know nothing about the aims of the Association, its organisation, history and traditions.

In reply to its critics, it is not sufficient for the W.E.A. to justify its continuing existence on the ground that there must be a voluntary consumer organisation. The relevant question is whether the principal voluntary organisation should or should not be the W.E.A. itself and whether the W.E.A. deserves support from public funds. There are not a few local authority officials for whom it is a superfluous irritant and who feel that the universities and the L.E.A.s between them are more than capable of meeting all possible demands.

Although conceding that its critics have a case to offer, it is difficult to see how the W.E.A. can be replaced without painful strife. There are indications, moreover, that, after several years of taking stock, it may well be on the threshold of a period of reform and expansion. In recent years it has produced several important papers. Its biennial conferences have been informed by a mood of energy, urgency and constructiveness. Nor is it by any means an elderly face that it puts on view. In the ultimate analysis, however, the future of the W.E.A. as a power in the land will depend upon its ability to sustain its oft-repeated claim to be keenly responsive to changing social demands. It must also revive its appeal as a dynamic national movement.

In January 1967 the W.E.A. released details of the findings of a Working Party report 'set up to investigate current practice and to suggest necessary reforms'.[12] The Working Party deliberately chose to make radical proposals of a general character designed to prepare the Association for the future and suggested that in order to develop at the speed and on the scale the times demand the W.E.A. would have to commit itself to:

'(i) translating our sense of social purpose into the language of our time;

(ii) mobilising the full strength of our student body and democratically directing a movement to which they feel they belong and through which they think they can express themselves;

(iii) demonstrating that we have a place of growing importance in a developing educational system, where adult education for mature people becomes more and not less essential as part of a continuing educational process;

(iv) identifying as precisely as possible new centres of opportunity for the W.E.A., and showing that we can respond quickly and enthusiastically to the opportunities;

(v) working alongside our partners, the Department of Education, the universities and the local education authorities, to extend the network and scope of adult education provision;

(vi) demonstrating that we have a valuable development role to play in relation to trade union education in a changing industrial context.'[13]

This statement of requirements is quoted in full because it could scarcely be improved upon. It remains to be seen what will happen in practice. One encouraging sign may be that the Working Party took a cold, hard look at the existing machinery for financing, administering and governing the Association. It also made no bones about recommending the addition of enlarged powers to the national committee and the central office. Earlier in this chapter it was suggested that the basic weakness of the W.E.A. is its 'confederal' structure. If greater influence can be exercised through a strong central executive, the W.E.A. may well again assert itself as a national organisation to be reckoned with.

In addition to the extra-mural departments of the universities and the W.E.A. Districts there is one other Responsible Body, the Welsh National Council of the Y.M.C.A., whose activities are described below on p. 184–5. Some confusion occasionally arises because in the past there were several other R.B.s, including the Educational Centres Association. The last organisation to give up this status was the Cornwall Adult Education Joint Committee, which did so at the end of the session 1965–66. The Cornwall Committee was a consortium of the L.E.A., Exeter University and the South-Western District of the W.E.A.

REFERENCES

1. Cf. Further Education (Grant) Regulations, 1959, Sections 19–20.
2. *Education and Science in 1967* (H.M.S.O.), p. 71.
3. R. Peers, 'The Place of English Universities in Adult Education' in *Jaargang 7* (December 1960), p. 92.
4. For full details cf. S. G. Raybould, *University Extra-Mural Education in England 1945–62: A Study in Finance and Policy* (1964).
5. 'The Universities and Adult Education' in *University Quarterly* (Vol. II, No. 1, November 1956), pp. 43–54.
6. *The Universities and Adult Education*, p. 1.
7. This is clearly brought out by B. W. Pashley in *University Extension Reconsidered* (Leicester, 1968).
8. *U.C.A.E. Report, 1959–60*, p. 9.

9. *The Universities and Adult Education*, p. 16.
10. op. cit., p. 21.
11. This fact began to cause alarm as long ago as 1949. Cf. S. G. Raybould, *The W.E.A.: The Next Phase* (W.E.A., 1949).
12. *Working Party on Structure Organisation and Finance* (1966), p. 9; see also *Action and Advance—the W.E.A. on the March* (The report of the Central Council for 1964–67, presented at the biennial conference of the Association in 1968).
13. *Ibid.*, p. 10.

Chapter Six

THE PUBLIC SERVICES

i. *Education in Her Majesty's Forces*

Of the small percentage of adults in the United Kingdom who are encouraged by their employers to continue their education up to all levels most are to be found in the armed forces. Each service has a full-time education branch; every serviceman is obliged to take part in some form of educational activity up to a certain level; and promotion usually hinges upon passing examinations.

A. *The Army*

'To give soldiers the mental alertness, skill and knowledge which will enable them to play their full part as members of their unit and as members of the community.'[1] Such is the aim of army education according to the official manual. The significant part of this statement is the reference to an obligation to the community, for the army seriously sets out to offer considerably more than vocational military studies.

Although the ultimate responsibility for education lies with the Adjutant General, it is, in fact, the Director of Army Education and the officers of the Royal Army Educational Corps who provide it. The Corps, which is now staffed entirely by officers, maintains close links with the State educational system, especially with the universities and local authorities, and invokes their aid as much as possible.

Army education takes the following forms:*

(i) *Preliminary Education.* This is designed for about 5% of those new recruits who, upon entering the army, need further training in the basic skills of English and Arithmetic. It is carried out at a special School of Preliminary Education, which copes each year with about 780 students.

---

* We are not concerned here, of course, with facilities for the children of service men or with such units as the Gurkhas. Nor is our concern with boys' units though these represent a major and fascinating part of the Corps' work; nor with the training of officers at Sandhurst and Shrivenham.

(ii) *Army Certificates.* All British other ranks who have not obtained several passes in the G.C.E. Examinations are obliged to attend education courses until they have gained at least a second-class certificate of army education. In the first place, they have to obtain the army certificate of education third class. The syllabus for this certificate deals not only with English and Arithmetic but also with what is described as 'Army and Nation (I)'. The latter is virtually social studies and is meant to have two objectives: '(a) to give the recruit a broad picture of what the army comprises and of its part in the defence of Britain and the Commonwealth; (b) to explain the place of Great Britain in the World, its relationship with the Commonwealth and our allies and the consequent effects upon the army's role and deployment.'[2]

Besides instruction in practical and written map reading the army certificate of education second class includes 'Army and Nation (II)'. According to the Royal Army Educational Corps, 'one of the main objectives of this syllabus is to give the soldier a knowledge of and pride in his country's ways and purpose'. Soldiers may rest on their laurels having acquired a second-class certificate, but if they seek warrant officer rank they must proceed to the first-class certificate. For this certificate English is compulsory and it is possible to choose three out of four examination subjects, of which one or two are selected by the soldier's Arm of Service and one is more or less vocational. The remaining subject or subjects are selected by the candidates themselves. Nevertheless, many of the subjects chosen by candidates come within the province of general and humane studies.

(iii) *Further Education.* Beyond providing courses for the first, second and third class certificates, the army offers a wide range of facilities for officers and other ranks who wish to undertake either professional or vocational courses or to pursue a special interest. The main forms of further education are as follows:

(a) *Education Centres.* Army education centres are primarily used for preparing candidates for various examinations, but they also serve as community centres where servicemen and their families can participate in a variety of activities, many of which broadly correspond to those that take place in evening institutes. These centres are especially valuable in overseas stations.

(b) *Local Authority Classes.* Within the United Kingdom servicemen are allowed to attend classes offered by the local education authorities and their tuition and accommodation fees are subsidised by the Army.

(c) *Correspondence Courses.* By arrangement with nearly all the reputable institutions the army enables its personnel to take correspondence courses at subsidised rates. On an average some 40,000 courses are taken each year.

(d) *The Universities.* The Army has a special relationship with the universities, which not only provide special courses but also give individual help to officers and men who are preparing for diplomas and degrees.

(e) *Library Service.* Every unit has a small reference library and a limited selection of books for borrowing. Every army education centre has a fairly large library. Command libraries provide full services, comparable with those provided by a large municipal library.

(f) *The Resettlement and Information and Advice Service.* This is organised by the Director of Army Education for all ranks. The two Higher Education Centres in the United Kingdom, at Aldershot and Catterick, are now known as Resettlement Centres.

(g) *Special Lectures.* These are given by visiting experts to troops stationed overseas.

To foreign languages and current affairs the army pays marked attention. Any officer or other rank may learn a foreign language either at a university or at one of the two special language centres at Beaconsfield and Singapore.

'Current Affairs is thus considered one of the most important educational commitments in the British army.' This was the view unanimously put forward at a conference of chief education officers held in 1962. Current affairs is a compulsory subject of study for all officers up to the rank of major and for all other ranks, and as a rule one hour a week is set aside for the purpose. The syllabuses are not strictly confined to topics that specially affect the army, but range extensively over the domestic and international field. Moreover, tutors, normally regimental officers, are encouraged to use the discussion method rather than to rely upon lecturing or formal instruction. In order to provide a sound basis for discussion the Royal Army Educational Corps provides *Current Affairs Briefs* which maintain a remarkably high standard in format, objectivity and comprehensiveness. It also supplies a variety of teaching aids.

Promotion for officers is controlled by examination in which

Current Affairs plays a large part. Thus, at one stage in his career, for a period of several years, every officer is obliged to make himself acquainted with the main problems and trends in international and national affairs. In 1964, moreover, regular courses, usually at monthly intervals, were introduced for young officers, conducted by the extra-mural departments of universities and mainly focussed upon the study of International Affairs. Since the last war there has been a special relationship between all the armed forces and the universities. There is a national Committee for University Assistance to Adult Education in H.M. Forces consisting of representatives of the three Services, the D.E.S. and the Universities Council for Adult Education. The function of this committee is to co-ordinate university assistance to the Forces and in general to act as a policy-making and consultative body. At the regional level committees also exist for the purpose of administering the scheme on the ground. As the volume of service work has tapered off since the last war, so the number and size of these committees have been reduced, but some still remain and Bristol and Southampton are notably active in the main areas of army concentration in the south of England.

A number of universities still receive grants from the armed forces equal to their expenditure on Forces' work. And a diminishing number of extra-mural staff tutors are still employed full-time on Forces' work and paid indirectly out of service funds. The unique value of the universities' connection is that it makes available a supply of expert lecturers in the controversial field of Current Affairs. For officers this facility is particularly important because the Current Affairs paper, which is obligatory in their promotion and Staff College examinations, is usually the one that they find most exacting to prepare. Apart from supplying lecturers the universities also give advice on general educational matters.

The main criticisms commonly levelled against education in the army can scarcely be attributed to the shortcomings of its education branch. They can be reduced to four. The first is that because of their many other training commitments senior officers cannot devote as much time to education as might be desired in ideal circumstances, though by and large officers today are much more progressive in their outlook than in the past. Secondly, commanding officers frequently regard time spent upon education as time lost to more urgent regimental duties. It is very often hard to condemn this attitude, for many units are under-manned. Thirdly, so many reductions have occurred in the size of the R.A.E.C. during recent years that young graduates are less likely to look upon it as providing a permanent and attractive career. Fourthly, there is a marked lack of continuity, a stop-go process of education; schemes are hatched, slowly brought to the point of implementation and then abandoned. The blame for this rests with the government rather than with the army, because it is the government's frequent changes of policy that prevent the army from working out long-term plans and sticking to them.

The techniques and ingenious aids of communication used by the R.A.E.C. are admirable and might well provide models for tutors in other fields. The Educational Corps has its own Research Department in the Institute of Army Education and conducts special surveys and enquiries, the findings of one of which concerned the reading habits of servicemen. Clearly surveys of this kind have an interest beyond the army itself. The experience of R.A.E.C. officers in teaching English to foreigners should also be drawn upon by anyone connected with basic adult education.

In conclusion, mention must be made of the Inspectorate of Army Education, which consists of senior R.A.E.C. officers organised according to schemes of instruction—languages, science, general education, individual education. They are based on the Institute of Army Education and advise, assess and report on educational work in the Army.

Judged by the highest academic standards a good deal of army education may seem elementary. But it has to be remembered that since the army is very often dealing with men whose educational level is low, it must willy-nilly devote a good deal of time to filling the gaps left by formal schooling. What is striking is the army's recognition that education is an integral part of its work and the comparative breadth of the studies that it prescribes. Earl Wavell was justified some years ago in making the claim:

> ... the Army seems to have been ahead of the Nation in the matter of Adult Education during the last century—and, I think, still is. The truth is of course, that the soldier, when he is not fighting, has much more leisure than the agricultural labourer or factory hand, and under wise officers can be induced or compelled to spend part of it on education.[3]

B. *The Royal Air Force*

In the Royal Air Force education is highly organised. A good deal of it is devoted to technical training* but a prominent place is also given to what is described as The General Education Scheme. In its handbook the Educational Service sums up the purpose of the scheme: 'It is an aim of the General Education Scheme to develop qualities of mind and character in officers, airmen and airwomen by encouraging the creative use of leisure time. As one means of achieving this, stations are required to provide facilities for practical activities such as handicrafts and hobbies of educational value, and for the encouragement of interest in cultural activities such as music, art and drama. It is the responsibility of the Station Education Officer to ensure that the facilities provided are adequate to meet the reasonable needs of the station'.

The Royal Air Force is, of course, customarily dealing with men who have reached a fairly high educational standard. All the educational arrangements are directly controlled by the Education Branch of the Royal Air Force, which has its own School of Education, and most of the teaching is carried out by its own education officers. For the rest, calls are made on the services of the universities, the local education authorities and part-time civilian teachers.

Some airmen have to take the Royal Air Force Education Test, but for most of them education is no longer compulsory. As in the other two services, however, officers must pass examinations if they wish to rise in rank. Education in the R.A.F. is concerned with four categories:

(*a*) Airmen who are taking promotion examinations or who require technical training for their work. The main effort of teaching is directed to preparation for the R.A.F. Education Test and the General Certificate of Education.

(*b*) Facilities for officers preparing for promotion examinations, Staff College Entrance or higher academic qualifications.

(*c*) The promotion of general cultural and intellectual activities for all ranks.

---

* Notably at the Royal Air Force College, the Royal Air Force Technical College and the Schools of Technical Training. General Education subjects are included in these courses.

E

(d) Resettlement education to enable servicemen to prepare themselves for their return to civilian life.

Facilities are provided in the following ways:

(i) In-service training for the G.C.E. examination and R.A.F. Education Test.

(ii) Correspondence courses.

(iii) Grants for attendance at courses provided by external bodies, particularly at technical colleges.

(iv) Courses arranged in collaboration with the University Services Education Committees. These are mainly for officers and are usually in the field of International Affairs. Courses in space research are also now offered.

(v) Short residential courses.

(vi) Courses for officers at the Institute for International Affairs, Chatham House, London, and special courses for senior officers organised by the University of Oxford.

(vii) Education centres. It is now incumbent upon all stations to provide facilities for recreational activities and nearly all stations have a special hobbies and crafts room.

(viii) The provision of libraries. The army and air force have recently begun to share library provision in specified districts.

(ix) Information rooms. Among other items, these display charts, maps, reports and diagrams about current affairs.

(x) Facilities for the study of foreign languages.

(xi) In overseas stations lecture series given by distinguished civilian visitors.

In nearly all the educational work of the R.A.F. there is a liberal studies content. In addition, the study of current affairs is compulsory; in so far as possible, one hour has to be set aside each week for this purpose. Some of the talks or lectures are given by external lecturers, very often university teachers, but the bulk of this particular teaching is borne by R.A.F. officers themselves.

Because of the run-down in staff during the last few years, the R.A.F. is now short of its requisite complement of education officers. As a result a decline has recently been noted in the volume of informal adult education being offered. Nevertheless, a good deal is still being done, particularly at overseas stations, and statistics show that there has been a large increase in the number of officers undertaking voluntary educational work. Moreover, it is the opinion of R.A.F. education officers, at any rate, that the level of the work is steadily rising.

C. *The Royal Navy*

Education in the Royal Navy is mainly technical. At the same time, in ascribing to itself three main functions the Royal Navy Educational Service distinguishes two of them as: 'to ensure that officers and men are well informed citizens; to provide facilities for officers and men to develop their cultural interests'.

Ultimately responsible to the Board of Admiralty, the Director of the Naval Education Service is also the head of the Instructor Branch of the Royal Navy. Instructor officers, mostly graduates and all of officer rank, are combatant officers who serve both ashore and afloat and also act as the Meteorological officers of the Royal Navy.

The training courses designed for purely naval purposes contain some general educational subjects.* In addition, special facilities are provided for general education, and, as in the Army and the Air Force, it is compulsory both at sea and ashore for each ship and establishment to set aside one hour each week for the study of current affairs. The syllabuses cover a wide range but are apparently treated with too much circumspection. Lectures and discussions are normally conducted by an instructor officer if one is available, but all officers may be called upon to conduct them.

The Navy divides its responsibility for providing general education into two parts, the educational and the cultural:

1. *Educational Facilities:*

(*a*) In-service education. All ratings must pass or gain exemption from an examination in English and Arithmetic before becoming eligible for promotion. Service personnel and their families can take the Forces' General Certificate of Education anywhere in the world.

(*b*) Correspondence courses.

* e.g., Cadets at the Royal Naval College, Dartmouth who are not destined to become engineers spend the whole of their third year studying science, history and languages.

(*c*) Short residential or non-residential courses usually in current affairs. The Navy provides some of these on its own but facilities are also provided by the L.E.A.s and the universities.

(*d*) Evening classes.

(*e*) Civilian examinations.

(*f*) Provision of short courses, especially for officers.

(*g*) Provision of films and film strips.

(*h*) Provision of literature.

(*i*) The study of languages.

(*j*) Lecture tours for overseas stations.

(*k*) Information rooms.

2. *Cultural Facilities*

(*a*) Drama. Most establishments have dramatic societies and these can obtain copies of plays from a central Drama Library. An annual R.N. Drama Festival is held in the United Kingdom, Malta and Singapore. Those who wish to do so may also attend drama classes.

(*b*) Music. Many establishments have music societies.

(*c*) Language records.

(*d*) Recreational Libraries. Each ship and shore establishment is entitled to a 'recreational library'.*

ii. *Education in H.M. Prisons*†

The accepted official view is that we must have a care for the future welfare of the 30,000‡ inmates of the nation's ninety prisons, that it is no longer reasonable merely to incarcerate them and make them do tedious routine jobs. So today one of the most important and exacting tasks in the whole field of adult education is to provide prisons with appropriate educational facilities.

The need has long been felt and was given formal recognition

---

* The pattern of education in the armed forces is at present under review and major changes are undoubtedly in the offing particularly in relation to the initial and in-service training of officers. However, there seems no point in making predictions at a stage when economic considerations tend to invalidate every scheme as soon as it is formulated.

† Though a number of the inmates are over 18, Detention Centres and Borstals are excluded from this brief account.

‡ This is an approximate figure. At the end of 1966 the prison population (including the inmates of Borstals and Detention Centres) was 33,776.

soon after the First World War, when, in 1922, education advisers were appointed to all but three of the prisons in England and Wales. Since that time special accommodation has been set aside and organised classes have been arranged for those prisoners who wish to attend them.[4] A sliding scale of so many hours per week, fixed to meet the particular requirements of each institution, is allowed to each prison for classes that take place very largely in the evening. In other words, within each prison there is the equivalent of an evening institute.

Today it is the duty of local authorities under the terms of an Act passed in 1948[5] to ensure that some educational facilities are available in every prison. They can reclaim all their expenditure on this form of education from the Prison Department of the Home Office (formerly the Prison Commission). By an arrangement made in 1963 overall responsibility for education within the Prison Department rests with the Chief Director but in practice direct supervision is carried out by the Assistant Commissioners in their respective areas of control. The Chief Inspector at the Department of Education and Science is recognised as the Prison Department's principal adviser in educational matters and within the Inspectorate there is a special prison and borstal panel. Apart from individual establishments there are also several regional training prisons which include recreational activities in their programmes. Inmates of open prisons and a few prisoners nearing the end of their sentences may be allowed to attend outside courses provided by the local authorities.

Each prison has a full-time or part-time tutor-organiser, appointed by the responsible L.E.A., whose job is to plan and supervise an educational programme. Full-time tutor-organisers are paid according to the Burnham scale, Grade B, with the addition in certain cases of a special allowance, and the part-time teachers they appoint are paid in accordance with prevailing local fees. In 1965 there were 82 tutor-organisers. Because their duties are onerous, tutors normally serve for a prescribed period of time, now five to seven years. Tutors belong to their own union ('Teachers in Borstals and Prisons') which is independent of the prison officers' association and affiliated to the Association of Teachers in Technical Institutions. Since tutor-organisers do not appear to attend induction courses, they are presumably expected to profit from their mistakes.

Very often the tutor-organisers are dealing with people who feel antagonistic towards society and its institutions, among which they often include the State system of education. Indeed, the great majority have left school at 14 or 15 and it is no secret that many of those who voluntarily attend classes do so not because they are actively interested in education but because they welcome the chance to escape from their cells for a few hours. Somehow they have to be made to realise that the object is to help them both to endure prison routine more easily and to prepare themselves for a socially constructive mode of life when they are released.

Four broad aims are pursued which are as much therapeutic as educational:

(i) to offer relief, if only temporarily, from the claustrophobic and deadening effects of the prison regime, from contact with other criminals, and from long hours of boredom caused by the all too short working day;

(ii) to introduce inmates to the 'normal' personalities of teachers;

(iii) to provide recreational and group therapy;

(iv) to enable prisoners to prepare for employment on their discharge.

On the whole, preparation for employment in the strict sense is the duty of trade instructors who do not form part of the tutor-organiser's department.

In practice, a good deal of attention is paid to the needs of illiterates and semi-literates and to helping prisoners to improve their use of spoken and written English. There is also an increasing stress upon technical education and preparation for such examinations as the G.C.E. Ordinary Level and those administered by the Royal Society of Arts. At the same time, non-vocational, liberal and recreational subjects are not neglected. There are a number of discussion groups as well as classes in literature, drama, music and the visual arts. Classes in current affairs, musical appreciation and carpentry appear notably popular. Besides attending classes, inmates may study by correspondence and take certain written examinations. The common experience of tutors is that attendance at classes awakens dormant interests and leads prisoners to discover that what they think about may well be the stuff of academic study. Education for them has usually meant mechanically learn-

ing the three 'R's and they are surprised to find that teachers may
be interested in such social problems as the rearing of children.

Organising an educational programme within prisons can be
extremely taxing, the degree of difficulty varying with the policy
of the institution.[6] The tutor is constantly coming up against the
paradox of punishment and reform. For one thing it is necessary
to interfere with the smooth routine of the prison regime. Yet
prison staffs may be obsessively concerned with discipline and
security and consequently suspicious of apparent interference.
It has been found, however, that prisoners who take full advantage
of the educational facilities usually become more co-operative as a
result. It is also often claimed that there has been a general
improvement in the atmosphere of prisons since educational
programmes were first introduced. Nevertheless, to judge from
their spoken comments, some tutors feel frustrated and isolated
by what they regard as the failure of governors and prison staff
to support their efforts through a failure to appreciate that education can reduce criminality. Another difficulty is that of recruiting
suitable tutors, for unusually warm human qualities and specialist
teaching experience are required in dealing with adults who have
had little education. In this field well-meaning but unqualified
philanthropists may do as much harm as tutors whose sole
concern is to earn extra money. Yet another difficulty is that
many prisons are located in such remote places that it is hard to
get teachers to visit them.

In an age when the aim is to reform rather than crudely punish
criminals it is essential that prison officers should have an enlightened and informed outlook upon their exacting work. Some
attention is paid, therefore, to the in-service training of prison
officers. At Wakefield Prison, for instance, the Leeds University
Department of Adult Education has for many years provided
intensive courses in aspects of criminology.

The educational opportunities available in prisons are plainly
less satisfactory than public statements would seem to suggest.
More than half the 30,000 or so prisoners do not make use of
them. Although it is true that many of these non-participants do
not want education, a good number are deprived of it because
the facilities are inadequate. A cut in 1962 in the number of hours
allocated per week to each prison was therefore a retrograde measure. Even less excusable was an attempt to reduce expenditure by

one-sixth that failed only because of a public outcry. If it is the declared policy to reform and not merely to punish criminals, the State must be prepared to spend far more money on their education and to set aside more time for classroom work. It is presumably necessary that sewing mailbags and recovering copper should absorb some of the prisoners' time, but these activities are perhaps less valuable than attending classes in social studies. One former tutor-organiser has observed, for example, that it is an urgent social task to make prisoners more aware of the functions and duties of parenthood, since many of them are the fathers of young children.

Nationally the gross expenditure on prison education and recreation during the year 1965–66 was £223,631. As an approximate percentage of total prison costs this represented a figure of 1%.[7] This level of expenditure is unjustifiably low even on economic grounds. After all, if we were to spend more money on prison education, we might have to spend less on locking people up.[8]

iii. *Other Services*

In addition to educational services provided in the armed forces and the prisons, mention should be made of the small amount of provision that is made in hospitals, the considerable amount of in-service training for police officers and the educational activities directly sponsored by the Civil Service Council for Education. Apart from the Ministry of Defence such Ministries as Labour and Social Security also provide at least some educational facilities for their employees.

It is desirable that patients in hospitals should be given an opportunity to pursue an educational interest but it is not easy to overcome the rigorous routine even in sanatoria where people are convalescing. In 1937 a scheme for introducing short courses into hospitals was started but abandoned on the outbreak of war. In 1947 the London County Council sponsored an educational scheme for six mental hospitals in the Epsom area. Little else appears to have been done. Despite the difficulties a positive effort to provide educational facilities in hospitals ought to be made wherever possible.

A large amount of in-service training takes place within the police service. Entrants to the forces have to undergo a period of intensive training; there are many refresher courses; and special courses are held at the staff college where no fewer than seven lecturers teach general studies. Though mainly for lack of time there used to be a heavy emphasis on technical requirements, more recently there has been a growing realisation that curricula should be broadened to include aspects of liberal and social studies. At the National Police College a good part of the syllabus is given over to general studies. The police forces up and down the country also send officers to attend courses provided by the L.E.A.s and university extra-mural departments.

The Civil Service Council for Further Education was founded early in this century and aims at providing educational facilities for civil servants. It is supported by the Treasury and the professional staff associations.

REFERENCES

1. *Manual of Education*, Part iii, paragraph iii.
2. *Education in the British Army* (BR. 4/1962 (AE2).
3. *Minerva's Owl or Education in the Army* (Birkbeck College, 1948). For further reading on the work of the R.A.E.C., cf. A. C. T. White, *The Story of Army Education, 1643–1963* (1963).
4. See the brief retrospective survey in *Report of the Commissioners of Prisons for the year 1961* (H.M.S.O.), pp. 25–7; see also *The Prison Rules 1964*, para 29, p. 10.
5. The Education (Miscellaneous Provisions) Act.
6. For details of the various classes of prison cf. *Report on the Work of the Prison Department 1965* (H.M.S.O.), pp. 64–9.
7. Cf. *Report of Prison Department (1965)*, Appendix No. 4, p. 57.
8. The announcement in May 1967 that the Prison Department intends to appoint a Chief Education Officer may perhaps be taken as encouraging. For further reading see: F. Banks, *Teach them to Live* (1958): H. Klare, *Anatomy of Prisons* (1960).

Chapter Seven

WOMEN'S ORGANISATIONS

The women of England and Wales join together in associations more readily than the men, and although their primary concerns are the enhancement of the status of their own sex and the mitigation of social evils, they give a high priority in their activities to education. Indeed, each of the three most powerful organisations stipulates that education must form an integral part of the programmes of its constituent branches. These three organisations—the Women's Institutes, the Townswomen's Guilds and the National Association of Women's Clubs—are the subject of this chapter.

First, however, it is important to note briefly the astonishing preponderance of women in almost every form of voluntary effort. Their domination of church activities and of the local work of political parties is as noticeable as their support for the great national women's movements. So also is their predominance in formal classes, as the figures below in Chapter 15 show clearly. The exact reasons for this predominance are insufficiently established but it is a fact which adult educators would be foolish to ignore in their thinking and planning and in formulating the terms in which a claim for further public support can be made.

It has sometimes been suggested that, generally speaking, working women are found in R.B. and L.E.A. classes whereas housewives flock to clubs and to T.W.G. and W.I. branches, the social needs of housewives being assumed to be greater than those of working women. This is, in fact, not the case. Housewives, especially those who are more comfortably off, attend evening classes in large numbers.

i. *Women's Institutes*

The popular view of a Women's Institute is false. It is not simply a place where countrywomen forgather to gossip and sip tea. On the contrary, the Women's Institutes are a remarkably strong, pragmatic and efficient organisation, and have done much to

improve social conditions in the countryside. If any current criticism can be substantiated, it is that too many honorary officers
seem to be chosen for their social rank rather than for their energy
and ability.

Nowadays the Institutes may have lost some of their former
zest and reforming urge but they can look back on a remarkable
achievement. The first Institutes were formed towards the end
of the nineteenth century to help overcome the inequality between
countrywomen and their menfolk. The fourfold object of their
founders was to emancipate women both socially and educationally, to enable them to express their individual personalities
freed from Victorian constraints, to elevate the status and influence
of women both locally and nationally and to improve the material
conditions of rural life. The measure of the movement's success
is that the initial aims of the founders are no longer the main
preoccupation of members.

The growth of the Women's Institutes has been spectacular and
despite the increasing spread of suburbia it continues. In August
1968 there were 9,006 Institutes and a total membership of
461,153, including a number of girls aged between fourteen and
eighteen. The most active parts of the movement are the local
branches, which elect representatives to the National Federation.
The movement very largely supports itself out of subscriptions
and fund-raising schemes but receives Department of Education
and Science grants for that part of its work directly concerned with
education (in 1967 £5,200) and some L.E.A. grants towards
administrative costs. It has a permanent headquarters staff as well
as salaried officers in the counties, but even so relies heavily upon
a large corps of Voluntary County Officers (V.C.O.s).

The principal aim of the Women's Institutes is social rather
than educational. It is social, however, in the widest sense, for
they seek to represent the views of their members upon matters
of public concern, to improve rural conditions and generally to
enrich the lives of women. In the belief that it is better to be
comprehensive than to arouse strong partisan feelings, they are
rigidly non-political and non-sectarian. This was no doubt a
correct attitude in the past when the essential task was to serve
the cause of all women regardless of their social and political
background. But now that the battle of emancipation has been
won, it is perhaps time for the Institutes to ask themselves whether

or not they should begin to tackle controversial problems which may necessitate strictures upon one or other of the political parties.

Though predominantly social in purpose, the Women's Institutes nevertheless lay claim to a specific educational function. Their own admirable handbook states: 'The first step towards the Women's Institute's aim of better conditions in the country is education.' They recognise four ways of carrying out this function: first, by enabling women as individuals to express themselves both through creative activities and through the acquisition of knowledge; secondly, like the Townswomen's Guilds, by regarding the organisation of branches and the administration of the whole apparatus of the movement primarily as tools which can be used to train women in the modes of citizenship; thirdly, by drawing their members' attention to rural and national problems and by encouraging them to discuss and campaign for particular reforms —at various times the Institutes have fought to ensure that we should have clean food, humane slaughter of animals, better educational facilities, railway hygiene, improved bus services, a ban on horror comics and so on; and finally, by insisting that their members should engage in some form of educational activity as an integral part of their regular meetings.

While it is true that by far the greatest part of the specifically educational work of the average institute is recreational and concerned with cookery and housecraft, it would be wrong to underestimate its utility. For the movement has wisely assessed the capacities and needs of women as they are and not as they might be in Utopia. It has seen, as a good secondary modern school teacher might see, that the way in which to give people an appetite for education is first of all to appeal to that side of their personalities which longs for creative expression and a mastery of practical techniques.

Every Women's Institute must hold a monthly meeting, and in the course of every monthly meeting a period must be set aside for education as well as for business and social recreation. This means in practice that every branch must plan an annual programme of at least eleven talks or lectures. The yardstick of the seriousness of this injunction is that the greater part of the expenditure of Women's Institutes is in payment of fees and expenses to visiting speakers. However, three comments have to be made about these educational periods. One is that half an hour, the normal span, is extremely short, though it may be, of course, that half an hour is as long as women who are unaccustomed to following a prolonged theme can be made to concentrate. Secondly, the programmes are extremely uneven, there is very rarely continuity and members themselves often describe them as 'snippety'; the standard of many lectures is also low. Thirdly, the subjects discussed are overwhelmingly concerned with domestic skills such as cake decoration, flower arrangement, cookery and soft furnishing, though it must be added that the technical standards attained are often extremely high. At the same time, the lectures are sometimes about social and economic problems; it is the policy of the movement to encourage the formation of discussion groups; before each annual conference some time is given to discussing the 'public questions' that are going to be raised; and very often out of a branch programme there arises a demand for a formal and intensive course to be provided by one of the established adult education agencies. The National Federation also organises one-day schools, speakers' training courses and exhibitions.

As far as possible the Women's Institutes try to provide their own speakers and instructors; apart from a national speakers' panel each county also has a panel. In addition, the organisation holds special training courses for its own members so that they may teach others. But the main sources of supply are the L.E.A.s. Indeed, the degree of collaboration between the W.I.s and the L.E.A.s is striking. In a private study which was made some 15 years ago it was shown that 1,757 out of 2,206 classes were provided by L.E.A.s It is apparent from statements made by both sides[1] that the L.E.A.s and the W.I.s in most counties lay particular store by mutual collaboration, this being the most fruitful product of that section in the 1944 Act which obliged L.E.A.s to extend aid and comfort to voluntary organisations. On the other hand there appears to be very little collaboration between the W.I.s and the Responsible Bodies.

The subject of residential colleges is dealt with elsewhere*, but it is appropriate at this point to draw attention to the special features of the Women's Institutes' own residential college. Denman College was founded after the last war and has accommodation for 61 students and tutors. It runs two types of courses known

* See above, chapter 4.

as 'A' courses and 'B' courses. 'A' courses are open to all members whereas 'B' courses are designed for those who will pass on their knowledge to others. The syllabus is specifically concerned with domestic crafts. In the 1962 prospectus, for example, no fewer than 67 of the courses dealt with cookery and domestic crafts as against a very small number of courses in the liberal arts. What is particularly interesting about Denman College is its recognition of the family and personal problems that often prevent attendance at educational meetings. Thus it has made special provision for four kinds of courses: (i) wives' and husbands' courses; (ii) mothers' and babies' week; (iii) family week; (iv) special facilities for handicapped members.

From the special angle of adult education, certain improvements in the operations of the W.I.'s readily suggest themselves. First, efforts should be made to extend the monthly education period. Secondly, more attention should be given to the value of continuity in planning a programme. Thirdly, the aid and advice of the Responsible Bodies should be sought more often. Fourthly, there should be a positive attempt to get away from the customary round of recreational courses and to launch out on liberal studies courses. Fifthly, the Institutes could do with some full-time education officers, who might pursue the four aims just mentioned and provide a means of liaison with other educational bodies. The difficulty is, of course, that in order to adopt this advice the W.I.s would be obliged to become more militant. That might not be a bad idea; otherwise sooner or later they will deteriorate into the gossip-parlours that some people wrongly think they have already become. The fact that in some areas new Institutes are being created alongside old ones, in order to satisfy the needs of women who are free only in the evenings, is perhaps an encouraging sign of the movement's responsiveness to change.

ii. *The Townswomen's Guilds*

Elderly and prosperous and consciously middle-class women living in the residential suburbs of, say, London or Manchester, do regularly attend local meetings of the Townswomen's Guilds but it would be wrong to view them as stereotypes. The total membership of the Guilds is over 216,000, and big enough therefore to contain a cross-section of society and a fair sample of younger women. The Guilds also form part of a vigorous, responsible and progressive movement. Until recently they had a gentlewomen's agreement not to overlap with the Women's Institutes, the working rule being that they should assume responsibility when the local population was greater than 4,000. However, two years ago the Women's Institutes asked that the convention be dropped since new towns were being established in rural areas. At the same time, the Guilds for their part felt that townswomen who had gone to live in rural areas were still more interested in town than in rural activities. Accordingly the arrangement is now flexible. Relations between the two organisations continue to be cordial, as witnessed by the fact that they encourage women to join either one or the other rather than any rival organisation.

Many members might be surprised to learn that they are being exposed to educational stimuli. But so they are. For from the date of their foundation in 1929, the primary purpose of the Townswomen's Guilds has been to educate:* to encourage women to become responsible and well-informed citizens, and to activate latent intellectual interests. They hope to achieve their aim in two ways: the first is by learning about contemporary affairs, democratic procedures and the duties of citizenship. Here the method is to give a good deal of time and thought to the organisational and procedural side of running a guild, so that members may acquire knowledge through practical experience rather than theory. Members are also deliberately encouraged to play an active part in both local and national affairs. In 1963, 205 members were active J.P.s, 215 were Borough Councillors and 17 were mayors, apart from a multitude of other members serving the community in various ways. The second way is by arranging classes in one of four major fields—arts and crafts, drama, music and social studies—or at least by encouraging the thematic treatment of a given problem and not merely dabbling in disconnected topics.

In 1966 the National Executive Committee decided that the time had come for the movement to bring its educational provision more in line with contemporary trends in adult education. Confin-

* The objects of the Guilds are explicitly described as: 'To encourage the education of women to enable them as citizens to make their best contribution towards the common good. To serve as a common meeting ground for women, irrespective of creed and party, for their wider education, including social activities.'

ing its attention to four defined areas inhibited it from dealing with other topics. It is too early at this stage to comment upon the changes that are foreshadowed but there can be no doubt that the reappraisal of function was timely.

For lack of staff and financial resources, the headquarters in London have few statistical records relating to educational programmes and limited means for ascertaining what is happening up and down the country. One is therefore thrown back upon generalisations. Though every Guild must include some lectures in its monthly meetings and devote time to the study of motions for the agenda of the annual national conference, its practical efficiency depends upon a number of factors, notably upon whether or not at least a few of the more energetic members are keen to stimulate an interest in educational activities. Thus in the best branches annual courses are arranged in collaboration with the L.E.A.s, the W.E.A., the residential colleges or university extra-mural departments;* there is a lively social studies section pursuing a carefully designed programme; language courses are popular; and there are a number of competent discussion groups. For example, in 1962 a small group in Leicestershire were preparing, with the aid of a County Library book-box, a survey and history of textiles. Out of 2,387 Guilds in 1962, only the following were without special sections: Music—699; Drama—432; Arts and Crafts—388; Social Studies—335. The National Union does all in its power to encourage debate and discussion by distributing occasional plans of study and by issuing notes for the guidance of honorary officials. In some branches, however, little more than token regard is paid to educational matters and a committee may content itself with inviting a few outside speakers to give 'little talks' either to the social studies section or the general monthly meeting on some topics of general interest that will not strain the attention of members. There is, of course, always the problem of dealing with heterogeneous groups of women whose formal education ceased at various stages, but it does not necessarily follow that a talk pitched at an easy, informal level is devoid of

---

* A good deal of the time of the W.E.A. tutor-organiser for East Kent is devoted to arranging classes for the Guilds. It is also noteworthy that of all the university extra-mural departments only Aberystwyth and Bangor do not provide a one-day conference or an extension course at the request of the Guilds. The Guilds make especially heavy demands upon the residential colleges.

educational value. As a former national social studies adviser once put it: '. . . (even with more statistical evidence) we shall still not be able to assess the imponderables—what windows have been opened for which members, what prejudices have been swept away and so on. In dealing with a membership of 207,000 we shall always have to speak in general terms, trying to evaluate trends rather than actual performance'.

At the end of 1967 there were 2,728 guilds annually increasing at the rate of approximately 70. The guilds are amalgamated into 107 Federations. Considering the size of its membership, the Union must be very nearly the most understaffed of all the voluntary educational agencies. Its headquarters, which receives an annual grant of approximately £4,600 from the D.E.S., is small. Until 1965 four national advisers were employed to organise not only national and regional conferences but also residential courses and one day schools in the four fields of study, conducted in the main part by themselves, but sometimes by suitably qualified outside lecturers. Aided by twelve area organisers, whose main task was to explain committee procedure and the techniques of running a guild, their general brief was to stimulate activity and to diffuse ideas and information. The reform of educational policy, however, has entailed the appointment of a full-time education officer and the creation of a single educational unit. Three of the educational advisers have been declared redundant. The initial task of the Education Officer is to arrange a series of national conferences at the regional level and generally to broaden the educational activities of the movement. In particular, he* will be expected to encourage the study in depth of a nation-wide theme, the first subject chosen being 'Communication'. Although most of the work undertaken by the Guilds is usually arranged in collaboration with the local authorities or one or other of the Responsible Bodies, some of it is done without outside help. In order to expand its own work in arts and crafts, the union is most anxious that some of its members should be trained up to the level of accredited teachers. In 1963, 44 members were known to be sitting City and Guilds examinations in Crafts.

Each year the Union holds a two-day national conference which is addressed by distinguished personalities on a theme connected with one of the four main subject areas. The object of this meeting

* The first education officer to be appointed is a man!

is to furnish each delegate with ideas for the framing of her own local programme, and it is reinforced by a series of follow-up courses in residential colleges. In various parts of the country the Guilds arrange occasional study tours and longer term schools, e.g. a traditional four-five day school is annually organised by Hampshire members in collaboration with the University of Southampton. Schools are also held on an area basis; for instance, an interesting experiment was recently tried in collaboration with Bournemouth Municipal Orchestra. Since 1960 the union has organised at least one annual foreign study tour.

The emphasis placed on education by the national organisers of the Townswomen's Guilds is not always fully reflected in the work of some local branches where the keynote is sometimes unequivocally social. Even so, the movement as a whole is entitled to claim that it has done much to meet the intellectual needs of women of all ages and social classes. If it had the means to employ more full-time organisers, particularly at the regional level, there is no question that there would be an immediate increase in the time and attention paid by branches to more purposeful education.

To judge the Townswomen's Guilds by the amount of formal education undertaken would in any case be to underestimate their essential value. For what they do is to educate by stealth, especially when dealing with women who lack experience of public life. Their greatest success lies in using indirect methods to encourage women to lead mentally absorbing lives. It is significant that their salaried organisers would like to have more time for helping inexperienced branches on the newest housing estates.

iii. *The National Association of Women's Clubs*

Some adult educators seem to think that whereas the Townswomen's Guilds and the Women's Institutes are mainly concerned to serve the interests of the middle classes, the National Associa- of Women's Clubs exists to serve the interests of working-class women. This is an over-simplification, but there is something in it. The Clubs sprang up during the period of national unemploy- ment after 1926. First formed to provide an outlet for women who were socially insecure, apathetic or lonely, they have steadily expanded since the thirties. For a long time they specifically aimed at providing new social opportunities and improving home standards. Currently they are preoccupied with the problem of loneliness, especially as it affects widows and those who are housebound. But nowadays they are also very conscious of having an educational purpose, and their national secretary is at pains to stress the educational function of the movement. According to its own prospectus, the aims and objects of the association are:

(i) to provide facilities for social life and opportunities for informal education within the means of all women, and, in particular, housewives;

(ii) to give members opportunities to understand their responsibilities and rights as citizens, and to encourage them to be of service to one another and to their neighbourhood;

(iii) to provide opportunities for members to develop their own gifts and talents, and to assist them to live a full and happy life.

It can thus be seen that education is given a high priority.

The work of the Clubs is co-ordinated and directed on a national basis by the National Association which in turn forms part of the complex of the National Council of Social Service. The National Association receives an annual Government grant (1966–67, £4,800) in recognition of its educational work. Its main task is to help in programme planning and to tender advice on such technical points as committee and financial problems. It also organises schools, training courses for organisers and an annual general conference, and generally works for the improvement of its members' living standards.

Below the National Association are a number of county or area federations. Below these again are the individual clubs. By the close of the year 1968 there were 870 affiliated clubs grouped together in 34 Associations with an approximate membership of 35,000: over 250 new clubs were formed between 1963 and 1967. Although some clubs own their own premises, most are compelled to hire them or to use premises provided by a local authority. Meetings are arranged both in the afternoon and in the evening and the practice is growing for a club to be divided in all essentials into two distinct afternoon and evening groups. An educational programme is arranged each year. In some cases teachers are supplied by the L.E.A.s and a few expert organisers are available to offer advice. The main concentration in subjects has traditionally been upon home crafts but the broad aim is to widen cultural interests. So music, play reading, choirs and seminar group activities form a major part of the teaching programme. Another subject to which the clubs pay notable attention is consumer education. The clubs also arrange exhibitions, festivals and concerts.

The National Association of Women's Clubs is an important organisation which receives less publicity than it deserves. Its contribution to the educational needs of women is particularly valuable in the most recently established residential areas. For its few officials there can be nothing but praise. Their work is characterised by a desire to experiment and a determination to tackle fundamental social problems.

REFERENCES

1. Cf. *Handbook*, p. 65: 'No County Federation Executive Committee should be satisfied until it has established close and friendly relations with the local education authority in its area and is receiving from it a full measure of assistance'.

Chapter Eight

INDUSTRY AND COMMERCE

'Industry needs, from top to bottom and in every part . . . the continual refreshment of new ideas. Its leading executives, no less than its managerial and technical personnel and the general body of workers engaged in it, need to be kept continually fresh in mind by mixing and meeting with others who can bring to them the invigorating air of different experiences and a different way of approach . . . adult education, as it is understood today, does not cover nearly the whole of what we have in mind. It does not cover the need for making regular and systematic provision of "refresher" courses for managers and technicians . . . the need of those already in high executive positions to broaden and deepen their outlook by contact with what is best in contemporary culture and scientific thought.' (Extract from a statement made in 1942.)[1]

'The use of the industrial community as a source of recruitment for classes became during the year an increasingly important side of the work of Responsible Bodies.' (Extract from *Education in England and Wales—Report* 1962.)[2]

i. *The Role of Employers*

For several years there has been much talk about the urgent need for management training on a nationwide scale: in 1961, for instance, our efforts to join the Common Market stimulated unprecedented interest among the business community in the study of foreign languages and economic problems. We are already analysing the initial effects of the Industrial Training Act. Day-release for young workers has become rapidly more widespread. But precisely how much organised education for adult employees is sponsored by industrial and commercial undertakings? Though it must be stressed that no one has yet taken the trouble to institute a comprehensive enquiry, the answer would appear to be not much.

Many firms, particularly the very big ones,* employ full-time

---

* e.g., I.C.I., Unilever, Shell, Pilkington Brothers. Among the 'giants' one must also include British Rail, the Central Electricity Board and the National Coal Board.

education officers and run extensive training programmes. A number are even prepared to recognise that they have a duty to help prepare their employees for retirement. A few have their own residential colleges. Indeed, training is often a disproportionately heavy charge upon the larger firms. Managers may attend courses at the universities, technical colleges, colleges of commerce or further education, polytechnics, the Administrative College at Henley-on-Thames, and short-term residential colleges. There are also several private organisations offering expensive courses for senior managerial staff.[3] From a scrutiny of prospectuses, however, it is obvious that virtually every programme is exclusively designed to improve working efficiency. Furthermore, although many education and training officers used to be teachers or educational administrators, they evidently consider that it is no part of their function to go beyond the arrangement and supervision of utilitarian training courses. Consider, for example, the following extract from a recent article by a Personnel Officer of I.C.I.:

'The purpose of training within a firm like I.C.I. is quite different from that in a university, technical college or business school. We do not train for training's sake, nor even for the individual's sake: the essential purpose of all our training is the better development of our business. Any benefit the individual derives is a welcome by-product.'[4]

Nor is there yet much indication that the great majority of employers, unlike a growing number of their American counterparts, can perceive any connection between sustaining the efficiency of their higher administrative staff and ensuring that they have broad social and cultural interests. Indeed, to suggest to the average employer that in the long run the usefulness of a top executive is likely to diminish if his range of activities is restricted to his full-time job and the playing of golf is to be met with incomprehension. For employers and managers, wholly immersed as they usually are in day-to-day problems, tend to see no further than immediate results, and some of them fail even to appreciate that long-term gains will accrue from running their own vocational training schemes. When an employer is aware of the relevance of liberal education to the performance of his employees, he may still have to overcome such problems as those created by shift work, and he may well be told by his managers and supervisors that the demands of work do not permit diversionary pleasures. Moreover, firms can only encourage employees to further their own education and provide the necessary facilities: they cannot exert compulsion on employees to use them. Not a few employers complain that their best laid schemes remain still-born because of the suspicion of their workers and the trade unions that 'they are trying it on'.

At the same time, the outlook is changing for the better. There is an increasing awareness that both management and workers are out of touch with social and economic realities. Some firms and trade unions feel strongly that one of the keys to greater efficiency is to improve inter-personal communications and for both sides of industry and commerce to pay special attention to the study of human relations. Many enlightened boards of directors recognise the importance of explaining to their employees what their policy is and where their enterprise fits into the national economic pattern. 'Retraining' is still essentially a new word, but there is no doubt that the need for regular refresher courses for employees at all levels is receiving increasing consideration. Furthermore, a rising proportion of education and personnel officers are pressing their firms not only to expand existing education programmes— and to institute them where they do not already exist—but to offer more than the typical, pared-down, functional syllabuses of the past. The chief personnel officer of Pilkingtons once stated: 'The firm is anxious to encourage all employees who wish to improve their knowledge and efficiency by further education.'

In the near future it is to be expected that the Association for Liberal Education, activists in certain extra-mural departments and W.E.A. districts, and the departments of management studies that have now been set up in several institutes of higher education will produce detailed surveys of the present scope of general studies in industry and commerce and recommendations about further developments. Meanwhile it may be helpful to sketch an outline of the existing forms of provision.*

To begin with, some firms encourage their staffs to take courses of study either by affording facilities for day release or by paying

---

* For what follows I am much indebted to Mr G. F. Stuttart, Staff Tutor in Industrial Relations in the Extra-Mural Department of the University of London, who has made a tentative enquiry into the amount of liberal adult education provided by industrial and commercial firms.

fees for their attendance at evening classes. It is true that more often than not they are hoping for enhanced professional skill in return for their financial outlay, but they are less prone than they used to be to complain when employees seem to be given instruction that has no direct vocational relevance. Other firms and some trade unions invite one or other of the providing bodies to arrange special courses on their behalf. This kind of collaboration is obviously most frequent in those places where the providing bodies themselves recognise the existence of a vast new field for development. At the present time, the departments of extra-mural studies in Birmingham, Leeds, London, Nottingham, Oxford and Sheffield, and several W.E.A. districts are most conspicuous as innovators.

Within industry and commerce arrangements for adult education vary a great deal. The following are the main ones:

(i) *General Provision.* Some of the traditionally progressive firms provide a whole range of educational activities including a strong liberal studies element. Firms such as Cadbury's, Metro-Vickers and Boots have their own day-continuation schools and 'induction to industry' courses; they also sponsor a wide variety of clubs and societies and arrange week-end and other residential courses, many of which are held in their own colleges.

(ii) *Special Training Courses.* There are firms which organise courses for different sections of their staff, particularly for apprentices and supervisory grades. Though primarily technical, these often deal with such topics as communications, human relations, and the historical and social background both of the industry in which they work and of their own firm.

(iii) *Induction Courses.* Induction courses for new employees are fairly common. Some are rudimentary but several firms organise residential weeks for all young entrants and these frequently have a high liberal content.

(iv) *Apprentice Associations.* Next there are 'Apprentice Associations': many of these arrange a social programme, which brings in liberal education in the form of industrial visits, lecture courses, debating and discussion groups. Some firms run award schemes which enable apprentices to travel abroad.

(v) *Trade Associations.* A few firms organise courses particularly for apprentices and new entrants through a trade association; especially interesting are those organised by the Wool Textiles Trade Association.

(vi) *Direct Experiments*. Some firms conduct direct experiments, such as 'Project Hercules', a version of a French scheme, which confronts apprentices and others with three challenges: solitude; intensive study followed by a report on a selected subject; and living hard for one month. Others run their own courses on a theme such as 'Widening Horizons' or 'The Use of Leisure'.

(vii) *Residential Colleges*. Many firms make full use of the facilities offered by external agencies. A large number of courses are arranged in conjunction with residential colleges. A high proportion of these are deliberately liberal in content and have no obvious connection with technical training.

(viii) *Voluntary Organisations*. Other firms make use of a whole range of agencies such as Outward Bound, Brathay Hall, the Y.M.C.A. Colleges at Kings Gate and other centres, The National Association of Boys' Clubs, Mixed Clubs and Girls' Clubs, which run a large number of 'adjustment to industry' courses, the Industrial Welfare Society and the British Association for Commercial and Industrial Education, the Duke of Edinburgh Award Scheme and the Economic League. A few firms also encourage support for voluntary services.

(ix) There are courses arranged by industrial consultants and by the professional associations, such as the Institute of Personnel Management and Institute of Industrial Supervisors.

(x) Finally, perhaps the most important development has been the recent introduction of 'factory-based courses' arranged by university extra-mural departments and W.E.A. Districts.

The number and diversity of the foregoing arrangements may easily give rise to a false estimate of the amount of general education already being provided. Considering the size of the working population it remains minute. Nevertheless, the scope for general education in industry and commerce is potentially immense. Now that there are a few enlightened pockets of activity it is to be hoped that there will be a contagious process of expansion, so that in the near future the kind of programme pioneered by Rubery Owen, Unilever, Glacier, and Pilkingtons, will have become commonplace. Whether the required degree of expansion takes place, however, will depend upon encouragement from the Government, trust between managements and workers, and upon the creation of joint consultative and planning committees consisting of employers, trade unionists and representatives of the various adult education agencies. Factory-based courses should multiply. Why not appoint resident tutors in the larger industrial complexes?

ii. *Industrial Training Boards*

Provision for the industrial and commercial training of personnel in management and on the shop-floor on the scale that the nation requires is grossly inadequate. For this shortage there are two principal reasons. The first is that in the past we have neglected the systematic training of manual workers, and workers, for their part, have not always seen the need for it. The second is that industrial methods and techniques are now changing so constantly that men trained once and for all to do a particular job soon find themselves redundant. Somehow the country has to find a way of producing the vast skilled work force now required by the economy and of devising a flexible training system that will enable it to anticipate future needs. The answer, proposed by H.M. Government, is the Industrial Training Act.

Passed by Parliament in 1964 the Industrial Training Act is designed to ensure that every firm will make suitable arrangements for the training of its employees. Significantly it is being implemented by the Ministry of Labour and not by the Department of Education and Science. The Act provides for the formation in every industry of a training board whose three main tasks are summarised as follows:

1. to produce an adequate number of skilled personnel at all levels;
2. to raise the quality and improve the efficiency of training programmes;
3. to share equitably among firms the financial cost of training.

Each firm is obliged to pay to the parent board a fixed levy for every employee on its payroll. The income accruing from the levies is then used both to reimburse firms already providing training facilities in accordance with their scale of expenditure and to arrange for the provision of such additional training facilities as the board considers necessary. In determining its expenditure each board is expected to take into account the national interest as well as the interest of the industry it represents. To date, the boards have been chiefly concerned with the training of manual workers but nothing in their remit debars them from also dealing with the training of managers.

By May 1968 twenty-two boards had been created covering a work force of approximately ten and a half millions. Eventually there may be as many as thirty-five boards. Already it is clear that at least some of the boards will command mighty resources. In its first year the Engineering Board, admittedly the richest, raised no less than £75 million on the basis of a $2\frac{1}{2}\%$ levy for each employee in the engineering industry. Never in history has such a glittering sum of money been made available for the education of adults. Naturally, there are those who are eagerly waiting to spend it. Numerous commercial firms have already flooded the market with text books and teaching aids for which there is not always a demonstrable need. An advertisement with a caption such as 'a new and intelligent approach to adult learning' may turn out to refer not to an innovation in teaching methods but to an item of classroom furniture. While existing educational institutions, notably Colleges of Further Education, have enlarged their programmes or revamped their syllabuses many entirely new educational institutions have sprung into being and several of the Boards have opened their own training centres. New journals have also appeared, their pages thick with advertisements for specialist training courses, sometimes held at residential centres, complete, in at least one case, with 'attractive cellar-bar', 'baronial dining-hall', and 'golf-course nearby'. Not all these courses and not all these teaching aids are meretricious. Indeed, as several educationists have judiciously pointed out, commercial firms may bring an original outlook to bear upon the educational enterprise and a refreshing realism about cost effectiveness. But when this concession has been made, the fact remains that some irresponsible firms are trying to obtain the lion's share of the unprecedented sums of money raised by the Industrial Training Boards.

No one ought to be one whit surprised that the proliferation of courses and materials has not been paralleled by the proliferation of good ideas. Sound syllabuses and competent teachers cannot be manufactured overnight. The distressing thing is that from first to last the bodies traditionally associated with the education of adults have scarcely been consulted during the process of framing the Act, forming the Boards and launching the initial training programmes. Never has there been such a salutary illustration of the strait-jacket within which adult education has been confined. Fortunately, it is not too late for the universities, the W.E.A. and the other long-established agencies to make a positive contribution, above all by insisting upon a regard for educational standards and by helping to train the trainers in industry.

The question which should be confounding the Industrial Training Boards is: 'where are we to find our training staff?' For every trainer in 1966 there were in the following industries the following numbers of employees:

Woollen	9,540
Shipbuilding	15,100
Iron and Steel	16,550
Engineering	20,450
Chemical	22,400
Construction	113,000
Distribution	211,000

These ratios show what a desperate shortage of training personnel there is. The problem is how to recruit suitable people and how to prepare them for their jobs. This is where the experienced adult educators ought to come in. Those departments of adult education in the universities already offering training courses can adjust them without too much difficulty to cover the requirements of trainers in industry, for there is a common body of knowledge and a common professional expertise required by any teacher of adults. Thus, existing courses need be only slightly modified.

By assuming some of the responsibility for the training of trainers in industry the traditional adult education agencies can also help to encourage a concern for standards. At the present time, the lack of quality in many industrial programmes is pronounced. By the terms of the Act, firms have only to show that training schemes are in operation; they do not have to show that their schemes are good ones. In the long run, it will be essential to introduce an objective system for evaluation. Meanwhile, there is hope that standards will be upheld if the trainers themselves are taught to hold academic detachment and integrity in high regard.

The most alarming development threatened by the Industrial Training Act is the further fragmentation of the already scattered field of adult education and further reinforcement of the divorce between vocational and non-vocational education. The Act itself distinguishes between Industrial Training and Further Education, which continues to be under the wing of the Local Authorities. A damaging split is bound to arise if the notion is allowed to take root that industrial training is rigorously utilitarian, the trainer's job being merely to impart the techniques required in a particular craft or industrial post. For this reason, it is absolutely imperative that the Industrial Training Boards should see their function as essentially educational and collaborate closely with the traditional adult education agencies. By the same token, it is also imperative that the latter should resolve to work with the Industrial Training Boards, whatever the difficulties and whatever the apparent indifference on the other side. It is painful to relate that by the end of 1968 there was relatively little co-operation between the Training Boards and the other adult educational agencies and ominous signs that 'Training' was being construed in perilously narrow terms.

For the first time in history great sums of money are being raised for at least one branch of adult education; in 1966 the amount raised in levies by the Boards was £102 million. The chance has arisen to spend generously upon physical plant and the training of teaching personnel. Already several boards have financed the creation of centres at enormous cost. Surely at least a portion of this uncovenanted windfall can be spent on promoting the traditional aims of adult education.

iii. *Workers' Education and the Trade Unions*

Since the nineteenth century the education of workers has been singled out as a distinctive sector of adult education, though there is a lack of clarity about the connotation of the word 'workers' and its precise meaning varies according to the beliefs and prejudices of the user. As has been seen, for the W.E.A. it is more or less synonymous with the educationally underprivileged. For the now defunct N.C.L.C. on the other hand, it referred to workers as an economic class in Marxist terminology. For middle-class dons it has meant those working-class leaders who might be expected wisely to exert their great influence with the trade unions. It would be less confusing to eschew such generalisations and to speak in terms of the needs of specific groups among the employed population.

The greater part of the education of workers, especially manual workers, is conducted either directly or indirectly under the aegis of the trade union movement itself. Its control was made explicit in 1963. Before that time the lead given by the movement had been a feeble one. To the outside observer two providing bodies seemed to be competing for its patronage. These two bodies were the W.E.T.U.C. (The Workers' Educational Association Trade Union Committee and the Trades Union Council) and the N.C.L.C. (The National Council of Labour Colleges). While the T.U.C. itself provided very little education, these two bodies were locked in a struggle for the affiliation of individual trade unions.

The National Council of Labour Colleges had a misleading title, for no colleges came under its control during most of its existence. Its title derived from the fact that the original founders of the movement were students who broke away from Ruskin College and in 1909 set up an independent establishment of their own which they called the Central Labour College. That College was soon closed and when the N.C.L.C. was formally dissolved in 1965 it was mainly a body for providing correspondence courses and classes.

The rivalry between the W.E.A.—operating through the W.E.T.U.C.—and the N.C.L.C. did serious damage to education within the trade union movement. It led to duplication of effort in some sectors and to no effort at all in others. It bewildered workers and officials anxious to know where their allegiance lay and caused them frequently to call a curse upon both rival houses. The feud was due to the confrontation of two opposing views of the nature of workers' education. Maintaining that the essential task was to educate citizens regardless of class antagonism, the W.E.A. welcomed assistance from the established organs of society. The N.C.L.C., on the other hand, argued that society was organised for the benefit of the property-owning bourgeoisie, so that if workers wished to improve their lot, they must behave as a class apart, determine their own educational needs and make their own unaided provision. At sixes and sevens themselves, the trade unions would not commit their support to one side or the other, and as a consequence there was internecine warfare. The N.C.L.C. was sustained by its deep convictions. The W.E.A. appeared inconsistent and reluctant to declare open war on the N.C.L.C. bantam cock.

By the beginning of the last war, if not before, the conflict had become meaninglessly sterile because many of the original grounds for conflict had disappeared. Time had mellowed the militancy of the N.C.L.C. and its more extreme beliefs had been dropped, but, unfortunately, in the popular view and particularly in W.E.A. circles the N.C.L.C. continued to look like a Marxist ogre. In fact, a careful analysis of the N.C.L.C. programme would have demonstrated that the subjects it taught and the syllabuses it followed were not startlingly dissimilar from those being employed by the W.E.A. itself. The irrationality of the conflict was steadily aggravated by the fact that individual trade unions began more and more to satisfy their own needs, to the extent that a position would eventually have been reached in which the struggle to provide educational services would have become three-sided.

Recognition of the folly of perpetuating the division, particularly in the light of changing social conditions, was bound to come sooner or later. In effect, the first measures to bring sense and order into the pattern of trade union education were taken in the early fifties. A working party set up by the W.E.A. reported that many things were wrong and recommended that intensive pilot studies should be carried out in three geographical areas with a view to pointing the way to a new system.[5] In due course, in 1958, a further report appeared based on the results of these three pilot experiments. The report was studied by the General Council of the T.U.C. and referred to its education committee. Three years later, after intensive enquiries and negotiations, a final report was prepared which was adopted by Congress in 1961. This foreshadowed a new scheme as from 1963, by the terms of which *de facto* control of trade union education would be vested in the General Council of Congress itself.

With the inception of this scheme it is now possible to classify the several arrangements for trade union education under the following five headings:

    (i) Courses arranged by the education department of the T.U.C. in the training college at Congress House or at weekend or one-week schools elsewhere, for example, at Ruskin College.

    (ii) Courses directly arranged by individual unions.

    (iii) An infinitesimal number of courses directly arranged by the Trades Councils.

(iv) Courses serviced by the W.E.A.

(v) Courses serviced by the universities.

By decree of Congress in 1962 every union now pays an additional 6d. per member out of general funds as an affiliation fee. Threepence of this constitutes a compulsory levy to meet the cost of the new rationalisation scheme. For the time being at any rate the T.U.C. pays grants to the W.E.A. and Ruskin College, respectively, equal to the total sum previously received from individual unions. All former W.E.T.U.C. and N.C.L.C. classes, correspondence courses and scholarships are made available to all trade unionists free of charge. Trade unions which already had their own educational schemes continue to maintain them in complete independence. The N.C.L.C. has been disbanded and its staff assimilated.* The correspondence courses arranged by Ruskin and the N.C.L.C. have been brought under unified control so that duplication will cease. It will take time to establish this new pattern, but in the long run the streamlining of administration is bound to save money and produce greater efficiency. Under the new arrangement educational courses are chiefly designed for officials but no applicants are barred. No fixed budget is earmarked, the T.U.C. preferring to spend according to the criteria of needs. Given an enlightened outlook at Congress House, this elastic arrangement may work well.

* The N.C.L.C. was always a magnet for hostility. Some of this may have been deserved because during its early phase it was militant and often rude to its opponents. At the same time it had a tenable case and displayed both courage and tenacity in upholding it. Furthermore its critics often failed to see, or at least to admit, that its assessment of workers' educational needs coincided with that of many workers themselves. They also underestimated the extent to which it was strongly entrenched within the Labour movement, not least within the Labour Party. The monthly journal *Plebs*, which its General Secretary, Mr James P. Millar, edited and used as a vehicle for unfolding his ideas, was year in and year out the liveliest publication not only within the Labour movement but within the whole adult education field.

There is a marked tendency to underrate the value of the N.C.L.C.'s educational work. Some of the criticism of its classes may well have been justified. Many lectures were given by organisers who, because of the heavy pressure of work, could hardly have been expected to have as much time for preparation as they should. But there is no reason to doubt that the correspondence courses were and remain of considerable value. An average of between 15,000 and 16,000 students used to follow these courses and at one point a peak was reached of 20,000 students. It was further claimed that 62% of the students regularly completed their courses. Moreover, with the passing of the N.C.L.C. the question arises, who will be responsible for education within the Labour Party itself?

For the purpose of supervising the new educational programme a special body was created consisting of members of the
General Council, nominees of the W.E.A. and Ruskin College,
and several co-opted members representing other organisations.
Its task was formulated as follows:

> to study the educational needs of trade unionists and to work out in
> co-operation with the W.E.A. the best means of fulfilling those needs;
> to provide opportunities for trade union members to undertake
> social, economic and political studies relevant to their trade union
> interests; to supplement the direct provision by trade union organisa-
> tions of facilities for trade union members; to remedy deficiencies of
> general education which might handicap them in their trade union
> work, and to provide both directly and indirectly opportunities for
> trade union students to acquire some knowledge of and experience in
> the techniques of study. The joint committee should also promote
> such measures as might be considered necessary from time to time to
> maintain and improve the standard of trade union educational
> facilities generally, having regard particularly to such factors as the
> supply of tutors and educational materials and methods being used.[6]

In the regions special committees have been formed with the task
of ensuring that an adequate educational service is available. These
Regional Advisory Committees meet at least three times a year
and inform the T.U.C. Education Service of the courses they would
like to see arranged.

Within the T.U.C. responsibility for education and training lies
with the Education Committee appointed by the General Council.
In addition, the T.U.C. Educational Trust proclaims three objects:
'to provide educational facilities for the study of economic history
and also of the history, principles and administration of trade
unions; to award scholarships for further education; and to assist
students to study abroad or students from abroad to study in this
country'. Its income is largely derived from the T.U.C. in the
form of annual grants.

The T.U.C. education department, which has only a small staff
and no full-time teachers, is not supported by a regional organisation and has had to rely in the past on the goodwill and administrative assistance of regional officials. At Congress House there is a
staff training college at which regular courses are held, largely concerned with the technical work of the unions—during the year

F

1966–67, 629 students from 57 unions attended 35 courses on such subjects as Social Security and Industrial Health, Industrial Relations and Negotiations. In addition, the education department now arranges regional courses, linked weekend schools, summer schools, and a special one-week school for women.* Increasingly it is specialising in courses for full-time officers and members of national committees. Presumably the work of the education department will increase once the teething troubles associated with the new scheme have been finally overcome.

Little evidence is available about the work of individual unions. It is well known, however, that some are much more interested in education than others. Thus, whereas several run their own training schemes and employ education officers, and one, the E.T.U., has had its own residential college at Esher, Surrey, since 1953, others are apparently unconcerned about the educational needs of their members. Again, some do a great deal for a few key personnel whereas others provide a general but necessarily superficial service. No doubt one of the main tasks of the new education body will be to try to stimulate activity in the backward unions.

It is not sufficiently realised that several trade unions have long been carrying out a good deal of education on their own account. Ten years ago in 1958, for example, the National Union of Mine Workers directly arranged a summer school (502 students), a number of weekend schools (1,198 students) and one or two day schools (60 students) at a total cost of £21,470. The Transport and General Workers' Union organised summer schools (500 students) and a number of weekend and day schools (1,352 students) at a total cost of £13,180. Other unions which were then making substantial financial contributions towards their own schemes were the National Union of Railwaymen, the Transport Salaried Staff Association, the Electrical Trades Union (£25,000), the Amalgamated Trades Union £(20,825), the Association of Engineering and Shipbuilding Draughtsmen and the Amalgamated Society of Woodworkers. In the year 1957, the total expenditure on all forms of education in unions, probably the most active, which answered a questionnaire sent out by the T.U.C. was £241,418. Of this sum no less than £142,334 or almost 60% was

* Statistical details about T.U.C. courses can be obtained from the Annual Report, which also contains an account of the year's work.

expended upon in-service schemes.* Compare this figure with the payment in the same year of £45,211 to the N.C.L.C. and £26,568 to the W.E.T.U.C.

The nature of the work done by individual trade unions is not much publicised. It would appear, however, that it is mainly limited to internal training in such practical matters as the techniques of communication, recording minutes, writing reports, and conducting meetings. The Transport and General Workers' Union, for example, arranges a home study course entitled 'The Union, its Work and Problems'. Post-war experience has shown that officials at all levels cannot function efficiently unless they not only fully understand the structure and problems of the industries with which they are directly involved but also perceive a relationship between the working conditions of their members and broad national issues.

Some trades councils organise lectures and classes on their own account. No statistics are available but senior trade union officials consider that the total amount of work carried out by this means is small.

Until the new scheme was introduced, the W.E.A. collaborated with the trade unions through the Workers' Educational Trades Union Committee (the W.E.T.U.C.), founded in 1919. At the national level three full-time officers were employed and it was considered an integral part of the function of district secretaries and tutor organisers to serve the interests of the trade union movement to the best of their ability. The W.E.A. is continuing to appoint special administrative committees to maintain close contact with the unions.

It is widely hoped that the new scheme will provide fresh outlets for the W.E.A., which was previously hampered not only by the rivalry of the N.C.L.C. but also by the difficulty of arousing enthusiasm in rank and file trade unionists. Complaints were often voiced about investing resources in trade union work to little purpose. Whenever direct comparison could be made with the effort expended and the achievement reached in the non-trade union field, it was found that the trade union work was disproportionately costly in time and money. Why was this so? Two reasons have been suggested. One is that trade unionists in general are either unwill-

* These figures have been extracted from a private survey undertaken by the T.U.C.

ing or unable to attend ordinary evening classes during the.winter months. The second and perhaps the more telling reason is that the kind of courses and methods used by the W.E.A. are inappropriate to the requirements of most trade unionists, many of whom want first and foremost to improve their proficiency in reading and writing. Various experiments have been tried to overcome these two problems but without much success. Unless the W.E.A. proves to be more skilful in identifying needs and adapting its methods than in the past, there can be little optimism about its ability to capitalise upon the new scheme.

Until comparatively recently the universities always assisted the trade unions indirectly through the Workers' Educational Association. For about 10 years, however, there has been an increasing tendency for a direct relationship to be established between a particular university extra-mural department and a particular trade union or a group of trade unionists concerned about a common topic such as collective bargaining. The first arrangement of this kind was made before the Second World War between the National Union of Mineworkers and Nottingham University. After the war the same union made an arrangement with both Sheffield and Leeds Universities. The feature of the courses arranged was that the N.U.M. paid selected nominees to take a day off from work in order to participate in an intensive course of study.

Elsewhere, isolated administrators in the extra-mural field have also discerned the possibilities of fruitful co-operation with the trade unions. The Oxford Delegacy for Extra-Mural Studies accord the highest priority to the study and teaching of Industrial Relations and to work with trade unions, two of their staff being employed full-time in this field. At both Nottingham and London the policy of the extra-mural departments has been to activate, but nevertheless to work through, the traditional W.E.A. machinery. The practice of organising both day-release and factory-based courses is rapidly spreading.

A few years ago, in an essay entitled 'Changes in Trade Union Education', Professor Raybould indicated that bi-lateral agreements between the trade unions and the universities might increase.[7] In the light of further experience this now seems doubtful. On the other hand, it is possible that the new controlling body in the T.U.C. will find it necessary more often to approach the universities directly in search of advice. The provision of external courses, however, looks as though it will remain predominantly in the hands of the W.E.A.

The trade union movement could well be on the verge of a notable expansion in educational activity. If it fails, then it will not be the fault of the full-time officials at Congress House. The danger is that the T.U.C. may concentrate too much upon the need for technical and procedural training to the detriment of liberal studies. While in the past all courses were frankly intended to serve trade union interests, they could at the same time have been accurately described as liberal studies with a sharply defined trade union function. Certainly there has always been some involvement in an academic discipline, and in nearly all courses students have acquired training in democratic procedure and have been taught that the trade union movement must try to serve the whole community. It would be a pity if these broad aims were to be abandoned. The words used by an American trade unionist at a recent conference are here germane: 'That education has been most successful which starts with the immediate problems of the workers and builds upon them. If it is conceived narrowly this principle can be self-defeating and workers' education can be reduced to training.'[8] Now that the Industrial Training Boards are rapidly expanding the facilities for training, it is more important than ever that the broad educational needs of workers should not be neglected. If the trade unions themselves must concentrate upon practical instruction then they should turn to other bodies for help in devising and servicing appropriate courses.

For providing bodies a large scale expansion in trade union demands will pose a challenge. Traditional teaching methods and forms of provision are not necessarily apposite to the requirements of the average trade unionist, to the education, for instance, of shop stewards. Again it will be necessary to overcome an unexpected shortage of tutors, for one of the many oddities in the recent history of adult education is that whereas there was once a surplus of tutors qualified to teach economics and industrial relations, there is now a pronounced shortage. It should be added that educational institutions, especially the universities, have almost as much to gain from engaging in trade union work as they have to contribute. Educationists concerned with the social sciences need to maintain contact with the trade unions and the whole industrial network if they are not to become sterile researchers. Furthermore, there are some university teachers who are hostile to the participation of the universities in adult education unless it is seen to have a marked social purpose.[9] Finally, certain officers in the W.E.A. and university extra-mural departments would presumably welcome increased work with the trade union movement, since it would represent a way of redressing two effects of post-war development which alarm and distress them. The first is the decline of working-class participation in adult education; the second is the general abandonment of the old ideal of training for social responsibility.

iv. *The Co-operative Union*

> Our general purposes remain the same, to equip our employees for the efficiency and the understanding of co-operative principles which the movement needs: to strengthen the attachment and participation of our members on all levels of co-operative democracy; and to engage for co-operative institutions and ideals, the mind and imagination of youth. . . .[12]

The Co-operative Union has always sought to provide an educational service. Its chief concern is to acquaint the members of its 517* societies with its principles, structure and work and to point out the advantages of consumer co-operation. At the same time, seeing education as the key to social progress, it has always related its aims to national needs. To this day its membership is largely working class and it continues to be affiliated to the Labour Party.

Every society allocates funds for educational purposes. Most of it is retained at source, but a small proportion is sent to the Co-operative Union. In 1966 the total amount of grants was £433,000, a decrease of approximately £25,000 from 1964 and £69,000 from 1962. Nearly every society has an education committee and in 52 districts there is also an education officer. The established policy is to appoint a full-time official whenever societies have a greater membership than 20,000. At the present time there are 153 such societies, leaving a shortage of about 80 education officers. Like many another organisation concerned with adult education, the Co-operative Union finds it hard to attract suitably qualified

* 680 Societies in the United Kingdom.

organisers and teachers at the salaries it can afford to pay. In addition to education officers, some societies employ part-time tutor organisers.

In 1948 the Union created the National Co-operative Education Association with the task of supervising and co-ordinating all educational activities. This association deals directly with the Department of Education and Science and the local education authorities, and is affiliated to the W.E.A. and the National Institute of Adult Education. It makes numerous grants of varying amounts for a variety of purposes, including scholarships to the residential colleges and payment of correspondence course fees. Linking the central organisation with the local societies there are seven sectional educational councils which elect representatives to the national executive.

The work of the Education Association is administered by the Education Department, which has its headquarters at Stamford Hall, Loughborough. This Department has a chief education officer and a small permanent staff. In 1966 its outlay was £77,981. The Department works through 6 channels:

   (i) making awards of various kinds;
  (ii) giving advice to local societies;
 (iii) providing a system of correspondence courses;
 (iv) offering direct provision of short-term courses held sectionally or nationally;
  (v) supervising the work of the youth movement (ages 15–20);
 (vi) administering and staffing the Co-operative Residential College at Stamford.

The Education Department seeks first and foremost to stimulate the interest of all members in the organisation and aims of the Union. To this end, it provides a flow of ideas and issues helpful publications such as study guides. Its recent publications have included three 'Tracts for our Times': *Consumers in the Community*, *Co-operators in the Common Market*, and *Values in Modern Society*.

The Co-operative College, near Loughborough, has room for about 110 students. In principle, the sexes are mixed, but during the session 1966–67 there were only four women in residence as against 89 men. It is unusually attractive and well-appointed. Between ten and fifteen of its students follow courses very similar to those studied at the other long-term residential colleges. But the College pays most attention to technical and professional courses for co-operative employees, for whom it offers both long-term and sessional courses.

Even in so far as its courses are designed to meet technical requirements, the Co-operative Union is necessarily, although often incidentally, dealing with aspects of liberal studies. In practice, moreover, it also deals directly with liberal and recreational studies. From time to time attempts have been made to arrange for all liberal studies courses to be provided by other bodies such as the W.E.A. and the universities, and some officials have always felt that money is gratuitously wasted by offering facilities already provided by other organisations. These attempts have invariably failed, so much so that liberal studies today constitutes more than 50% of the Union's total education programme.

In recent years, the Co-operative Union has been making a determined effort to intensify its educational work. In 1957 it commissioned Mr. Brian Groombridge to undertake a detailed study of the co-operative auxiliaries, the Women's Co-operative Guild, the National Guild of Co-operators, the National Men's Guild, and the British Federation of Young Co-operators, and to make recommendations designed to increase their efficiency. He produced a comprehensive and challenging report which the Union might have chosen to ignore. On the contrary, most of his recommendations were adopted.[11] In 1956 the Union launched a five-year educational campaign. The reward for this self-questioning and enterprise has been an overall expansion in the amount of work being carried out, though the annual returns reveal that a peak of achievement seems to have been reached in the year 1960–61.

Despite the recession over the last seven years, however, it is clear that there has been a marked increase in student participation since the last war. The most striking advance has been made through the Women's Co-operative Guild, an organisation that has much in common with the Women's Institutes and the Townswomen's Guilds. An important innovation has been the spread of courses about consumer education. Some years ago a full-time tutor organiser was appointed to stimulate interest in the subject and to devise ways and means of making it not merely immediately interesting in a utilitarian sense, but a vehicle for examining the universal problem of standards and values. Other organisations might well profit from a study of the Union's experience in this special field. Unfortunately, this appointment had to be abandoned for lack of funds, with a consequent decline in the interest of members. It is, incidentally, the general feeling within the Union that both the level and quantity of work could be raised if only there were more full-time staff to stir up enthusiasm and to keep educational groups alive.

The total membership of the Co-operative Union in 1967 was 11,448,704.* In practice, of course, very few of these actually participate in its educational programmes. In practice, too, some societies are plainly much more active than others. Indeed, so far as can be gathered from annual reports, the burden of activity is carried by a minority of societies. The Education Department itself sees the membership as being divided into three concentric bands. The outer band consists of those members who have no interest whatsoever in the Co-operative Union except as a retail organisation. The intermediate band embraces the vast number of people who take occasional advantage of the facilities provided. Finally, there is a narrow inner band of members who take a sustained interest in the educational activities of the Union.

The Union distinguishes between in-service training courses for employees and the general educational activities of members. Over 10,000 employees attend day-release courses that are overwhelmingly technical in content. Members' activities are as follows: social and co-operative studies; subjects other than social studies; short lecture courses; cultural groups; and other educational activities. The attendance figures for 1966/67, excluding Scotland and Ireland, were:

(i) *Social (including Co-operative) Studies.* 1,784 students (1965–66—1934) took part in these studies with women exceeding men roughly four to one. About a third of the classes were provided by the W.E.A. More classes were provided by the branches themselves. There was a pronounced decline in attendance by comparison with the previous year.

(ii) *Subjects other than Social Studies.* These subjects correspond pretty closely to the sort of classes provided by evening institutes. It is not, therefore, surprising that almost half of the classes should

* 13,065,402 in the United Kingdom.

have been provided directly by the L.E.A.s and conducted by evening institute staff. It is also obvious that the bulk of these classes are for women, for in a total of 3,065 (1965–66—3,698) they outnumbered men in the ratio of five to one. More than half of the classes were provided independently by the Co-operative Societies.

(iii) *Short Lecture Courses.* Though these attracted 14,273 students (1965–66—13,915) there was a significant fall in attendance by comparison with previous years. Half these classes were provided by the local societies, the other half by the W.E.A. The Union itself ascribes the decline in numbers to the reduction of classes organised by the W.E.A., which had been obliged by a shortage of funds to restrict its normal programme. That their judgement is sound would seem borne out by the fact that the subjects to suffer most are those dealing with economic and social problems, and history.

(iv) *Cultural Groups.* By cultural groups the Co-operatives mean drama and choral societies, orchestras and bands, film societies and a miscellany of various groups. 217 groups containing 9,055 members and representing 86 societies were active. There was apparently a slight increase in the number of societies and groups but a slight decline in the number of members.

(v) *Other Educational Activities.* These activities, which include schools for members, concerts, film meetings and dramatic presentations, seem to attract fairly large numbers, but are so loosely organised and so marginally educational that the Union itself does not see fit to regard them on the same level as the other four categories.[12]

Excluding the last category, the total number of students taking advantage of the educational provision made by the Co-operative Societies was 28,597. More than half of these participated in classes arranged independently by the Union itself. Commenting on statistics of this order in its report for 1962 the National Education Association observed: 'there can be little reason for complacency in the total given in the above table. Persuading people to attend to serious adult liberal studies has always been difficult and the session 1960–61 represents the peak of achievement at the end of the first five years in which the "plan and challenge" scheme was operating'. That self-criticism was commendable and alas remains justified. The truth is that the leaders of the Co-operative Movement have splendid aspirations and are full of goodwill, but they do not provide adequate funds for a healthy education programme. There is a serious shortage of qualified staff, especially of organisers. Yet, here is a constituency ripe for development. For by and large the members of the Co-operative Union belong to that segment of the population which, though most in need of further education, is neglected by the traditional organisations. What is lacking is effective collaboration between the Union on the one side and the L.E.A.s and the Responsible Bodies on the other.

v. *Working Men's Clubs*

By tradition Working Men's Clubs have an educational as well as a social purpose. But today their educational purpose has become so indistinct that those who see them simply as convivial centres where working men can enjoy a pint of beer and play snooker are probably very near the mark.[13]

3,900 clubs are affiliated to the Club and Institute Union and in all there are approximately 2,000,000 club members. Though officially no pretence is made that education is a *raison d'être* of the Union, yet there is a national education committee and a full-time secretary who divides his responsibilities between education and recreational activities. Interposed between the national executive and the individual clubs there are also branch committees which have some care for education.

At both the national and the branch level the clubs are affiliated to the W.E.A. and sometimes to the Co-operative Union. They also award scholarships to members attending Ruskin College. Two national one-week schools are held annually at Vaughan College and Ruskin College respectively. Several one-day schools are also arranged and the small number of members who take correspondence courses can recover half of their fees.

In the small amount of educational provision made by the Clubs there is not much that is consciously oriented towards liberal studies. Thus, as a rule, one-day schools are divided into two parts: the first part is about committee procedure and the problems of running and financing a branch; the second part is concerned with wider social problems.

The fact that the Working Men's Clubs pay scant heed to education is no reason why they should be ignored as a point of penetration. Dotted about there are groups and individuals struggling against the prevailing demand for fun and relaxation. The W.E.A. in particular might well hold courses in conjunction with the clubs.

vi. *Pre-Retirement Courses*

During recent years it has been increasingly recognised that those who face impending retirement ought to be given some information about the problems they are likely to face and how they may best overcome them. The firm of Rubery Owen, the Glasgow Retirement Council and the City Literary Institute have acted as pioneers in the organising of pre-retirement courses. Now many L.E.A.s and a number of W.E.A. branches pay special attention to this problem.

Created in 1964 the Pre-Retirement Association operates as a consultative and servicing agency. In its publicity it states as its purpose: 'to enable people to make the most of their retirement: to prepare for a completely new pattern of living and avoid the sudden limitations of interests, the loneliness and sense of uselessness which engulf too many in their later years.' Firms and other bodies interested in developing pre-retirement schemes may turn to it for advice and assistance. It publishes pamphlets and reports on aspects of retirement and organises conferences on request.

So far most pre-retirement schemes have been designed for those on the brink of retirement. The real need, however, is for schemes spread over a long period, since people have to be conditioned to accept retirement and such conditioning cannot be achieved overnight.

Concern for those on the road to retirement should not lead to the neglect of those who have already retired. Some agencies, such as the Welsh Y.M.C.A., go out of their way to arrange appropriate programmes for the retired, but by and large the needs of this section of the community are not satisfied. Yet another argument for the spread of independent adult educational centres is that they could arrange morning and afternoon classes for the benefit of the retired.

The demand for educational facilities sponsored by industry and commerce seems bound to expand. Both manual and professional workers will require frequent re-training courses as the methods and techniques used in their work become obsolescent. Increasing numbers of married women are seeking part-time or full-time employment as soon as their children are no longer a tie. The danger is that attention will be focused so exclusively upon utilitarian training that general education will be neglected. Above all, it is now a matter of national concern that employees at all levels and in every branch of industry and commerce should perceive the importance of playing a full part in their factory, shop or office in strengthening the national economy. To this end employers should be more generous to employees over the age of twenty-one, as opposed to young people, in allowing time off for attendance at day-release classes.

REFERENCES

1. *Industry and Education: A Statement* (O.U.P.), p. 2.
2. p. 70.
3. Cf. British Institute of Management, *A Conspectus of Management Courses* (1963).
4. K. B. Robertson, 'Training for a Purpose' in *New Society*, 30 June 1966, pp. 12–13.
5. Cf. *Trade Union Educational Facilities* (Reprinted from the Report of the T.U.C. General Council to the Trades Union Congress 1960).
6. T.U.C. Report, 1961.
7. Cf. S. G. Raybould (ed.), *Trends in Adult Education*, pp. 49–51.
8. L. Roger, 'AFL–CIO and Union Schemes for Workers' Education in the United States' in Papers presented at a Conference held in Rewley House (Oxford, June 1965), p. 6.
9. For further reading cf. H. Clegg and R. Adams, *Trade Union Education* (W.E.A., 1959); A. H. Thornton and F. J. Bayliss, *Adult Education and the Industrial Community* (N.I.A.E., 1965).
10. *Report of Education Executive* (1961), p. 1.
11. B. Groombridge, *Report on the Co-operative Auxiliaries* (1960).
12. Cf. National Co-operative Education Association, *Education Executive Report* (1967), pp. 21–4.
13. In an article entitled 'Adult Education in Working Men's Clubs' in *Adult Education*, Vol. xxviii, 1955–56, pp. 260–72, Mr John Levitt gave a summary account of the work and attitudes of Working Men's Clubs. Though he was careful to emphasise that the amount of work done was extremely small, he nevertheless conveyed what was probably an optimistic view of its value.

Chapter Nine

OTHER NATIONAL ORGANISATIONS

Aside from the relatively powerful and highly structured organisations so far considered, there are a number of national bodies which exist either primarily or at least partially for the purpose of providing educational services and which are entirely or almost entirely financially self-supporting. In this chapter it will be possible to deal only with those that seem particularly important. They are divided into three groups:

(A) Organisations for which education is a primary aim.
(B) Organisations for which education is a secondary aim.
(C) Other organisations including a specific educational aim in their programmes.

(A) NATIONAL ORGANISATIONS WITH ADULT EDUCATION AS A PRIMARY AIM

i. *The National Adult School Union*

'Adult Schools are groups which seek on the basis of friendship to learn together and to enrich life through study, appreciation, social service, and obedience to a religious ideal.'[1]

This is a small and lonely voluntary organisation with a history of more than 150 years which, in the words of its secretary, is 'terribly poor and terribly unimportant'. During the early years of this century there were no fewer than 100,000 members. The advent of the First World War reduced that figure by half and since 1919 there has been a steady fall in membership. In 1966 the Union had about 5,000 members divided into roughly 320 groups of approximately 15 each. Since 1954 a few new groups have been formed. But though the number of groups shows a slight increase, the number of individual members continues to decline; the loss during 1962–63 for instance was 261 members.

The groups are organised into twenty County Unions which in turn send representatives to the National Council, a body of 110 members meeting twice a year. The entire association is run by a secretary and one assistant, aided by five committees including a handbook compilation committee. Individual members pay 6s. per year and their subscriptions amount to two-sevenths of the total income. In addition, the Union receives interest upon its fairly substantial capital, derived mainly from bequests.

The work of the groups is based upon a Handbook which is published every year and of which by 1967 there had been fifty-seven editions. The syllabus is changed each year, concentrates upon a subject that seems to be of topical concern, and seeks to offer a basis for discussion at exactly 52 meetings. In 1963 the subject was 'One World', in 1964, 'Living in the Sixties', in 1965, 'A Sense of Purpose', in 1966, 'Leading and Following'. About 80% of the groups, especially those more recently formed, make use of the Handbook. As a rule, they meet weekly in private houses for a period of one and a half hours. The remaining 20% of the groups, broadly corresponding to those first founded, assemble for 'Bright Hours' usually in Union premises. For them, as for all the members of the Union in the past, the purpose of these meet-ings is primarily religious.

The Central Office annually plans about thirty week-end schools and two summer schools, each of one week, which are attended by between thirty and forty people. It also publishes a monthly journal entitled *One and All*.

Since no money is available to pay either lecturers or teachers, the groups following the Handbook rely upon the discussion method. There is a shortage of group leaders. All the groups mainly consist of working class people with a leavening of lower middle class members, particularly in the newer groups.

The academic standard of the work is necessarily low. This explains why the Union has made several vain requests to the Department of Education and Science for a grant. The D.E.S. has rightly pointed out that the activities of the groups are not supervised by accredited teachers under sufficiently serious con-ditions and that the syllabus is not only sometimes unsound academically but also contains too much material—each section designed for two meetings ought to extend over a much longer period.

It may be there is no place for the Adult Schools in modern society. One passage in the Presidential Address at the Annual

Conference in 1964 would seem to suggest that some of its own members are dispirited: 'There are those who think our Movement is dead, and too many have never heard of its existence. Even within its ranks there are those who see no future for it.' Nevertheless, the movement represents a striking example of the instinct for survival. It might even yet take on a new lease of life by revolutionising its methods, for example, by borrowing ideas from the Great Books Programme in the United States or the Kit Scheme in Australia.

ii. *The Seafarers' Education Service and College of the Sea*

Here and there an independent and self-contained educational organisation can be seen admirably and quietly fulfilling an exemplary public service. Such an organisation is the Seafarers' Education Service and College of the Sea. Founded in 1919 under the inspiration of the ubiquitous Albert Mansbridge, it was intended to help serve the educational needs of men leading a life at sea. Today it has four main functions: to provide a library service; to supply films; to offer correspondence courses; and to guide and advise seamen who ask for help in educational matters.

The Seafarers' Education Service is a voluntary society governed by representatives of ship owners, seafarers' associations, voluntary societies connected with the sea, and distinguished educationists. Though a non-profit making organisation, largely subsisting on its income from trust funds, members' subscriptions and donations, it receives grants from the Department of Education and Science (1967–68—£3,135 + £1,630 for the library account) and the local education authorities (in 1967–68—£3,783). Its budget is small, however, and leaves little room for experiment and manoeuvre.

The main purpose of the Seafarers' Education Service is to provide libraries for British merchant ships. At the present time it is supplying about 1,500 ships—the bulk of Britain's ocean-going fleet. Some 40,000 new books, apart from paper backs, are purchased every year. The aim is to provide each ship with a collection of books likely to please all tastes, to supply specialist books on request and to change stocks sufficiently often to ensure that would-be readers can always find a new volume to interest them. Cultural and educational films are also supplied to supplement the provision of popular films to ships and shore establishments.

About 1,500 seamen take correspondence courses which are provided by the college and marked by a team of 800 honorary tutors. Some of the courses impinge upon professional studies, but the majority are of a general kind. Languages are among the most popular subjects. This is no doubt a small service but the standard of achievement is apparently high and for keen students who have the strength of will to overcome the difficulties of working at sea, the courses are invaluable.

One of the functions of the College is to provide educational advice to those who need it. In recent years the annual number of enquiries has tended to be little short of 2,000. An innovation in 1966 was the holding of an experimental residential course for seamen who were about to retire. In 1967 the College published jointly with the N.I.A.E. a book entitled *Modern Teaching Methods and the Merchant Navy* and written by Mr A. Carver. This important monograph examines the various ways in which seafarers may learn. The College of the Sea publishes a quarterly journal entitled *The Seafarer*.

iii. *The Rural Music Schools*

This splendid body, the only teaching organisation in adult education solely concerned with teaching music, is the offshoot of an unusually successful experiment. The Schools are not educational establishments as such but independent organisations with administrative centres from which itinerant teachers are sent out to conduct music classes either for groups or for individuals. They also organise concerts and musical groups.

The first school was founded in 1929 as a branch of an education settlement in Hertfordshire and today there are eleven* schools. They were created in order to meet the demand for musical education in rural areas, which was rightly felt to be serious and widespread, though, as their distinguished founder Miss Mary Ibberson has pointed out, the methods adopted could easily be applied, and subsequently have been applied, in urban areas. The

---

* Buckinghamshire (1963), Cornwall (1956), Dorset (1947), Hampshire (1934), Hertfordshire (1929), Holland (Lincolnshire, 1962), Kent (1948), Norfolk (1939), Suffolk (1945), Sussex (1934), and Wiltshire (1934).

emphasis was originally upon string playing, but now all branches of music are dealt with. Five desiderata are considered essential for each School:

(i) Teachers who combine professional efficiency with sympathy for the amateur's outlook.
(ii) A director responsible for the standard of teaching, who must be a musician as well as an organiser.
(iii) A centre or administrative headquarters.
(iv) A council representing the general public to help with organising and to raise funds.
(v) A council or advisory board of eminent musicians.

Each School has a director and a permanent staff, which may be large or small according to the range of its commitments, forming the nucleus of a musical community. A much larger panel of part-time teachers is also used, though there always remains a shortage of teachers. Collaboration is maintained with the county music organisers of the L.E.A.s, and indeed the directors of some of the Schools are doubly employed as County Music Organisers. The council of each School contains local authority representatives.

Though each of the Schools is autonomous, a good deal of planning and co-ordination is carried out by the headquarters of the Association, which is based in Hitchin. This headquarters, which consists of administrative offices and a small residential music centre, supplies a reference library and a gramophone record service and is prepared to help the Schools financially if they should run into difficulties. It also publishes a periodical, *Making Music*, three times a year and runs a small residential college at Little Benslow Hills, Hitchin. In addition it provides training courses for teachers.

Broadly speaking, the teaching costs of the Association are met out of public funds, voluntary subscriptions and students' fees. The local authorities make grants to the Schools individually, Kent being notably generous. The Association also has capital funds and a small income from subscriptions. But the bulk of its money comes from the Department of Education and Science. The D.E.S. has made a grant to the Association of more than £4,000 per year for the last seven years (£5,166 in 1966) and this has been supplemented by generous grants from the Gulbenkian Foundation Fund. Nevertheless, lack of money is a handicap despite the fact that an appeal for a Development Fund in 1964 had brought in £10,000 by the end of 1967.

Facilities in the Schools' centres vary greatly. Some can accommodate classes and musical performances, whereas others are no more than administrative offices. Each centre has been deliberately located in a town that is the natural focal point for a wide area. The first centre, for example, was established at Hitchin, a small market town in Hertfordshire. Population movements and transport changes have altered the pattern in the countryside since the first School was founded but the guiding principle still remains to serve areas in which there is no urban centre large enough to offer reasonable musical facilities.

It is a striking fact that all but one of the Schools are located in the south—in Kent, for instance, there are centres at Maidstone, Canterbury and Tonbridge. This is because no request for Schools has come from rural areas in the north and it is the policy of the Association not to try to set up a new School unless there is a clearly articulated need for it. It is, of course, to be borne in mind that in some areas, such as North Lancashire, the county authority sponsors its own musical activities. Nevertheless, the demand for this type of musical education can scarcely be confined to the ten counties in which the Association now operates.

A fair proportion of the students served are still in full-time education. Even so, during the Session 1965–66, over 2,500 adults took advantage of the facilities provided by the Schools, whose creed is that musical education should be a continuous all-age process. The work is conducted mainly in the late afternoons and evenings.

The achievement of the movement is substantial. Between 1963 and 1967 its numbers rose from 14,500 to almost 28,000. It has brought music to a vast number of people who would otherwise have remained deprived of it. It has been remarkably successful in getting professionals and amateurs to work together and in engendering a spirit of camaraderie. Some measure of its achievement is afforded by the fact that when its founder and first director retired in 1962, a concert was arranged at the Royal College of Music in which all but four of the 500 performers had passed through one of the Schools at one time or another.

iv. *The Field Studies Council*

The Field Studies Council, an independent organisation, was founded in 1943 as the Council for the Promotion of Field Studies, with the object of stimulating interest in and providing facilities for studying every branch of field work, from art to geology, from archaeology to geography, and from natural history to meteorology. At the present time there are nine fully established residential centres, two of which were opened in 1967 and 1968 respectively. The intention in 1966 was to provide a total of fifteen centres by 1976, but a shortage of capital now makes this an unlikely prospect. Each centre is situated in the heart of the countryside so as to afford easy access to the practical work which is the basis of the Council's approach. In a policy statement put out in 1966 the Field Studies Council made this important statement of purpose: 'The Council intends that the centres shall be research as well as teaching organisations. Effective teaching is itself promoted by active participation in research.'

Until March 1963, the D.E.S. provided an annual grant with the aim of helping the Council to become a going concern. On that date, however, the grant, which had been gradually scaled down year by year, was finally withdrawn. So far, the L.E.A.s have given little in the way of direct financial help, though they have been generous in grant-aiding students. Apart from grants from universities and occasional grants from industrial organisations, the council subsists on fees from students which must necessarily be fixed at an economic rate. If capital grants were available, however, there is no question that the council could substantially extend the range of its work.

Each centre is directed by a warden-tutor, assisted by two other graduate members of staff and, from time to time, by visiting experts. Laboratory, library and other essential facilities are provided. The centres close from November to February but are fairly full throughout the rest of the year and much over-subscribed during certain peak-periods.

During the session 1966–67, 12,538 students attended courses at the centres, of whom 871 were described in the annual report as amateurs. These amateurs were, in fact, adult students as opposed to students still in full-time education.

The Field Studies Council caters for a small but high quality minority of the population. Its work is obviously sound and received very favourable endorsement from a Ministry inspection some years ago, and the inspectorate continues to give it the strongest support. For this reason, it would seem entitled to a reasonable allocation if more public funds should become available for adult education.

(B) NATIONAL ORGANISATIONS WITH ADULT EDUCATION AS A SECONDARY AIM

i. *The Young Women's Christian Association*

Not much liberal education of a formal kind is carried on under the auspices of the Y.W.C.A. Informal educational activities, however, are arranged independently by each club, the quality and amount of what is done depending upon local circumstances.

As can be seen from the general statement of aims given in its *Handbook* for 1961, the status given to education is vague:

'To unite Members in groups for fellowship, service and activities which promote their spiritual, intellectual, social and physical welfare, including opportunities for prayer and bible study, *informal**
education, recreation and the provision of clubs, hostels, and other amenities, . . . To stimulate in Members a sense of membership based on Christian teaching.'[2]

Though the reference here to education is unspecific, it is only fair to say that the Y.W.C.A. would consider that group meetings for any constructive purpose provide in essence an educational experience.

The informal work undertaken assumes a variety of forms. There are talks and demonstrations, film shows, discussions, quizzes and visits. There are also many recreational activities. But the key feature of all these informal activities is that there is no continuity and no attempt to pursue a special theme.

A minority of clubs do organise formal classes. These are normally taught by teachers supplied by the L.E.A.s following a formal application submitted in the summer before the class is due to begin. From a report of activities in Y.W.C.A. membership

* My italics.

groups and centres in 1960, it is possible to work out the subject areas and the number of courses in each as follows:

	No. of Clubs
History (broadly defined)	3
Sociology and General Social Studies	6
Philosophy and Religion	34
English Language and Literature	53
Foreign Languages, Literature and Culture	8
Music	38
Visual Arts	16
Recreational activities (miscellaneous groups)	61

Considering that at the time there were altogether 180 clubs in the United Kingdom, this was an insignificant amount of work. One experiment which the Y.W.C.A. might consider is organising day-time classes for young married women.

But in criticising the small provision for education by the Y.W.C.A., it is important to emphasise that it pays much attention to religious and social training, a good deal of which is bound to be educational in the broad sense. Furthermore, it has recently been making successful efforts to develop day-release courses for young girls, especially in the London area.

ii. *The Young Men's Christian Association*

Throughout its long history the Y.M.C.A. has taken its educational obligations very seriously. One sentence in its statement of aims reads: 'The educational opportunities of such a movement are obvious, and have been recognised by its leaders from the earliest days of its history.' Naturally it gives the highest priority to moral training but it also tries to assist its members to come to terms with society and to understand the world around them.

Institutionally, it is organised in three tiers: local associations, divisions and a national council. The National Council has a large and distinguished education committee and employs a full-time education officer. Though subsidised by the D.E.S. (in 1967 £3,380), some of the local authorities, the Carnegie United Kingdom Trust and a number of other bodies, this committee runs its programme at a loss, its annual deficit of approximately £6,000 being met out of general funds. Its annual budget is of the order of £50,000.

The educational work of the Y.M.C.A. is provided by three bodies:

(i) the local associations,
(ii) the Youth in Industry Department,
(iii) its own residential colleges.

(i) *Work of the local associations*. The National Council have no exact information about the standards and quantity of the educational provision sponsored by the local associations, but there is evidently a gap between what they consider desirable and what is actually done. Precisely how much work is undertaken depends upon local conditions and upon the special interests and degree of enterprise of individual secretaries. At the principal centre in London, there is a regular programme of lecture and discussion groups pitched at a high level. A number of associations both directly provide and sponsor classes, schools, conferences, research projects and multifarious informal activities.

What this all amounts to is hard to assess since there are no reliable statistics. The most recent indication dates back to the years 1961–62 and 1962–63 when the following figures were estimated from the national survey returns:

1960–61	1961–62	
36	45	Terminal and One-Year Classes
57	58	Bible Study
76	83	Discussion
54	67	Dramatic Societies
54	68	Photography
73	83	Record Recital
43	43	Music and Music Appreciation
30	43	Art and Art Appreciation
28	40	Debating Societies
27	35	Modelling
19	23	Choirs
19	17	Radio Clubs
19	11	Orchestras
11	23	Speech Training
7	11	Stamp Collecting
6	9	Operatic Societies
31	38	Holidays Abroad
590	697	

It is plainly difficult to estimate the quality of such activities. They give the impression of being concerned with random informal studies rather than sustained and serious work. At the same time, it is the belief of the Y.M.C.A. that in order to make an impact on young people one must be prepared to seize and exploit their ephemeral interest in what may be a kaleidoscope of subjects. In other words, it is the ethos of a hostel or centre that counts. It is probable, therefore, that a great deal of fruitful discussion about social and political problems takes place which is never recorded and whose value is intangible.

(ii) *Youth in Industry Department.* In 1960, the Y.M.C.A. set up a department specifically to deal with young workers. Its basic aim is 'to help young people to grow up as persons as well as workers and to have a sense of responsible citizenship in our modern society'. Six full-time area secretaries and one part-time secretary have been appointed with the initial task of establishing relations with industrial firms and obtaining agreement to hold weekly, fortnightly or monthly meetings for employees during the firms' own time and on the firms' premises. These meetings are generally devoted to examining the problems of growing up in contemporary society and to studying current affairs and 'basic questions concerning the meaning and purpose of life'. This scheme has brought the Y.M.C.A. annually in touch with over 1,000 young workers and obviously has great merit. In its early stages it was financed partly by the Carnegie United Kingdom Trust and partly by industrial firms and local education authorities. Some L.E.A.s have been particularly generous: Gloucestershire provides £750 a year and Cumberland finds the whole salary of one of the area secretaries. The scheme is now almost self-supporting.

(iii) *Programmes arranged in residential colleges.* The Y.M.C.A. has three residential colleges* and maintains close links with two more.†

Formed in 1918 and a Responsible Body, the Welsh Y.M.C.A. has been concentrating in recent years upon terminal and short courses and breaking away from its traditional practice of offering

---

* Dunford College, Sussex; Kingsgate College, Kent; Coleg-y-Fro, Glamorganshire.

† International Centre, Castle Mainau, Germany, and Cheshunt College, Cambridge.

single lectures. During the year 1965–66 its programme was as follows:

29 short terminal courses   (1961–62—37)
27 terminal courses   (1961–62—18)
63 other lectures   (1961–62—76)

The total of students attending was 2,781. Welsh history and language was the most popular subject; psychology, philosophy, sociology and international affairs came next; and there were a few classes in Bible Study and Christian Ethics. An outstanding feature is the programme of courses for hospital patients and old age pensioners. The Welsh Y.M.C.A. also runs its own independent Youth in Industry programme.

The Education Committee of the Y.M.C.A. is confident that with more money it could immediately expand the scope and volume of its work. It is a deserving case, for it shows a willingness to experiment and uses original methods in dealing with young people. If there is to be more continuity in the educational process, then closer cooperation between the Y.M.C.A. and the leading adult educational bodies would seem required.

(c) OTHER ORGANISATIONS INCLUDING A
SPECIFIC EDUCATIONAL AIM IN THEIR PROGRAMMES

There exists a whole host of organisations for which education is geared to a special purpose. For convenience these purposes may be classified under six heads: social, political, aesthetic, scientific, commercial and religious.

Social

Of all the organisations with a social purpose easily the most important is the National Council of Social Service. It is concerned with voluntary social work in town and country and shelters under its capacious wing a large number of bodies having a greater or lesser care for education.* Its overriding objective has been to develop in the population a sense of social responsibility. For this reason it encourages voluntary service, believing that service not

---

* Organisations sponsored by the National Council of Social Service are referred to elsewhere in the text, e.g. Community Associations, pp. 72-5.

only benefits society as a whole but the person who undertakes it. This may be viewed as education through action. Because the countryside is so badly serviced, it has concentrated especially upon starting and sustaining educational movements in rural areas. Not the least valuable of its general functions is the co-ordination of the activities of voluntary bodies both at the national and the local level.

Other organisations having a social purpose are concerned with health—the Central Council for Health Education, National Marriage Guidance Council, Family Planning Association, Red Cross; with the problems of particular groups—the Pre-Retirement Association, Housewives' Register, Ratepayers' Associations; with educational matters—Parent-Teachers' Associations, Association for the Advancement of State Education; with buying goods—the Consumer Association; with planned recreation—the Central Council of Physical Recreation. The list is long. Some organisations meet primarily for social purposes but arrange an educational programme, e.g. the Rotarians, Soroptimists, Business and Professional Women.

Political

Each of the political parties provides a loosely constructed educational programme. Associations attached to the parties are often more purposeful as witness the Fabian Society and the Bow Group. Other bodies try to raise the level of political understanding, e.g. The Hansard Society for Parliamentary Government. Others, again, promote regional and international co-operation, *e.g.* the United Nations Association, whose branches nearly always arrange an annual programme of lectures and debates; the English-Speaking Union, a powerful organisation which through its headquarters in London and its various branches runs a substantial educational programme; the Commonwealth Institute, as its name suggests, spreads knowledge about the countries in the Commonwealth. At the local level, there are numerous debating societies.

Aesthetic

The Arts Council received a new charter in 1967 and a steep increase in its financial allocation (1968–69=£7,750,000—including Scotland). Its aims are:

'to stimulate public interest in Music, Drama, Art, Poetry, Opera and Ballet; to encourage active participation; to ensure the greatest possible accessibility of the Arts'.

Though its annual grant is made by Parliament and administered by the Treasury, the Council is free to distribute its resources as it sees fit. There is a separate council for Wales as well as for Scotland.

A substantial portion of the grant goes to the 'national' opera and theatre companies. Nevertheless, significant sums of money are given in support of auxiliary adult education activities. Thus subsidies are awarded to local arts centres to enable them to engage professional lecturers and performers, to art clubs and art galleries for mounting exhibitions, and to music societies for arranging concerts. One of the more noteworthy subsidies is that given to enable parties of country dwellers to attend theatres and concert halls in the major towns.

The Society for Education through Art seeks to encourage interest in the arts. Inaugurated in 1957, the Civic Trust seeks 'to promote beauty and fight ugliness in town, village and country-side', using as its chief methods of communication travelling exhibitions and films. Besides the Civic Trust a number of bodies are concerned about the preservation of amenities, for example, the Council for Preservation of Rural England. The British Drama League tries to foster native drama, acts as a co-ordinating agency for local branches and arranges festivals, competitions, exhibitions and lending library facilities. Bodies concerned with music are legion, for example, the British Federation of Music Festivals. The English Folk Dance and Song Society supplies teachers and lecturers to local groups and offers vacation courses.

Scientific

Several organisations seek to develop an interest in science and technology. We may note the British Association for the Advancement of Science, the Scientific Film Association and the Society for Science Education in Film and Television.

Commercial

Apart from the commercial correspondence colleges referred to elsewhere* there are many profit-making organisations that offer

* See below, pp. 224–5.

classes. The British Association for Commercial and Industrial Education (BACIE) is a national body which has done much to arouse public and official concern for vocational education and to raise standards.

Religious

Last but by no means least of the organisations that use education as a means to an end are the churches. Indeed, in conspectuses of the field of adult education published in the past it was often the practice to devote a whole chapter to the educational work of the churches.

The borderline between pure evangelicism and education is hard to define. What is certain is that the churches are tending to use up-to-date methods both in training clergy and providing facilities for the laity. The Church of England, which prides itself on being a pioneer in adult education, has now organised its educational programme in a formal way. At the centre there is a special Adult Education sub-committee of the Church of England Council for Education and most dioceses now have local committees. It is also felt that religious education should be developed in collaboration with the L.E.A.s and other bodies. Southwark recently purchased a house to use as an educational centre. Many parishes now plan programmes of study; in one parish in Liverpool about one hundred people meet in small groups in private rooms. Much use is also made of residential colleges. There are several associations such as the William Temple Association. Many dioceses have appointed full-time education officers.

The Free Churches, of course, have always set great store by informed discussions among the laity. Apart from Bible classes and adult Sunday school classes there are often mid-week discussion groups about current social and political problems. How much and what sort of work is done depends upon the interests of individual congregations.

It is well known that the Catholic Church jealously guards control over the teaching of children. The same is true of its teaching of adults, which is very largely designed to reinforce a knowledge and understanding of church doctrine. At the same time, the Newman Association for graduates, the Grail for women and the Catholic Social Guild are concerned to have an educated laity in the broad sense. The Newman Society points out that between 10% and 20% of those who attend the regular programmes of lectures arranged by its branches are non-Catholics.

Like the Catholic Church the Jewish Church is anxious to buttress the faith of its adherents and trims its educational programme accordingly. The Central Jewish Lecture Committee plans a number of programmes.

Locally we also find Men's Fellowship groups, the Mothers' Unions, Young Wives' Leagues, and church discussion groups. Toc H continues to arrange lectures and discussion groups.

iv

The organisations mentioned in this chapter are only the better-known ones. For some idea of the number that might have been referred to, it is convenient to consult the annual directory of the N.I.A.E., where no fewer than 68 organisations are listed. And even that list is incomplete, especially as there are certain organisations that perform an educational role of which they are unaware. The need here is for professional adult educators to be alert to detect such organisations and to persuade them to control the educational component in their programmes in a more purposeful way.

In order that the maximum number of people should continue their education it is important that organisations for which education is a secondary or incidental interest should treat it more seriously. There are two measures they might consider adopting: the first is to plan sequential programmes; the second is to set up, wherever possible, special committees to promote the educational aspect of their work.

REFERENCES

1. Minute of Education Committee of the movement (1948).
2. *Handbook of the Y.M.C.A.*, p. 7.

Chapter Ten

SOCIETIES AND CLUBS

. . . many clubs set out deliberately to instruct their members as well as to entertain them. This is true not only of specialist organisations such as scientific societies, but also of more general groups such as the Women's Institutes or youth clubs; a large proportion of even the purely social clubs find time for periodical talks and discussions. The contribution thus made to what we may call "informal education", although difficult to measure, is undoubtedly very great.[1]

It would be wrong to assume that the extent of public participation in adult education has been exhausted with the enumeration of the various forms of provision described in preceding chapters. Apart from attending classes organised by public or private institutions people also educate themselves either by solitary effort—reading, attending concerts, visiting galleries, listening to the radio*—or by taking part in unofficially sponsored social and cultural activities. Clubs and societies of all kinds abound throughout the country. Some are affiliated to a national co-ordinating body whereas many are exclusively local. No one knows how many there are or how significant is their impact but they cannot be overlooked. Although a few special studies have been made here and there and passing reference to their activities has been made in works largely concerned with general sociological problems or the sociology of particular communities,[2] the total stock of evidence remains meagre.

Speculative inferences can be drawn about the nation-wide educational value and influence of societies from subjective impressions, but it is impossible to put forward any reliable conclusions. To carry out a detailed national survey would be unduly burdensome, complicated, and prohibitively expensive. In the short term, therefore, the only expedient is to make detailed studies of special areas. For the purpose of this present survey

---

* It is plainly extremely difficult to estimate the extent and significance of such individual efforts. The task has not been attempted here but is obviously very important.

such a study was made of the City of Liverpool. Further evidence was then gleaned from other studies.

The method adopted for ascertaining the number and cultural impact of societies in Liverpool was to set up a working party consisting of men and women prominent in various spheres of civic life. The task of this working party was threefold:

(i) to ascertain how much social and cultural activity was taking place in Liverpool;
(ii) to determine how far this activity contributed to the fundamental social and cultural needs of the City;
(iii) to make recommendations.

For convenience the survey was confined to the City of Liverpool although in fact the amenities of Liverpool are used by many people residing outside the municipal boundaries. Despite its drab and even unsavoury reputation Liverpool is far from being a cultural desert. On the contrary, it compares favourably with most cities in the country outside the metropolis. In other words, any conclusions based on the vigour of its cultural activity should not be assumed to understate the situation in most provincial cities but perhaps to overstate it.

The population of Liverpool is approximately 750,000. In density it is unusually high. High also is the number of children and young people under the age of 18. There is a large working class population and during times of economic recession the level of unemployment rises well above the national average. Only the poorer people tend to live in or near the centre of the city. Communications are good, however, so that in the evening, when the volume of traffic has slackened off, it is possible for almost anyone to reach the centre in under or little over half an hour. This means that social and other activities can conveniently be centralised.

At the very beginning of any enquiry of this kind it is more necessary than ever to determine what should and should not be defined as adult education. In the loosest sense almost any activity may have some educational content. For example, a member of the working party was frequently at pains to point out that for *aficionados* keeping homing pigeons is educative as well as relaxing, since fanciers not only learn about the habits of their birds but through them become aware of the principles of flight and the practices of predators, whether of the human or animal species. There are also degrees of intensity of educational activity. Some societies care about educating their members more than others. For this reason it was decided to construct a classification for informal educational activities which would have as wide an application as possible. Six categories were separated out as follows:

(i) Associations having some kind of educational activity as an integral part of their programme (e.g. Historical Societies).
(ii) Professional associations that exclude laymen, having some kind of educational activity as part of their programme.
(iii) Associations having specific intellectual or cultural aims (e.g. debating societies and music societies).
(iv) Associations having basically social aims, but including some educational provision in their programme (e.g. community associations).
(v) The affiliated clubs of commercial or semi-commercial undertakings.
(vi) Certain hobbies societies.

Whether or not this classification is universally valid, it has at least the merit of ensuring that no group having any pretensions to educate its members is likely to be overlooked. If anything, it errs on the side of being too comprehensive.

To work out a classification is comparatively easy: to apply it is more difficult. In the first place it is impossible in almost any English town or city to lay hands upon a complete and authentic list of clubs and societies. It is true that most local authorities publish directories of one kind or another, but these invariably contain many irrelevant and misleading details and in any case leave out a good deal of essential information. The working party decided to tackle this problem by invoking its members' experience and intimate knowledge of the city. Thus, the directory officially published by the municipal authority and other handbooks were carefully sifted in order to determine which of the societies listed were entitled to belong to one of the six selected categories. When this had been done, the names of other societies known to the group were added, a notice was published in the press inviting people to submit the names of societies to which they belonged or with which they were familiar, and several officials in federal associations were asked to submit further lists. In spite of all these precautions, some societies may still have slipped through the net. It seems safe to assume, however, that all the really important ones were identified. The list was further adjusted by means of a questionnaire which had the dual purpose of determining the validity of societies' claims to be educational and eliciting information about their aims and their members.

The next task was to summarise the general characteristics of the societies that had survived the sifting process and to ascertain their differences and their educational value. To this end four methods were adopted. First, we drew upon the knowledge and suggestions of the members of the working party themselves. Secondly, we studied previous reports about the life of the city. Thirdly, we distributed a questionnaire to all the associations on the list. And finally we invited a number of distinguished citizens to give their views, purely subjectively, upon the vitality of the intellectual and cultural life of Liverpool.

A pilot questionnaire was distributed to 12 societies. In the light of their replies and the trouble they experienced in answering particular questions, that questionnaire was redesigned. It was then sent out to each of the 124 societies in the selected list. Of these societies, 94 (or 76%) replied. It may well be that of the 30 societies failing to reply, a number were either completely defunct or temporarily suspended. At any rate, no reply was received from this group to even a third letter of reminder. There is significance in the fact that all the well-known societies in Liverpool replied promptly and in detail.*

The number of members in each society varied from under 20 to over 1,000. Two out of five societies have a membership of over 1,000. The majority of societies (37) have a membership of between 100 and 500. One society has under 20 members. 18 societies have 50 members or less and 17 have between 50 and 100 members. 9 societies have between 500 and 1,000 and 7 societies have over 1,000 members.

The total membership of all the societies is 7,690. Of this, 4,081 are women and 3,609 are men. Membership of many societies is rigorously restricted to one sex. But this factor seems to balance itself out.

---

* One striking fact is that over a third of the societies which replied were founded before 1914 and that very nearly two thirds were founded before 1939.

G

About 500 members are in the age group 18–25, 676 are in the age group 26–39, 1,000 are in the age group 40–59 and 560 are over 60. These figures refer only to those societies whose secretary had some idea of the ages of his members. It will be noted that this age pattern is similar to that found in publicly organised classes.*

Of course, the size of membership gives no accurate indication of the actual attendance at meetings. Several clubs, especially those in which members share a common interest, report a high rate of attendance, e.g. the Aquarists Club has a membership of 48 and an average attendance of 30. On the other hand, another club with a membership of 140 has an actual attendance of 35. A third club with 122 members has an average attendance of 35. Seen as a percentage of the membership attendance figures seem to vary from about 65% to about 20%.

As a general rule, societies hold a regular number of meetings in each year, usually from October to June with a summer recess of two or three months. Regular meetings are essential if clubs wish to stay healthy.

A number of societies evidently take great pains in preparing their annual programmes and some are able to attract distinguished speakers. Although most societies rely, of course, upon local personalities giving their services for no lecturing fee, quite a few build their programme around the capacity and experience of their own members, upon whom they depend for talks.

Most societies are content to make ends meet and require only sufficient funds for the hire of premises, payment of speakers and their personnel and secretarial costs. One club has an annual subscription of £21 and another has a subscription of five guineas. For the rest, subscriptions range from about 5s. to about 30s. Few societies have reserve funds but a small though significant number receive grants of varying size. The Dante Alighieri Society receives a subscription of between £80 and £120 per year from the Sede Centrale, Rome. 17 Societies occupy rented premises, 13 own their own premises, 22 obtain accommodation free of charge and 39 hire premises for their meetings. A number of societies complain that their main difficulty lies in finding accommodation and in paying for it. It is, in fact, perfectly clear that the

*See below, p. 318.

success of a society depends largely upon its ability to secure attractive and comfortable premises for its meetings.

The overall impression formed from this survey is that voluntary clubs and societies answer a vital cultural and social need. In a city the size of Liverpool, it is possible to find a group of people who have come together in pursuit of almost any interest that comes to mind. In short, no one can legitimately complain that he cannot find a group of like-minded people with whom to converse and exchange ideas. At the same time, clubs and societies attract only a small percentage of the population. Even if it be assumed, and it is a far-fetched assumption, that the proportion of members in the societies which did not reply was of the same order as those who did, it would still mean that all the clubs and societies in Liverpool combined have no more than 9,000 members. When these further facts are considered—that many people belong to more than one society, that a considerable proportion of members must reside outside the city and that some societies have a membership of over 1,000—it is clear that something like 95% of the city's population do not belong to any association having even a marginal educational purpose.

It is possible to supplement the above account by reference to the situation in Wolverhampton.* There some 26 societies with a total membership of 4,195 can reasonably be described as pursuing an educational objective. The first striking fact is that only 6 societies or rather less than 25% were founded before 1939; the inter-war period was either unfavourable to the founding of clubs or clubs were then founded and failed to prosper, for only two date from that time.

51% of members regularly attend meetings. 51% are women and 49% are men. Half of the total membership in all societies is to be found in the Literary and Scientific Society, which has the distinction of being the first to be founded, in 1880. The most striking fact about this society is that it commands a regular attendance figure of 58%. Presumably the pull of tradition and prestige is very powerful.

As a percentage of the local population roughly three times as many people belong to societies in Wolverhampton as compared

---

* The raw material for this short section was generously provided by Mr Ingram, Principal of the Adult Institute. He is not responsible, however, for either the comments made or the percentages quoted.

with Liverpool. It could be, of course, that it is much easier to form societies in a small town, though naturally the larger town can offer more variety.

One important fact about the position of societies in Wolverhampton is that their role as auxiliaries of adult education is formally recognised by the Local Authority. They are given free publicity by having their aims and programme described in a general prospectus entitled *Fanfare*. They are allowed the use of a large house, specially adapted as a cultural centre, for a nominal hiring fee. And they may be given small grants to enable them to secure the services of distinguished lecturers.*

In a recent survey of voluntary organisations in Halifax, Lady Morris found 193 societies in a town of one hundred thousand people, approximately half of them being concerned with some kind of social service (defined as 'founded by some for the benefit of others') and half concerned with the use of leisure. Of the latter the 'cultural' societies were tending to decline and had an ageing membership, while those concerned with sport or combining social intercourse with some kind of informal education (e.g. Rotary, T.W.G., Soroptimists) were on the up-grade. There was little evidence of overlapping between the two types of voluntary organisations.

What general conclusions can be drawn from this summary treatment of the activities of voluntary local societies? Quite clearly, with varying degrees of intensity, they do supplement the work of the publicly supported providing bodies. At the same time they deal with similar social strands in the population and are no more successful in attracting the support of the lower income groups and the less well educated. Indeed, it is the impression of some adult tutors and administrators that precisely the same people belong to cultural clubs and societies as attend their classes.†

*The Borough of Leicester is even more generous. It pays 50% of the approved teaching or lecturing costs of societies.

† Further complementary as well as reinforcing evidence, based on a study of Derby, may be found in Cauter and Downham, *The Communication of Ideas: a study of contemporary influence on urban life*. Their relevant conclusions were as follows:

> (i) 'While the main emphasis is naturally on the social and recreational facilities provided by clubs, there are few organisations (with the possible exception of sports clubs) that do not make some effort, however informal, to educate as well as to entertain. Although only a minority of people join clubs whose primary objective can be classified as cultural, the

number of people who do so is quite impressive by comparison with the number currently engaged in what we have called further education.' (p. 75.)

(ii) 'Whereas over a quarter of the people interviewed belonged to a social club of some kind, taking the latter in its widest sense, only about 1 in 9 belonged to a club whose primary purpose was "intellectual" (again in the widest sense).' (p. 68.)

(iii) '. . . a comparatively limited number of people in the population are responsible for a large proportion of total membership'. (p. 66.)

(iv) 'Most hobbies . . . have a strong utilitarian basis and they are practical rather than utilitarian.'
'The proportion of intellectual or cultural hobbies cannot amount to more than about 15 per cent of the total hobbies activities mentioned.' (p. 87.)

(v) 'Cultural clubs appear less popular among the under 35's.' (p. 66).

(vi) 'Cultural clubs . . . have a disproportionately large number of non-manual workers and a strong element of people not in employment (mainly housewives, but also some retired people)'. (p. 66.)

REFERENCES

1. Cauter, T., and Downham, J. S., *The Communication of Ideas: a study of contemporary influence on urban life* (1954), p. 62.

2. For example, Rowntree, B. S., and Lavers, G. R., *English Life and Leisure* (1951); Ruddock, R., and Wilson, D., *After Work: Leisure and Learning in Two Towns* (1959); M. Morris, *Voluntary Organisations and Social Progress* (1955). The Principal of the Adult Institute in Wolverhampton recently completed a thesis that took the form of a survey of the activities of clubs and societies in Wolverhampton (University of Leicester Library.)

Chapter Eleven

THE RURAL AREAS

It is extremely difficult, even for a trained person, to ascertain exactly what Further Education facilities are available in a given rural area.[1]

It is well known that the social contrast between country and town is much less marked than it used to be. The motor car has facilitated movement, labour conditions and housing have improved, and television has broadened tastes and interests. The composition of the rural population is also steadily changing. What were once strictly agricultural districts now frequently contain an infusion of professional and well-to-do people, and men who once worked on the land are often found working in factories in nearby towns. But if the disparity between town and country in terms of customs and outlook has largely vanished, from the point of view of adult educators an important demographic difference yet remains.

Whereas in a town it is relatively easy, given adequate civic concern, to provide educational facilities, in a small place or any sparsely populated area it can be extremely difficult. Thus the obligations of the L.E.A. in the City of Oxford, say, can be discharged by offering a variety of classes in a number of separate establishments and leaving the public to choose what it will. Serving the needs of the inhabitants of North Oxfordshire is another matter, however. Even a town of the size of Banbury affords little scope for a selective programme and outside Banbury there are only small villages scattered over a wide area. Nor is North Oxfordshire untypical, for a surprisingly large part of England and Wales still consists of very small towns and innumerable villages, many of which remain more or less self-contained.

In any case, it would be a mistake to assume that we have to deal only with a 'rural' problem. Many people now live in areas which are neither strictly town nor country, though they are certainly the product of urban sprawl. Take the case of Leicester and its environs, for example. An administrator might reasonably argue that any person living within reach of the public transport system ought to be prepared to go into the centre of the city in order to attend classes. But what of the people who gain their living in and from the city but who choose to live outside it? How are they to be served?

Some administrators believe that with the extension of private car ownership it is sufficient to organise classes in the larger centres of population, arguing that if people are really interested in a given subject, they will gladly drive a long distance to a class centre. All the evidence indicates that this is not so. Inquiries by the Yorkshire Council for Further Education revealed that the population of the neighbouring countryside made scarcely any use of the facilities at hand in Beverley.[2] The several surveys in other parts of the country, described below in Chapter 15, substantiate this finding. On the whole people will not travel very far in search of classes; what is more, townsmen appear willing to travel longer distances than country dwellers. In many families, too, the car is not at the disposal of the housewife at the only time of day when she is free to attend classes. In any case, many people still do not own cars or are reluctant to venture far from home on unpleasant winter nights. Many parts of the countryside are worse off for public transport than they were even ten years ago. For various reasons, including competition from private cars, a number of local authorities have curtailed their public transport services, especially in the evenings. In some areas, the situation is so bad that since Dr Beeching's axe fell for the last time a considerable section of the population has been immobilised after 6 or 7 p.m. In short, if administrators confine their programmes to large centres, they will be denying a majority of country and suburban dwellers the right to attend classes.

The problem of providing facilities outside urban areas is tackled in a variety of ways. Cambridgeshire has its village colleges; Leicestershire and Oxfordshire have adopted somewhat similar centres. Some country authorities appoint organisers— Lancashire made its first appointment as long ago as 1928; others have one or two tutor organisers, the universities have their resident staff tutors, the W.E.A. their tutor-organisers. The Women's Institutes, as we have seen, cater for women's needs with some degree of success. A few residential colleges, such as Attingham Park and Dillington Hall, operate more or less as local education centres. Even before the last war Gloucestershire had set up a community council to oversee the needs of the whole county. Young Farmers' Clubs provide a notable public service. The British Drama League is very active. Above all, the work of Rural Community Councils deserves special mention.

Rural Community Councils are yet another offshoot of the National Council of Social Service. They employ salaried officials in each county, who are, as usual, underpaid and overstretched. Most of their work is organised through Parish Councils. Their overriding aim is to improve the conditions of rural life, and they are giving increasing attention to developing more and better facilities for the use of leisure and to preserving indigenous crafts and customs. To this end they arrange week-end schools and conferences. Their greatest achievement has been to stimulate the erection of village halls and the foundation of clubs. They can rightly claim to be pioneers in the field of informal adult education.

Despite the admirable record of a few counties existing facilities in the countryside are far from adequate. Many areas are poorly served and have always been neglected. Other areas enjoy short-lived periods of activity. A survey carried out some years ago by a member of the Southampton Extra-Mural Department showed that it is the villages having a population between 100 and 1,000 that are chiefly neglected. This is scarcely surprising; a resident staff tutor from a university extra-mural department may find upwards of 200 villages in his area; in the whole country there are fewer than 90 tutor organisers employed by the W.E.A. Districts. In any event the W.E.A. is not very effective, since it concentrates upon urban and industrial groups and is handicapped in some areas by its working class connection. But the basic trouble is the lack of suitable accommodation. Many villages have no accommodation at all and such premises as are available may be totally unsuitable. Schools, for example, are usually too small and seldom have chairs and desks of the right size. In this respect the newly built residential estates near the towns are more fortunate because the schools built since the war tend to be pleasing and comfortable to meet in.

There are, admittedly, serious obstacles to be overcome in dealing with the needs of the countryside. As a rule, the population is too small to allow a wide choice of activities. The universities are in a special difficulty here because of their determination to maintain high standards; indeed a class of long duration and

demanding a high degree of educational attainment is often unsuitable for a village group. The choice of subjects is also rigidly
circumscribed. A common complaint is that people read so little
that there is no basis for study and discussion. The feeling that
education is exclusively for the young is also more deeply rooted
than it is in the towns. Still more serious is the deep-seated ignorance of the aims of adult education and the kinds of facilities
that could be made available. Finally, there is the lack of interest
shown by men. If countrywomen are fairly active, countrymen
are lethargic. 'Yes, I shall come to a class but I'm afraid my
husband is not interested in that sort of thing', is a stock response
to class organisers.

What can be done? First, administrators should accept two
propositions:

(a) that it is essential to distinguish sharply between the needs
of people living in large centres of population and people living
outside them. This is primarily but not exclusively a rural problem. It affects all those people who cannot reach classes in the
large centres whether they happen to reside in dormitory suburbs
or deep in East Anglia.

(b) that, especially in the countryside, it is essential to distinguish the needs of the great majority of the population from
those of the small educated minority.

Given these two propositions, there are several measures
which could be adopted, according to local requirements and
resources:

1. Every village with a population of more than 500 which does
not possess a multi-purpose school should have its own hall.
Halls should be comfortable, warm in winter and fully equipped
for holding classes.

2. In each village or each group of villages the needs of the
people should be carefully studied and proper facilities provided
accordingly. Since the traditional form of adult class will usually
prove to be inappropriate, emphasis on short courses, single
lectures, and informal methods will be called for. The subjects
commonly studied in evening institutes are likely to be in most
demand. An initial course in local history is usually calculated
to arouse interest.

3. More public support should be given to the Rural Community Councils, the Women's Institutes and Young Farmers' Clubs, respectively. In particular, more full-time organisers are required.

4. Provided the W.E.A. can overcome the handicap of its name and adopt more flexible methods and techniques, it should find scope for expansion in country areas. Of course, it would have to recruit many more tutor organisers and therefore require greatly increased financial support from the Department of Education and Science.

5. In some of the more thickly populated villages it is possible to organise classes for the better educated. In general, however the needs of this group can be met only by establishing centres in a large catchment area. On the whole, the universities seem to play their part effectively, although most resident tutors would guarantee to double or treble their present programme if enough qualified teachers were available. For the rest, however, too little is being done. More centres are required where high level classes can take place alongside recreational and craft classes. Such centres might be new schools of any type, grammar schools, comprehensive schools, community centres or people's colleges.

6. Wherever a new school with decent amenities exists, it should become an adult education centre, at least during the evenings. Ideally, every new school should have an adult wing.

7. Much greater use should be made of the grammar schools, which are usually strategically placed and carry a certain social prestige. Furthermore, lively parent-teacher associations might well form the nucleus of adult groups. This would entail overcoming the lack of sympathy towards adult education of some grammar school headmasters and their staffs.

8. In general, school teachers occupy a key position in small communities. It is essential that they be cajoled into supporting and indeed sponsoring schemes for the education of adults.

9. Community centres are especially useful because of their comprehensive appeal and the informality of their ambience.

10. It would be helpful to have several residential colleges in every county, especially those which are sparsely populated. Such colleges could not only cater for residential students recruited from a wide area but also serve as education centres for the immediate neighbourhood.

11. A few enterprising county councils might well consider the

advantages of setting up people's colleges on Dutch and Danish models.

12. The L.E.A.s hold the key to expanding facilities. Aside from providing suitable accommodation they should be stimulating demand. For this purpose they need to appoint organisers and tutor organisers on a large scale, particularly men and women who are qualified to teach art, music and drama, and who are adept at using informal methods.

13. Seeing that the availability of cars and buses frequently governs the rate of attendance at classes, local authorities should take a leaf out of Cambridgeshire's book by providing public transport to take students to and from classes.

14. Local broadcasting stations could be of great value by deliberately addressing programmes to rural audiences.

15. Something like the Australian Kit scheme might also be tried. This is a scheme for supplying local autonomous groups with all the materials they need for conducting courses on their own account.

16. Finally, and above all, joint planning and consultation on the part of providing bodies and local organisations are essential if many areas are not to be neglected through default. All the interested parties should hold regular meetings in order to co-ordinate planning and to ensure an equitable distribution of facilities. Voluntary local committees, backed by the L.E.A.s, should be formed in every district. Leaflets and posters advertising the programmes of all providing bodies should be given the widest possible circulation.

REFERENCES

1. Yorkshire Council for Further Education, *Further Education and the Countryside* (1950), p. 27.
2. *Ibid.*

Chapter Twelve

BROADCASTING AND FILMS[1]

(A) THE ROLE OF BROADCASTING IN ADULT EDUCATION

i

It seems hardly necessary to say that the educative influence of broadcasting is enormous. No other medium of communication, whether it be the press, films, or paperback books, can stand comparison with it. While many people seldom read at all or lightly scan the sports' or women's features in popular newspapers, nearly every family has a television set and there are now more radio receivers than ever before. At one time or another during each day about 30,000,000 people watch television and over 18,000,000 people listen to the radio; even in the evenings there is still an average radio audience of one and a half million people.

Television has made a much greater impact upon social habits than sound broadcasting, itself a revolutionary force in its day, and there is reason to suppose that its specifically educational influence will continue to increase as existing techniques are perfected and new ones are introduced. Though only the more sophisticated section of the television audience may consciously register information and mental stimuli, all who view are exposed to a steady stream of ideas and impressions. Whether it is their intention or not, the broadcasting authorities cannot avoid affecting people's thoughts and attitudes. As the Hadow Committee[2] observed in 1928: 'Even if no single item labelled educational ever appeared in the programmes, broadcasting would still be a great educational influence.' It does not follow, of course, that the total influence of broadcasting is socially or educationally a good one and there are not a few educationists who consider its effects to be injurious.

The present and potential uses of television as an instrument of education have been discussed *ad nauseam* during recent years. The publication of the *Pilkington Report* in 1960 followed by the Government's White Paper arising from it, the inauguration in

1964 of a second television channel by the B.B.C., the controversy about the advantages and disadvantages of setting up a separate educational channel, and the plan to launch an 'open university' in 1971 have kept interest alive. The result is that little remains to be said on the subject. It is necessary, however, to try to define the function of television and sound broadcasting in the particular field of adult education and that is what this chapter will attempt to do.

ii

In the United Kingdom the State officially designates broadcasting a responsible public service. The British Broadcasting Corporation, by the terms of its charter dating from 1 January 1927 and the Independent Television Authority, by the terms of the Television Act 1954*, are required to maintain high standards and to serve the common good. To provide an educational service is taken to be an implicit function. Thus from its foundation the B.B.C.† proclaimed three aims: to disseminate objective information, to entertain, and to *educate*. And to its educational commitment it gave the highest priority during its formative years. It is now almost forgotten that *The Listener* was initially published as the educational journal of sound broadcasting.

Since the educational effects of broadcasting are intangible, attempts have been made to draw working distinctions, as for instance between 'educative' and 'educational' programmes or between 'generally educational' and 'narrowly instructional' programmes. In an unpublished report the Broadcasting Sub-Committee of the Universities Council for Adult Education reached this conclusion:

A rough distinction can, in fact, be drawn between three types of programmes, the *instructional* (offering preparation for an examination or qualification of some kind, or similar intensive and limited studies, including training for a skill), the *educational* (explicitly

* Renewed in 1964.
† Whereas the commercial television companies tend to preserve a discreet silence about their responsibility, the B.B.C. frequently stresses the fact that it offers a public service. It is mainly for this reason that the B.B.C. is cited more often in this chapter than the commercial television companies. However, on most points concerning the educational uses of television what can be said of the B.B.C. can now equally be said of the commercial television companies.

aimed at encouraging serious attention and study in the field of liberal education, sustained over a period, but without concern for qualifications), and the *educative* (covering a wide range of programmes which to a greater or lesser extent enlarge the knowledge or understanding of the viewer without necessarily calling for a serious study).

This distinction closely parallels that made by the Pilkington Committee. To begin with, that Committee recognised that nearly all the programmes may have a diffused educative effect.* Thereafter, excluding school broadcasts, it distinguished two categories: (i) particular programmes that are unquestionably educative; (ii) programmes that are directly educational.

One thing is clear. There is a risk in seeking too rigid a classification of functions. The B.B.C. has consistently argued that it would be wrong to separate its educational function from its other functions by running an educational programme independently of its general services. To do so, in its opinion, would be to ensure that the vast majority of people would never tune in to the educational programmes. The only way of influencing most people's attitudes, of enlarging their experience and of stimulating their thoughts, is by means of programmes having no overt educational purpose. The case for the rejection of a separate education service was put to the test some seven years ago, when the Independent Television Authority suggested that there should be a special channel for educational television. Nearly all the educational organisations which gave evidence to the Pilkington Committee sided with the B.B.C.'s traditional view. One of their many now familiar reasons has been summed up by Professor Richard Hoggart: 'the principle of comprehensive broadcasting is too important, too variously valuable, to be weakened as it would be weakened if you added a direct teaching channel—

* The B.B.C. has officially reinforced this point: 'A full half of the B.B.C. output during the week is of educational value in the sense that it makes a demand upon the intelligence of the viewer' (*Education in Broadcasting*, B.B.C., 1961, p. 4). In the same publication (p. 3) there also occurred this statement '. . . while reflecting as their starting point existing levels of tastes and interest, they (its programmes) should also contribute to a progressively wider enjoyment of the arts, a progressively deeper interest in the contemporary world and an increased awareness of human possibilities. Broadcasting as a means of communication with a universal pull can do much to bridge the gap between experts and plain men and create a general common culture.'

because that channel would inevitably milk off certain educative programmes from the main channel'.[3] The second major objection to a special channel was that it would be economically wasteful. The Pilkington Committee itself, while strongly recommending the expansion of 'adult education' programmes, was opposed to creating a special channel, and its view was subsequently endorsed by the Government in its White Paper.[4] It would seem, therefore, that aside from a limited amount of time formally allocated to educational programmes during off-peak hours, and until the inauguration of the Open University, the broadcasting agencies in the United Kingdom will continue to offer an educational service mainly through general rather than through particular programmes. The ex-Director General, Sir Hugh Carleton Greene, once expressed the B.B.C.'s policy in this way: 'radio and television are, however, mass media with an almost universal appeal. We believe that their main educational impact is, and should be, made through the general programme output.' At the same time, critics of both the B.B.C. and the Independent Television Companies would welcome the presentation of specifically educational programmes not merely late at night or on Sunday mornings, as at present, but also during peak viewing hours.

iii

In April 1964, the B.B.C. launched a second television channel (B.B.C. 2), which had spread to most of the United Kingdom by 1966. This channel complements the provision being made by Channel 1 and enables the B.B.C. to pay more explicit attention to its educational function. The B.B.C. and the Independent Television Companies between them now contribute to the education of adults in the following ways:

(1) *Educative*

(*a*) They consciously strive to help make the United Kingdom an educated democracy, not only by providing a full coverage of news and information but also by enabling people to see for themselves what is happening in Britain and in the world at large. Programmes such as *Panorama*, with a weekly audience of six million, and *This Week*, reinforced by special documentary programmes, must clearly have some influence. On B.B.C. 2 there are edited versions of political and scientific conferences as well as open-ended discussions. Each evening at the end of the day there is a programme explaining and interpreting the day's news. It may well be, as some commentators have observed, that the decline in attendance at current affairs classes given by the universities and the W.E.A. is due to the fact that television coverage of this subject is so comprehensive and compelling that they cannot compete with it. Certainly it has made millions of people aware of the world's major problems and familiar with the personalities and policies of the leading international statesmen to an extent that would have seemed beyond the reach of possibility even a decade ago. Without television, international crises in the Congo or in Vietnam would never have aroused so much public interest and concern: without television, the issues and personalities involved in presidential elections in the U.S.A. or France would have been a closed book except to that small section of the population which reads the 'quality' newspapers and periodicals: as it is, national leaders such as De Gaulle and Johnson are better known than most of our own cabinet ministers.

The work of the late J. Trenaman[5] showed clearly that today people gain nearly all their political knowledge and understanding of Home Affairs from what they see and hear on television. For instance, the issues involved in a general election are put before the electorate with a clarity and immediacy that were undreamt of in the pre-television era. Television may not alter people's party allegiances, but it certainly stimulates them to think more politically and gives them at least a modicum of relevant evidence to take into account when casting their votes.

(b) If only fortuitously television can greatly extend the range of people's cultural and intellectual interests*; once the switch has been turned on for a crime feature, it is likely to remain switched on for the documentary or science programme that may follow.

---

* 'Interests' is the operative word. During the 1962 annual general meeting of the Standing Conference for Television Viewing, Mrs Wyndham Goldie, Head of Talks and Current Affairs Programmes, observed: 'we like to think we are creating these programmes out of a feeling for what will interest the viewer, not because they are educational . . . . If they happen to be 'educative' that is splendid, but let us not, for heaven's sake, label them educational or they will die.' (*Pilkington and After*, p. 17.)

The size of the viewing audience for *Monitor*, which eschewed the temptation to talk down to its audience, was remarkable. Since its opening in 1964 B.B.C. 2 has undoubtedly helped to heighten interest in special subjects by presenting programmes designed to appeal to minority tastes.

(*c*) Television introduces people to the conventions of the theatre. It is true that many plays on television deal with shallow themes and are clumsily constructed, and that limitations of time sometimes reduce their effectiveness. Nevertheless, thanks to television millions of people who would never have thought to see a live play at the theatre have come to know a little about dramatic conventions, have seen great plays performed and, through perceptively written scripts, have caught a glimpse of unfamiliar human problems. The presentation of plays and serials on television has also inspired a new public to go in search of books. If the B.B.C. presents a serialised version of *The Forsyte Saga* or *Les Misérables*, it can confidently be predicted that all over the country people will besiege libraries and bookshops in search of copies of the novels.

(*d*) Television can bring laymen in touch with the specialised work of members of the learned professions, particularly the work of scientists. There is no question that many viewers have learnt a little at any rate about the major scientific developments of recent times as a direct consequence of viewing television programmes. This function of television was memorably described by Mr Raymond Williams in a broadcast in the General Overseas Service of the B.B.C. as 'the making of bridges of new kinds between originators and specialists and the general life of the nation'.

(*e*) Because of its resources, television can provide musical and visual entertainment of a superlatively high order. Performances by the New York Symphony Orchestra or by the Royal Ballet Company are two examples of what can be offered. Viewers can also eavesdrop upon rehearsals by the great opera and ballet companies of the world and by the outstanding musical virtuosi.

(*f*) In addition, television can be educative in a multitude of diffuse ways. It can help to remove—and sometimes, it must be admitted, to strengthen—prejudices. It can awaken a regard for the eloquent use of language, and sharpen critical and aesthetic perceptions.

(2) *Educational*

(*a*) While also meant to entertain some programmes are designed to be primarily educational. A good illustration of such programmes was the series of half-hour lectures on Social History given in 1966 by Mr A. J. P. Taylor.

(*b*) Certain programmes are deliberately grouped under the rubric of Further Education or Adult Education. The B.B.C. offers Further Education programmes on Channels 1 and 2, which usually go out on Sunday mornings with repeats on week nights or the following Saturday morning. Certain programmes are put out during the afternoons. Each weekday evening on B.B.C. 2 there is a Further Education programme from 7.30 to 8.00 p.m. Subjects covered in the period 1966–67 included: Working with a Computer, Science of Man, Industrial Archaeology, 100 years of Marxism, and The Social Workers.

Of late the Independent Television Companies have been taking their educational responsibilities seriously. They have introduced a number of special adult educational programmes, usually presented on Sunday mornings with repeats on Saturday mornings. Programmes produced in one region are often repeated in another. Among the subjects dealt with during the period 1966–67 were: Psychology for Everyman, Say it in Russian, First Steps in Physics, The Struggle for Peace, and Sociology—The Middle Years.

(*c*) Some educational programmes are worked out in collaboration with learned bodies and adult education organisations. Full authorisation for such programmes was given by the government in its White Paper of 1962, though it was recognised that the additional hours allotted to such programmes would have to fall during the off-peak periods. The government did intimate, however, that it hoped for increased provision when more television time was made available, and in the event the number of programmes has notably increased.

iv

The B.B.C. sees television and radio as complementing each other in providing a general educational service. Despite the competition of television, sound broadcasting still commands a surprisingly large audience, especially during the day-time. Because of the greater amount of time at its disposal, its Reithian traditions and its range of four programmes, sound broadcasting offers many more facilities for educative programmes than television and is especially strong in serving the needs of minority groups. Even Radio 2, which is designed almost exclusively for light entertainment, nevertheless has its more serious moments, and besides presenting stimulating programmes like *Any Questions* also consciously uses a serial such as *The Archers* as a medium of instruction and information. Radio 4 carries a few essentially educational programmes and a high proportion of material which is educative, while the Third Programme deliberately appeals to the cultural and intellectual tastes of educated minority groups, even if, in practice, it draws its audience from a surprisingly wide cross-section of the population. Finally, Network III, through its Study Session, offers a number of educational programmes, though it is not designed as a systematic educational service.

Sound broadcasting attempts to educate adults in the following ways:

(i) *Educative*

(a) It provides news and current affairs features. Such programmes as *At Home and Abroad, 10 o'clock, Radio Link* and *Letter from America*, sustain a remarkably high standard.

(b) It is especially strong in music programmes. In an average year the B.B.C. devotes as many as 9,000 hours to music of all kinds. In recent years it has made a point of giving a hearing to new music, especially in the Third Programme. In consequence of a government decision taken in 1962 Network III now provides 'good music', that is, classical music, throughout the day-time on the frequencies allotted to it.

(c) Drama is also strongly represented. The B.B.C. seeks to provide something more than a fortuitous sequence of plays. By concentrating on particular historical periods or by planning a season of plays by a certain author it attempts to convey some impression of the international scope and the various forms of drama.

(d) Periodically there are lecture and discussion series. Thanks to the wide publicity they receive, the Reith Lectures, for example, often have the effect of drawing public attention to such topics as World Order and Family Problems.

(e) School broadcasts attract a large adult audience. It is estimated that between 50,000 and 500,000 adults, according to the nature of the subject, regularly listen to school programmes.

(ii) *Educational*

(*a*) There are special instructional programmes for agricultural-ists, students in technical colleges and other vocational groups. Some programmes addressed to these groups are really a mixture of the direct and the indirect method.

(*b*) Study Session is expressly designed to provide programmes on special educational topics.

In 1957 the B.B.C. so far departed from its resolve not to provide a separate educational programme detached from its general service as to set up a special service called Network III for the purpose of presenting systematic courses aimed at specific audi-ences. Network III, now known as *Study Session*, is planned in conjunction with Radio 3, and in an average week is on the air for between thirteen and fifteen hours, of which strictly educational subjects occupy four or five hours at most. The other two-thirds of the time are devoted to programmes ranging from 'Christian Outlook' and 'Science Survey' to 'In Your Garden' and 'Jazz Session'. Programmes in Study Session are sometimes repeated on Radio 4, which also has a few educational series of its own.

Study Session makes a feature of modern languages, the presen-tation and discussion of historical and current problems, and the appreciation of music, and works in close collaboration with the principal educational agencies. It also supplements its broadcasts with tastefully designed explanatory booklets, publishes bi-annually a programme of forthcoming items entitled *B.B.C. Further Education Programmes*, and issues a leaflet before each academic year listing those impending programmes which may be of use in the field of further education. Among its recent offer-ings there have been 'Understanding Music', a language course in Russian, and 'The Celts'. Its audience frequently exceeds 50,000, which means that it is able to command for a single course an audience far beyond the reach of any other educational body. An indication of the response to these programmes is provided by the fact that the sales of explanatory booklets range from 15,000 to 20,000 for history series to over 60,000 for language courses.

Controlling the educational programmes in Study Session is the

Further Education Unit, first formed in 1952. Its staff includes a small liaison section and three regional education officers. This unit has been at great pains to forge close links with all the adult education organisations and to consult them about the planning and conduct of its programmes. For this purpose it employs four full-time liaison officers. The Unit considers that while, on the one hand, it has the nucleus of a ready-made audience created by the work of adult educators, on the other hand, it can serve the interests of adult educators by advertising their facilities to all its listeners. Even Study Session cannot explore most subjects in the same depth as a tutorial class or indeed a university extension course, and for this reason the Unit seeks to ensure that listeners to a particular series will pursue their studies by attending an appropriate adult education class.

Since Study Session now performs an essential service, the B.B.C.'s Further Education Unit should be regarded as one of the key providing bodies in the adult education field. It is to be hoped that the B.B.C. will gradually expand its resources.

v

In 1967 the B.B.C. opened its first local broadcasting stations, seven years after the Pilkington Committee had recommended their creation. From the point of view of adult educators there is every reason for satisfaction that such stations are being established. They will be of immeasurable value as a means both of reaching a bigger audience and of stimulating interest in such topics as local government: it is particularly to be hoped that time for adult education programmes will be set aside during peak listening hours between 7.00 p.m. and 10.00 p.m. During the first year of operations Nottingham University's Department of Adult Education mounted a series of four programmes supported by a correspondence course. Important for the future was the imaginative decision of the D.E.S. to recognise for grant aid courses undertaken for local radio stations by full-time tutors.

vi

Audience research has not received as much attention in this country as it deserves. Nevertheless, the B.B.C. has carried out several notable enquiries and published much information which is valuable not only for its own purposes but for the purposes of all those engaged in adult education. Most of the enquiries and surveys undertaken by its Audience Research Section have been about the comparative audiences for general programmes. J. Trenaman devoted a good deal of his time during the period 1948 to 1955 to exploring the nature of audiences for educational broadcasts, and his reports are preserved in the B.B.C.'s archives. In 1964 four B.B.C. education officers undertook a comprehensive inquiry into public interests.[6] The Further Education Service also justly claims 'that broadcasts are preceded by a professional study of adult needs, and that some objective assessment is sought, where possible, of the educational achievement of these broadcasts'.

vii

Some Jeremiahs have suggested that the range of interest and mass appeal of television have rendered irrelevant much of the work of the adult education agencies. While not dissenting from several of the comments frequently made, for instance, that the presentation of current affairs on television is so vivid and so immediate as to lessen the need for tutorial classes in current affairs, it is not difficult to refute their main arguments. For one thing, attendance at classes provided by the L.E.A.s and the Responsible Bodies seems to have been expanding at about the same rate as television viewing. Indeed, there is plentiful evidence that certain television programmes may well create a popular demand for follow-up classes. Thus the striking expansion in the number of archaeology classes during the last ten or twelve years has owed not a little to the B.B.C.'s *Animal, Vegetable and Mineral* programme and its team of personable archaeologists.

About broadcasting and particularly about television those engaged in adult education can take three things for granted. The first is that there is a widespread and articulate demand for a larger educational content in television and sound programmes and that this demand seems bound to increase. The second is that through its educational programmes broadcasting is able to touch an audience many times greater than that which can be touched by the adult education organisations. Furthermore, producers have devised techniques for arousing and holding the interest of a large section of the population which adult education, using traditional methods, has not succeeded in attracting to its own classes. In other words, in at least one respect broadcasters are entitled to claim that they are more influential than the professional adult educators. The third thing is that since broadcasting is constantly helping to change the nature of contemporary society, adult educators must be alert to identify and analyse its effects on their work.

Adult educators have accepted the challenge of television by reappraising their policies in the light of its impact and by seeking liaison arrangements with the television companies similar to those already made with B.B.C. Sound Broadcasting. The Universities Council for Adult Education set up a broadcasting sub-committee in 1960 which has since been extremely active. The W.E.A. has also given much thought to the new problems and prospects created by the rapid development of television. In a working party report published in 1960 they expressed the view that 'the task of adult education is to develop impulses generated among minorities by the mass media'.[7] The National Institute of Adult Education, which has always had close relations with the B.B.C., has also established contact with the independent television companies, besides for a time taking under its wing an organisation, 'The Television Viewers' Council', whose main object was to bring the providers and viewers together.

In its White Paper (1962) the Government empowered the B.B.C. and I.T.A. to allow more television time specifically for adult education transmissions but stipulated that any programmes launched should be planned in conjunction with the existing adult education organisations according to an agreed formula. The B.B.C. and the independent television companies have since demonstrated their willingness to collaborate with the adult education organisations. A Further Educational Advisory Council has been set up by the B.B.C. and an Educational Advisory Council has been formed by the Independent Television Authority (1964).* The membership of the two committees conveniently overlaps. As for the agreed formula, it was quickly worked out by the B.B.C.

* This committee consists of 20 members and 3 assessors (among the agencies represented are: The W.E.A., U.C.A.E., N.I.A.E., T.U.C., N.F.W.I., T.W.G., and the Association of Tutors in Adult Education).

as follows: 'Educational television programmes for adults are programmes (other than school broadcasts) arranged in series and planned in consultation with appropriate educational bodies to help viewers towards the progressive mastery or understanding of some skill or body of knowledge. The definition shall be held to include programmes primarily designed for class use, e.g. in technical colleges or centres for adult education, as well as those primarily designed for the home viewer'. The important thing is to ensure that all the agencies engaged in adult education are consulted and that there is not too much concentration upon the few most prominent organisations. Many problems arise in operating an effective liaison scheme. In particular, adult educators have to take care not to press their views too hard, for in the last resort producers often know best how to seize and hold the attention of viewers.

Among the reasons why adult education must take note of broadcasting the following may be singled out as the most important:

(i) It is a social phenomenon affecting nearly every aspect of their work and therefore demanding constant attention both in the planning of programmes and in the conduct of classes. Students acquire much of their knowledge from it.*

(ii) It is a direct medium of instruction in the home and can supplement correspondence courses and classroom instruction, particularly if tutors are prepared to recommend programmes.

(iii) It can be a direct medium of instruction in the classroom.

(iv) It is an additional teaching aid. Certain television programmes can be used to illustrate aspects of courses taught in the classroom.

(v) A few television programmes aimed at the general public are already in essence directly educational. This is particularly true of a few of the programmes put out by the B.B.C. on its second channel.

(vi) It has now been made possible for adult education organisations to join with the programme companies in designing and presenting systematic courses similar to those already put out by Study Session. In this kind of collaboration it will always be a question of bringing together the specialist knowledge of the

---

* It should never be forgotten, however, that a surprising number of people are seldom able to watch television because they either cannot afford to buy or hire a television set, or live in a room where it is inconvenient to install a set.

educationists and the technical expertise of the broadcasting experts.

(vii) Particularly in more informal organisations, groups can be assembled to study various facets of television. In a community centre, for example, a group might come together to study the content and social import of *Coronation Street*.

(viii) Adult educators should try to persuade the television authorities to emulate Study Session by making the public aware of the adult education resources that are available.[8] Long advance notice of plans is essential.

(ix) Those who work in adult education have a special duty to ensure that television maintains high aesthetic, social and intellectual standards. In a small way they can contribute to this end by seeking to sharpen the critical faculties of those students whom they serve. But they can help even more positively by acting as a responsible pressure group and by encouraging the spread of consumer organisations. Adult educators might also consider undertaking inquiries into the effects of television upon people's attitudes and habits. Through their classes and their special connections they are particularly well placed to undertake this kind of research, for if it is true that broadcasters have had unprecedented success in awakening the dormant interests of the mass audience, adult educationists have had far more experience of dealing with individual members of the public face to face.

Consumer organisations could well become not only the public watchdogs of broadcasting but also valuable instruments of adult education. Nothing could be more fruitful as an intellectual and civic exercise than that groups of people should regularly meet for the purpose of studying the implications of television and, firmly but objectively, publicly expressing their views about its virtues and vices. At the present time there are several organisations in the United Kingdom which have been set up to represent the interests of the listener and the viewer.

(x) Television companies could keep a bank of videotape recordings of educational programmes for loan to or purchase by adult education agencies.

(xi) In densely populated areas there is much to be gained from the use of closed circuit television. Programmes can be transmitted either by cable or microwave link. Hull University has its own television station. The University of Leeds intends to offer educational programmes by this method, which has two distinct advantages over programmes transmitted on the national network: it is cheaper, and it is more effective simply because each programme can be designed for an identifiable local group.

viii

Because the emphasis has been upon its educational function, the evaluation of broadcasting, and more especially, of television, presented in this chapter has been essentially favourable. There is, of course, another side of the coin. Much of the material shown on television is cheap and superficial. Even in programmes clearly meant to be serious, topics are seldom explored at length or in depth. News and information are given in fragments, thereby leaving in the mind an impression of disjointedness. Few demands are made upon the viewer who may, if he is so disposed, sit with eyes focused upon the screen from six in the evening until nearly midnight without making a moment's effort to reflect constructively upon what he sees. Worst of all are the escapist programmes shown at peak-viewing times which give the public what the programme planners think they want as indicated by the TAM ratings. The effects of such programmes may well be anti-educational.

The defence of the mass-viewing approach is that television caters for a mass audience and not for select minorities. When watching television most people are seeking relaxation. Put on more than one or two serious programmes in an evening and they will switch to the rival channel. If education is to be provided it must be provided stealthily or in programmes presented outside peak-viewing hours.

Even if the *vox populi* argument be accepted, it does not follow that standards need be as low as they sometimes are. Is there really such a species as the average viewer? Should it be assumed that the viewer's commitment is unalterably passive? More evidence is required before the popular argument is allowed to pass unchallenged. Even then, there is still the problem that non-educators are mainly responsible for determining what the public wants and what it can be induced to respond to.

This caveat about the effects of television having been made, the conclusion is that the overall influence of broadcasting is for good. It can and does supplement the work of the providing bodies and for the uneducated it is an indispensable source of information and an occasional stimulus to mental activity. At the same time, despite its pervasive power, broadcasting will never be a complete substitute for face-to-face classes, for they alone involve personal engagement and guarantee sustained effort. If broadcasting is to be even a partial substitute for adult education classes, then it is necessary to arrange for more effective feed-back than we have at present. There is still also a crying need for more intensive research into the nature and effectiveness of broadcasting as a means of education. The B.B.C. and I.T.A. ought to spend more money on research and adult educationists should regard the study of the influence of the mass media as a high priority.

(B) THE CINEMA AND FILM SOCIETIES

i

An interest in the cinema as an art form was first aroused in the early twenties and from an early stage film societies were being formed. In the thirties, thanks largely to the work of Dr Roger Manvell, some adult educators began to treat film appreciation as a subject for serious study. With the advent of nationwide television coverage, however, serious interest in the cinema declined until 1962 when a recovery began.

At the end of 1966 nearly 100,000 people in England and Wales belonged to over 450 film societies, varying in size from about 100 to 1,500 members. Membership is steadily expanding. The societies share in common three broad aims:

(i) to enable members to see, at a low cost, films that are not exhibited on the commercial network;

(ii) to revive the classics (e.g. *Ivan the Terrible, Intolerance*);

(iii) to stimulate interest in the cinema as an art form and in film-making as a skilled craft.

In addition to those societies whose sole purpose is simply to show good films, there are a number of societies which specialise in scientific and religious films or in the techniques of film-making. A few groups also produce films on their own account.

Co-ordinating the activities of existing societies and constantly encouraging the formation of new ones is the Federation of British

Film Societies. Founded in 1945 and at present serving a membership of about 45,000, the Federation has its headquarters in London and is sub-divided into nine regional sections. It offers advice about starting and running a film society, publishes a magazine entitled *Film*, which appears three times a year, a publication for members only entitled *Film News*, which contains reviews of films and details about how to obtain them, and an annual yearbook. The Federation also keeps a library of programme notes.

Film societies have value even if they exist only to show films. The minority that encourage detailed study of such subjects as the history of the cinema, that seek to relate the cinema to the other arts and that encourage a critical assessment of films and the total impact of the cinema upon society, are fulfilling a particularly useful function.

For adult education generally the cinema holds an interest from three aspects: as an art form; as a social phenomenon; and as a teaching aid. A number of adult education agencies organise courses in film appreciation often presented in conjunction with a local cinema or a local film society. Nowadays the cinema exercises much less influence than it did before the coming of television. Nevertheless, its social impact remains significant and educating film tastes and urging people to be discriminating about what they see is still something which ought to concern adult educationists. In the United States and France, for instance, far more attention is paid to the study of the cinema and its social effects than in this country.

It is no longer as difficult as it used to be for people in the provinces to see good films. At the same time, there are many areas in which only popular films are exhibited. Ideally every town ought to have a repertory cinema. Until that time comes, adult education organisations could do much to meet the need.

ii

The British Film Institute was founded in 1933 and describes its aims as:

> To encourage the development of the art of the film, to promote its use as a record of contemporary life and manners, to foster study and appreciation of it from these points of view, to explore and promote new or extended uses for film and to encourage, support and serve other bodies working in the same field.

To foster study and appreciation of films for television and television programmes generally, to encourage the best use of television, to explore and promote its new and extended uses and to encourage, support and serve other bodies working in the same field.

It is the official national archive for film and television recordings and runs the National Film Theatre.

The Institute receives an annual grant of £100,000 from the Treasury, and approximately £7,000 from the Cinematograph Fund. In addition, the D.E.S. now makes a grant of £19,000 per annum in support of the activities of the Education Department. This department consists of a head, an assistant, and a lectures officer. These three officers spend most of their time in lecturing and their efforts are supported by a large panel of part-time lecturers. (The salary scale of the full-time officers compares favourably with, for example, that of staff tutors employed by the university extra-mural departments.)

The Institute as a whole is engaged in educational work. It publishes three periodicals—*Sight and Sound*, *The Monthly Film Bulletin* and *Contrast*—aimed at encouraging the spread of high critical standards. It guides and assists the work of the film societies, particularly by loaning films from its Distribution Library and by circulating lecture notes and other teaching aids. Recently it took the Federation of Film Societies under its wing.

The education department operates through three channels. It stimulates an interest in the study of films by a variety of methods. It devotes the greater part of its resources to running a lecture agency. Most lectures are run in collaboration with other bodies but the department directly organises two annual residential courses. Finally, the department provides services and teaching material and organises conferences.

The department labours under three difficulties. In the first place, it is short of lecturers, particularly to meet demands from outside the Home Counties. Though each of the staff lecturers gives about 100 lectures a year, there are usually about 500 more lectures to be provided. Secondly, the small permanent staff are obliged to surrender time to lecturing that they would often prefer to spend upon study, upon seeing and evaluating films and television programmes. Thirdly, the department is very short of materials. It particularly needs an enlarged stock of film extracts for illustrating lectures.

REFERENCES

1. To describe the role in adult education of Broadcasting and Films, Libraries, Museums and Art Galleries, the apt term 'auxiliaries'was coined by Sir W. E. Williams when he was Secretary of the British Institute of Adult Education (cf. W. E. Williams, ed., *Adult Education in Great Britain and the United States of America* (1938). Cf. also W. E. Williams, *The Auxiliaries of Adult Education* (1934).
2. *New Ventures in Broadcasting* (B.B.C., 1928), p. 1.
3. Cf. *Pilkington and After* (N.I.A.E., 1962), p. 6.
4. *Memorandum on the Report of the Committee on Broadcasting 1960* (H.M.S.O., 1962), p. 5.
5. Cf. J. Trenaman and D. McQuail, *Television and the Political Image* (1961).
6. Cf. *The People's Activities* (B.B.C., 1965).
7. *Aspects of Adult Education: A W.E.A. Working Party Report*, p. 10.
8. Cf. E. H. Hutchinson, *Pilkington and After*, p. 21: 'Those of us who are concerned directly with organised provision of adult education know that our biggest limitation is public ignorance of what is available. To reduce that ignorance is the biggest service that television can perform for adult education.'

Chapter Thirteen

EDUCATION THROUGH HOME STUDY

Must students attend regular classes in order to learn? Is class-room instruction the only truly effective method of communication between teacher and taught? Can students study effectively at home? Some educationists are in no doubt about the answers to these questions. They argue vigorously that study at home is desirable and should be actively encouraged by the D.E.S. and the L.E.A.s. By home study they mean study not necessarily by correspondence alone but by a combination of methods, including the use of radio, television, tape-recorders and, whenever practicable, face-to-face tutorials. There seems little doubt that the practice of studying at home, already by no means negligible in volume, is due for expansion.

i. *Education by Correspondence*

After almost a century of low repute the organised provision of education by correspondence through the post, sometimes described appropriately as postal tuition, is suddenly approaching respectability. Its past neglect stemmed principally from two causes. In the first place, the educational establishment regarded it as an inferior method of instruction; to this day neither the D.E.S. nor the L.E.A.s show much enthusiasm for the method. Secondly, correspondence education has been and still is associated in many minds with the sharp practice of certain institutions with as little claim to provide education as to peddle soap.

Several developments have now occurred, however, which may lead to correspondence education becoming an honest woman. To begin with, educationists in Britain have at last taken account of the extensive and apparently successful use of the method in other countries, especially in Russia, the United States, Sweden, Australia, and several of the developing countries. Of special appeal to the public authorities is the discovery that these pioneering countries have succeeded in reaching out to a large public at a relatively low cost per capita. A second development is the explosive demand for post-school courses from would-be students. A third development is that the growing preoccupation of educationists with new media has led them to see that instruction by correspondence can be made effective if supplemented by other methods. Finally, the D.E.S. has found it impossible to go on turning a deaf ear to the allegations of malpractice levelled against some of the more unscrupulous commercial colleges.

Students who wish or who are required to study by correspondence fall into four categories:

1. Those who can study by no other method. This group includes servicemen, seamen, patients in hospitals, housewives, shiftworkers, and above all, people who live at some distance from a suitable educational institution.

2. Those who are traditionally expected to study for professional examinations by correspondence, for example, accountants.

3. Those who cannot get a place in a recognised institution or whose local institution does not offer all or some of the courses they wish to study.

4. Those who positively prefer working at home to attending classes.

No reliable estimate can at present be made of the number of people taking correspondence courses. For one thing, some of the commercial firms are reluctant to publish annual statistics for fear of losing custom. Inspired guesses suggest that the total enrolment in the United Kingdom, excluding enrolments from overseas, may well exceed 300,000. What is certain is that the total is rapidly rising from year to year and seems to know no ceiling.

The common motive of students for studying by correspondence is vocational. A large number are preparing for external degrees, G.C.E., O and A levels, and a host of professional examinations. It is difficult to estimate how many have no vocational interest. In a recent report, the figure of 30,000 was suggested. Undoubtedly there are a good number of students taking G.C.E. and external degree courses not so much to better themselves as to prove their worth to their own satisfaction. Furthermore, many of the subjects studied are anything but technical; many army officers, for instance, are taking courses in current affairs provided by the Metropolitan College. It is only necessary to scan through the advertising columns of both the serious and the popular press to see what a wide selection of subjects may be studied, all the way from bee-keeping to advanced English studies.

Institutions offering correspondence courses are of four kinds:

1. Some set their own examinations and make their own awards.
2. Some prepare students for national examinations.
3. Some are institutions supported by the State.
4. Some provide a particular service, e.g. the T.U.C.

Most of the institutions are run for profit. Commercial undertakings include such long-established and respected institutions as Wolsey Hall, International Correspondence Schools, and Cleave Hume Ltd. To avoid being contaminated by disreputable institutions this leading group recently set up a working party under the chairmanship of Dr Gurr, a retired H.M.I., to recommend ways of preventing sharp practices and maintaining academic standards.[2] The main product of the Working Party's Report was the foundation of the Association of British Correspondence Colleges.

The best known non-profit making institutions are the T.U.C., which now provides the postal courses previously arranged by the N.C.L.C. and Ruskin College, Coleg Harlech, the Co-operative College, NALGO, and the College of the Sea. The most recent and dramatic entrant into the field is the National Extension College, pledged to give a second chance to those who have been unable to obtain all the help they need within the framework of the education system.[3]

The domination of the field of correspondence education by commercial institutions is a matter for concern. The fact that some of them appear to offer an efficient service is not enough to cancel out the shortcomings of the remainder. Whatever else happens, the Government ought to take powers to inspect the work of all the institutions. More constructively, the D.E.S. and the L.E.A.s must recognize correspondence as an acceptable teaching method and give financial support to accredited agencies. This is a question not only of launching the Open University but of backing the efforts of non-profit-making institutions and awarding grants to students who study by the correspondence method.

It is also clear that we need to have much more information about existing arrangements for correspondence education. We

H

should also examine the techniques being used successfully in other countries and see to it that they are adopted in England and Wales.

ii. *An Open University*

It is often urged that the universities should offer part-time degree courses. Most of them are reluctant to do so, their main objection in recent years being that they have insufficient staff as it is without having to cope with more students. The Government has now proposed to deal with the problem by establishing, in 1969, an entirely novel kind of university, a university that will make full use of the new educational media.

The idea of an Open University, initially and imprudently termed a University of the Air, was set out in the White Paper Cmnd. 2922 of February 1966. The Government envisages the Open University awarding its own degrees, and having its own independent charter as well as its own vice-chancellor, registrar and full-time staff. It will be located at the new town of Milton Keynes.

The Open University will have three purposes:

(a) to contribute to the general improvement of educational, cultural and professional standards in the United Kingdom;
(b) to enable keen students outside the existing universities to undertake disciplined study with a view to acquiring degrees or other qualifications;
(c) to contribute to the educational needs of students in other parts of the world, more especially in the developing countries.

The degrees will be at the general rather than the honours level and to begin with it is probable that no more than ten subjects will be offered. Students will spend three years on major subjects and two years on minor subjects. The whole course will probably take at least four years and in most cases very much longer. Enrolment will be open to all regardless of academic qualifications.

Courses will be conducted by a combination of national television programmes and correspondence courses centrally organised by the Open University's own staff.[4] It is further hoped that university extra-mural departments, the W.E.A. and the L.E.A.s will supplement these methods by arranging locally based tutorial classes and seminars. The central provision may also be supported in certain areas by programmes put out by the newly established local radio stations.

The Open University may employ all or some of the following methods of communication between the enrolled students and the teacher:

   (i) correspondence teaching requiring individual correction and guidance to ensure critical thought and independent investigation;

  (ii) study groups in areas where it is possible to collect sufficient students to have face-to-face discussion;

 (iii) short residential courses or seminars for more intensive study. Seminars could be held throughout the year. Residential courses will be held during University vacations;

 (iv) regular news-letters and tutorial letters giving advice on study, listing appropriate reading and drawing attention to new research findings;

  (v) opportunity for personal interviews or tutorials with tutors to resolve difficulties that arise in the course of study;

 (vi) a telephone service for enquiries;

(vii) some provision of library facilities.

Several universities outside Britain, through their extra-mural or extension departments, have experience of providing external degrees either by correspondence or television or a combination of both. For example, the University of New England at Armadale, N.S.W., conducts most of its extension work in this way and has a system whereby it is part of the duty of internal staff, according to their terms of appointment, to undertake correspondence work. Extensive schemes exist in the U.S.A. and Canada embracing all the methods described in the preceding paragraph. The University of South Africa is another institution with a slightly different experience of correspondence education and residential tuition. Teaching by a combination of television, radio and correspondence is also plainly going to become commonplace in the developing countries.

To assist the Open University such adult educational agencies as university extra-mural departments and W.E.A. will probably require:

(a) A member of staff to co-ordinate any tuition provided, to supervise course material, arrange residential courses, make local tutorial and library arrangements, and collaborate with other bodies in the area also participating in the scheme.

(b) Lecturers in several disciplines willing, for a fee, to mark scripts, to offer guidance and help. The number could be quite large depending on the number of registrations for the Open University.

(c) Permission to arrange and pay for small group seminars which would probably consist of fewer students than the existing regulations for adult classes allow. Lecturers would be required to tutor these groups.

(d) Authority to reserve for study groups accommodation in university halls of residence and residential colleges during vacation periods. In some cases students would be able to attend courses on Saturdays and Sundays but these would require the presence of caretakers and catering staff.

(e) Authority to arrange with university libraries and with city and county libraries for the loan of books.

It is likely that initial interest in the Open University will be considerable but that in a short time the numbers coming forward will taper off as ill-equipped and dilettante students fall away. This process would certainly be in keeping with the experience of those North American universities which have been offering degree courses by television for several years.

The R.B.s and other adult educational agencies should have little to fear from the introduction of the Open University. They will not be directly involved in its provisions except in so far as they choose to supplement its work by arranging seminars, tutorials and residential schools for the students dwelling in their regions. Their problem will be to decide to what extent they are prepared to alter the balance of their present programmes in order to be co-operative. As for the universities, they should welcome the establishment of the Open University since they will be under less pressure to meet the rising clamour to provide external degrees on their own account. The Open University may be expected to siphon off both actual and potential discontent.

The main risk in establishing the Open University is that it will become so costly to maintain that the Government will try to economise by reducing its financial support to other forms of adult education. Not a few adult educators are already chagrined to note, after years of struggling to obtain relatively small increases in their grants from the D.E.S., that in its first year the Open University will receive four times the total amount being given to all the Responsible Bodies. It will also be regrettable if the B.B.C. and the Independent Television Companies cut back on their adult education services on the ground that they have become superfluous.

REFERENCES

1. Committee on Accreditation of Correspondence Colleges, *Report* (1966), p. 5; see also W. J. Harris, 'Education by Post' in *Adult Education*, vol. 39, No. 5, pp. 269–73, p. 277. This is altogether a most valuable article.
2. The section on 'Correspondence Colleges' in the report of the NUS (*Adult Education*, pp. 12–16) compresses into a short space a good deal of data about the correspondence colleges.
3. Cf. B. Jackson, *National Extension College 1967, Four Years' Work, and the Future* (1967).
4. For a recent survey of the aims and potentialities of the linked television/correspondence course method of instruction see H. Perraton, 'Why Use Television' in *Adult Education*, vol. 39, No. 5, January 1967, pp. 267–8.

Chapter Fourteen

LIBRARIES, MUSEUMS AND ART GALLERIES

i. *Libraries*

Many people obtain most of their education from private reading. Thus merely by keeping large stocks of books to satisfy all tastes and providing an efficient lending system at virtually no charge to the users, public libraries perform an indispensable public service. The question that concerns adult educationists, however, is how much more can and should they do?

Very few libraries carry out a programme of adult education in the narrow sense of that term. At Swindon, where the borough librarian superintends multifarious activities, and perhaps ten or so other libraries up and down the country, there is a substantial educational programme, including a number of systematic courses, but in the main the amount of provision fluctuates between occasional lecture series and special exhibitions and nothing at all. Moreover, there is great variation in policy from one local authority to another and from branch library to branch library, depending upon the degree of interest and energy possessed by the local librarian and the backing he receives from his committee. It may also happen that when one librarian has introduced and developed extension activities, his successor will choose to abandon them.

In the wider educational sense, however, many libraries do far more than lend books. Mr. Jolliffe,[1] the late Swindon Borough Librarian, stated in a recent work that 236 out of 585 library authorities were organising some kind of extension work. Most officers consider that their libraries ought to be cultural centres for the communities which they serve, and many libraries set aside accommodation for local societies and give a warm welcome to classes organised by the Responsible Bodies. Others arrange music concerts besides providing facilities for art displays and public lectures.

The Local Government Act of 1948 authorised a 6d. rate for 'entertainment'. While some local authorities use this rate for expenditure on such things as sports facilities, a number have allocated the funds raised by this means to their libraries for the promotion of cultural activities. Libraries may also receive grants for this purpose under the terms of the 1944 Education Act. For some cultural activities it is also possible to obtain a subsidy from the Arts Council. In addition, libraries are able to augment their incomes by charging admission fees to concerts and public lectures.

Several libraries have theatres or auditoria; others have lecture halls and a few rooms for group meetings; some have art galleries for exhibitions; and some have separate buildings specially designed for extension activities, e.g. Dagenham Library. Even where there is no lack of good will on the part of local authorities and librarians, it is nevertheless often difficult to offer much in the way of cultural activities because of a shortage of accommodation and staff. With regard to staffing, it is usually a big enough problem to find sufficient people to keep the library functioning from the point of view of book service, leave alone for supervising ancillary activities. Nevertheless, some librarians take the business of extension provision so seriously that they either supervise it themselves or second a member of their staff for the purpose.

Whenever possible, libraries ought to play an important part in the provision of adult education in such ways as the following:

(a) by providing books to R.B. classes;
(b) by providing an auditorium or small room for *bona fide* educational groups such as W.E.A. tutorial classes;
(c) by providing a quiet study room for adult students;
(d) by giving free publicity to the programmes of adult educational bodies;
(e) by providing a home for local cultural societies;
(f) by offering their own lecture programmes, especially celebrity lectures; such programmes are less popular than they were and have been abandoned by certain libraries;
(g) by presenting music concerts. At Sheffield, for example, weekly record concerts are arranged during the lunch hour throughout the winter months;
(h) by organising arts festivals as does St Pancras Borough Library;
(i) by providing a meeting place for film societies and facilities for the showing of films. Many libraries now have regular

showings of good films and keep their own film collections. The documentary has had a particular vogue in libraries;

(j) by organising exhibitions of paintings, shows of the works of local artists, shows of loan collections, and shows of specific local art groups. There is a spreading practice, too, of showing exhibitions of local photographic art;

(k) by arranging exhibitions to illustrate an educational theme, e.g. the British in the Far East.

Though many libraries are willing, and indeed anxious, to collaborate with the Responsible Bodies and adult education centres in providing meeting places for classes, the majority offer no accommodation. Increased collaboration is undoubtedly possible and desirable. Moreover, libraries in general could successfully pay more attention to extension activities. According to Mr Jolliffe 'not a great deal has been done to foster the work nationally in the United Kingdom although there are signs at the present time of a greater awareness of the Library Association of the need for central advice and assistance'.[2] The erection of many new buildings with more space and better facilities than the old ones may well lead to a pronounced expansion in the adult educational activities of libraries.

ii. *Museums*

Museums and education—museums are education. They exist only to further it, they can be neither provided, maintained, nor utilized without it.[3]

In the popular mind too many museums might as well be mausoleums, store houses of unexciting exhibits in sombre cases, to which children should be dutifully taken from time to time and where an hour or two may be heroically endured on a rainy afternoon. This dismal image is undeserved. For one thing, it is out of date. While it remains true that some museums continue to warrant all the harsh strictures of their critics, the great majority are nowadays lively and experimental. Moreover, curators are fully aware of their educational possibilities. For another thing, museums can appeal to an unusually large public and ought to be regarded as an integral part of the pattern of adult education. This fact is not as widely appreciated as it should be, even among educationists, despite the fact that in 1956 the N.I.A.E. published a special study of the functions of museums in adult education.[4] It is to be hoped that the recent report of the Rosse Commission will have a greater effect.[5]

Apart from the great national institutions such as the Science Museum, which alone attracts almost two million visitors a year, the university and the diminishing number of private institutions, museums are usually controlled by civic authorities. They range from sizeable establishments with at least adequate staff through medium-sized institutions to one-room displays. A museum can also take several forms. For example, it may be a folk museum or an arts and craft museum or simply a period house. The term is even applied sometimes to open-air archaeological sites.

As a general rule, a museum is considered to have four principal functions. Its primary function is to collect and preserve items. Deriving from this its second function is to undertake research. Its two other functions are: to provide a means of education, particularly of visual education, and to operate as a cultural centre. In fulfilling these functions, museums experience widely varying degrees of success. Some of them concentrate upon one or two functions at the expense of the rest.

The blame for a tatty museum should by no means necessarily be pinned on those who direct them, for all too often there is such a shortage of money, staff and accommodation that curators are unable to implement any plans they may have for reform and expansion. Their poverty is a byword. They draw such finance as they receive from their allocation of the 6d. rate, and though some municipalities make fairly generous allocations, in the main they tend to be parsimonious. Considering the high qualifications and devotion to duty demanded from them, keepers and assistant keepers are very poorly paid, their salaries comparing most unfavourably with those received by similarly qualified staff elsewhere in the educational field. And until recently there was no attempt to work out a national policy.

When museums are criticised it is also frequently the case that the beam is in the eyes of the critics themselves, for many visitors have not the least idea how to make use of them. For instance, curators often deplore the habit of trying to take in all the exhibits in a single rapid tour. They also complain of the inability of many people to discern any continuity in the order in which exhibits are displayed, even when maximum attention has been paid to this feature. Curators themselves recognise that given sufficient funds and adequate space they could give much more help to the visitor. But there is always a limit to what they alone can do. In the last resort, other educational bodies have to point out what to look for. Of course, some institutions do need to put their own houses in order by seeing to it that their opening hours are sensible and that rooms are well illuminated and reasonably warm.

Though of comparatively recent origin, the idea of deliberately using museums as instruments of education appeals to most curators. While it is not easy to particularise, museums can play their part in serving adult needs in some or all of the following ways:

DIRECT

(i) *Permanent Exhibitions.* Though their impact may be pronounced, museums are not in themselves an 'education': they cannot evoke an active response from insensitive visitors. But when exhibits are carefully labelled and arranged in an arresting form they can widen people's intellectual horizons by yielding up the story of the past and relating it to the present, by illustrating the variety and complexity of human achievement, by displaying examples of consummate skills in craftsmanship in an age when individual craftsmanship is fading out, and by creating more international understanding. It is significant that UNESCO is particularly interested in the power of museums to stimulate curiosity and to inform.

(ii) *Special Exhibitions.* These can be used above all to seize on topical interest in a particular subject.

(iii) *Local History.* Museums are obviously well placed to deal with local history.

(iv) *Conducted Tours.* These are of outstanding value and it is a pity that they are not a regular feature of all museum programmes.

(v) *Lectures.* Many museums offer single lectures or series of lectures. Their staff are also in demand as lecturers to other bodies.

(vi) *Courses.* A few museums offer systematic courses on their own account. Many more present courses in collaboration with outside bodies.

(vii) *Film Shows.* If a suitable auditorium is available, the showing of films is an effective way of arousing interest.

(viii) *Projects.* Museums may organise field projects which involve working externally as well as internally.

INDIRECT

(ix) *Centres.* Many museums try to be something more than repositories for exhibits by also providing small libraries and reading rooms, lounges, a meeting place for societies and so on. 'The Museum, as a community centre, has to keep in mind three things: what its resources can reasonably do, what the surrounding community needs, and which of its needs are being adequately met by other bodies or institutions.'[6]

(x) *Extra-Mural Activities.* Museums can provide extensive facilities by inviting television companies to put on programmes about their exhibits, by lending their exhibits for demonstration purposes to those who conduct adult classes, and by preparing slides, films and charts about their exhibits.

Several adult education organisations already exploit museum facilities by holding courses in conjunction with and in museums, by arranging visits and by borrowing exhibits. But, on the whole, adult education organisations have not gone out of their way to make full use of them. This is surprising in view of the remarkable increase in public interest in such subjects as archaeology and local history since the last war. In rural areas in particular it would seem desirable for more attention to be given to the possibility of arranging visits to museums.

If museums are to play their full part in adult education, it will be necessary for them to create constructive displays, in many cases to provide more guidance, perhaps by appointing tutor-curators or special consultants, to offer more comfortable and friendly surroundings and to improve their publicity methods. Perhaps above all more efficient publicity is the essential need, for the main problem facing museums is how to overcome the handicap of the 'stuffed-animal' image and make people aware of the wide range of their offerings. Besides general purpose museums there is a need for special institutions concentrating on such subjects as agriculture and local history. On their side, adult education organisations should make bigger efforts to utilise museum facilities. More adult classes might well be held within the museums themselves and greater efforts should certainly be made to draw upon the skill and knowledge of curators and keepers by inviting them to act as tutors or lecturers for adult classes.*

iii. *Art Galleries*

First of all, art galleries educate merely by exhibiting pictures, though their effectiveness clearly depends upon a number of related factors, of which the most important are the size, quality and representativeness of the permanent exhibition. A small gallery with a small number of undistinguished paintings collected according to no particular plan is scarcely likely to wield much influence. On the other hand, a large gallery that has taken the trouble or simply had the good fortune to acquire a selection of old masters and which is able to present paintings illustrating the various phases in the history of art is well equipped to educate public taste. It does not follow, of course, that large galleries are always successful. Unless pains are taken they do not attract great numbers of visitors—indeed, gallery-going was on the same scale in the late nineteenth century as it is today—and they do not provide adequate stimulation.

In England there are not many galleries with large, diversified collections and the difficulty now is that good paintings are so highly priced in the world market that few boards of trustees can afford to purchase them. Few distinguished collections exist outside the major towns. Nevertheless, there are a number of small town art galleries which are enhancing their usefulness by emphasising the history of local paintings and crafts in a more integrative way than in the past.

Art galleries may serve the interests of adult education both directly and indirectly:

* On 18 September 1968 the Minister for the Arts announced that she had commissioned a 1968–69 survey of the educational work of museums.

(a) *Directly*

   (i) by arranging regular single lectures or lecture courses about the permanent exhibition. Lunch-hour lectures often attract sizeable audiences. *Ad hoc* lectures or courses are especially necessary when special exhibitions are being shown;

   (ii) by offering guided tours;

   (iii) by showing films about art;

   (iv) by arranging practical art classes.

(b) *Indirectly*

   (v) by organizing special exhibitions;

   (vi) by arranging their exhibits so as to ensure that their collections illustrate the history of painting;

   (vii) by serving as a focus for the study of visual arts in a given area;

   (viii) by encouraging Art Societies;

   (ix) by organising circulating exhibitions;

   (x) by offering lecture courses in conjunction with university extra-mural departments or other agencies;

   (xi) by lending exhibits or teaching aids.

Small and large towns should perhaps give greater attention to the development of civic art galleries featuring local traditions and providing adequate space for travelling exhibitions sponsored by such bodies as the Arts Council. More study should be made of the use of galleries and of the policies now being pursued in other countries such as the Netherlands. Finally, those who direct galleries should recognise that their function is not merely to exhibit paintings but also to educate public taste. So as to implement that function galleries should, wherever possible, appoint a full-time organising lecturer.

REFERENCES

1. H. Jolliffe, *Public Library Extension Activities* (Library Association, 1962), pp. 20–38.
2. *ibid.*, p. 4.
3. D. A. Allan, *Museums and Education* (Royal Society of Arts, 1949).
4. *Museums and Adult Education—the report of a Working Party.*
5. *Survey of Provincial Museums and Galleries* (H.M.S.O., 1963).
6. *Report of an International Seminar on the Role of Museums in Education* (UNESCO, 1954).

Chapter Fifteen

ADULT STUDENTS
AND THEIR CHARACTERISTICS

Most of the current generalisations about the characteristics of adult students are based upon personal impressions or the findings of inquiries limited to relatively small groups. The one inference now commonly made with some confidence is that students who bother to attend organised courses are atypical of the population as a whole in that they have attained a level of education well above the national average. For the rest adult educators are left to guess the answers to such questions as: do the characteristics of students differ from region to region or from class to class? Do providing bodies unwittingly compete for the same groups of students?

Most of our knowledge has been accumulated about motives for participation, particularly for attending long-term courses. To begin with, those who attend courses must have had not only the necessary urge but also the necessary information. They have nearly always exercised a voluntary choice since social and economic pressures are slight or non-existent. These two facts already say something about adult students. They show that, in the absence of mass advertising and the kind of counselling services so dear to American educators, these people are tolerably well educated and enterprising. What are their motives? They vary considerably and any one person may have mixed motives. Evidence points to the following:

> to develop a personal interest;
> to engage in an activity that has society's approval;
> to join in a group activity;
> to deepen understanding of perennial and current problems;
> to serve the community;
> to escape from routine;
> to make friends;
> to acquire a skill or information of vocational value.

Even about motivation our knowledge is largely subjective. What we really require is a nation-wide study of adults taking part in a variety of educational activities. But such a study would call for the services of a team of researchers, a large sum of money, a long period devoted to planning and to processing data, and an unprecedented amount of goodwill and co-operation on the part of harassed administrators. Given the shortage of money available for research and the continuing fragmentation of the adult education field it is a remote prospect.*

The best alternative to a nation-wide survey is a sample survey based on an analysis of returns from the chief providing bodies in a number of contrasting areas. In 1963 the present writer carried out such a survey simultaneously in a number of different places. In undertaking the survey some assistance was already forthcoming from two sources. In the first place, from routine records; several well established institutions record a good deal of evidence about their students. Various devices are also used for obtaining particular items of information and the practice is growing of keeping more or less elaborate card index systems. Secondly, there was the information contained in previous studies. Though comparatively few and restricted in purpose, these studies have yielded a basis of reliable and objective data upon which to build. They have also led to a steady improvement in the techniques of inquiry and analysis.

Unfortunately, up to the present time, a shortage of funds has forced researchers to confine their attention to particular institutions or, at best, to particular geographical areas. Thus, while we know a little about students in W.E.A. and university classes, our knowledge of students served by other agencies is minimal. Comparisons between students in different kinds of classes and in different parts of the country have yet to be made. The relationship of adult students to the adult population as a whole remains unexplored.

The aims of this particular survey were as follows:

1. to analyse key characteristics of students in a selection of extra-mural classes, W.E.A. classes and evening institutes, in a large centre, in representative residential colleges;

* At the time of writing, 1968, the National Institute of Adult Education is conducting a major enquiry into the adequacy of adult education facilities in certain selected areas. This will greatly help to increase our knowledge.

2. to select areas in various parts of the country which should represent respectively, the Metropolis, a few large cities, a large borough, a mixed urban and rural region, a residential 'suburb' in the Home Counties;

3. to compare and contrast students in similar institutions but in different parts of the country;

4. to compare and contrast students in different institutions within the same area;

5. to ascertain if different subjects attract different kinds of students.

The findings of the survey were based upon a questionnaire distributed among students attending classes under the following sponsorship and in the following regions:

The City Literary Institute, London.
University of Liverpool, Department of Extra-Mural Studies—Liverpool.
W.E.A. West Lancs. and Cheshire + Liverpool.
Leeds Education Authority—Evening Institutes.
W.E.A. South Gloucestershire
University of Bristol, Department of Extra-Mural Studies—South-West Gloucestershire.
W.E.A. Sheffield.
University of Oxford, Delegacy for Extra-Mural Studies—South Bucks.
Burton Manor Residential College.
Grantley Hall Residential College.

The questionnaire was designed to elicit information regarding age, sex, marital status, socio-economic ranking, number of young children, educational background, method of travel and length of journey to classes, motives for attending and regularity of attendance. Planned to ensure a maximum response, the questionnaire was anonymous, short, easily answerable and posed few problems either to students or tutors (see pp. 242–3). In general, there is some distrust of questionnaires. At least one head of an extra-mural department expressed the view that they had no practical value and were calculated to do more harm than good. Other administrators thought that questionnaires elicited information which could more readily be obtained by simpler methods and that great numbers of students would refuse to complete them. In the event very few students raised objections, the number of questionnaires returned representing a high percentage of average attendances. Indeed, in several instances, there was a return of one hundred per cent. The questionnaires were all sent out at the same time, namely in the month of February.

ii

Here it will be necessary only to summarise the general inferences that were drawn from the survey. For those who are interested comparative statistical tables for all areas in which the questionnaire was administered are given in Appendix 2(i)*.

What stood out prominently was the high socio-economic status† of students in all areas except Leeds. The administrative, professional and managerial group formed the majority in all but two places (W.E.A. South Gloucestershire and evening institutes, Leeds). There were significant differences between students in W.E.A. classes and students in extra-mural classes, but the fact remains that both agencies were drawing their students from the higher ranges of the socio-economic scale.

---

* See below, pp. 318–20. Full details of this survey, including a description of the methods used in conducting it, are contained in an unpublished report submitted by the author to the Nuffield Foundation in 1963.

† All references to socio-economic status relate to the 14 point scale used in the 1951 census as amended in the 1961 census.

Socio-Economic Groups:
Non-Manual
1. Higher administrative, professional and managerial
2. Other administrative, professional and managerial
3. Shopkeepers and shop-managers
4. Clerical
5. Shop assistants
6. Personal service
Manual
1. Foremen
2. Skilled
3. Semi-skilled
4. Unskilled
Other
1. Armed Forces—other ranks
2. Farmers
3. Agricultural workers
4. Unclassifiable

CONFIDENTIAL

THE UNIVERSITY OF LIVERPOOL

Questionnaire No.

Department of Extra-Mural Studies

Survey of Students in Adult Education Courses—Feb. 1963

The object of this survey is to secure much-needed information about the characteristics of students at present attending adult education classes in England and Wales. 20,000 questionnaires have been distributed simultaneously at various evening centres and in several university extra-mural and W.E.A. districts.

The information that you provide will be treated as confidential and used only for purposes of research. *Do not give your name.*

In response to each question, except questions 1 and 7, all you have to do is to put a *circle* around the number that applies to you. In the case of questions 1 and 7 (and possibly 13 and 14) please *write* your answers as briefly and accurately as possible.

If you are still a student in full-time education or have already completed a questionniare in another class please do *not* complete this form.

---

1. Title of class (or course) at which . . . .
   this questionnaire was issued : . . . .

Personal Details (Do *not* give your name)

2. *Age* last birthday	18–24	1		3. *Sex*	Male	1
	25–34	2			Female	2
	35–44	3				
	45–54	4		4. *Marital*	Single	1
	55–64	5		*Status*	Married	2
	65 plus	6			Widowed/Separated	
					Divorced	3

---

5. Have you any children of your own or under your
   care who are living at home aged under 11?   Yes 1   No 2

---

6. *Present employment position:*

In paid or voluntary work full-time	1
In paid or voluntary work part-time	2
Retired	3
Unemployed	4
Housewife	5
Housewife, in part-time work	6
Any other	7

---

7. *Occupation* (please write in): . . . .
   . . . .

   Notes (i) please give brief details if there is any risk of doubt, e.g. not just 'Engineer' but 'Leading Hand Fitter' or 'Civil Engineer'.
   (ii) if you are a *married* woman please give your husband's occupation.
   (iii) if you are *retired* please give your occupation before retirement.

Travel

8. Do you normally go home from work before coming to this class?   Yes 1   No 2   Not applicable 3

---

9. How far is it from your home to the place where this class meets?	10. Do you travel home from **this class** most frequently?	
under 2 miles 1 10–20 miles 4	by public transport	1
2–5 miles 2 more than 20 miles 5	on foot or bicycle	2
5–10 miles 3 Don't know 6	by private car or other private vehicle	3

---

11. What is the normal travelling time from   Under 30 mins. 1
    this class to your place of residence?   30 mins. and under 1 hr. 2
    1 hr. or over 3

Education

12. *Age* on completion of *full-time* education?	15 and under	1	18	4
	16	2	19	5
	17	3	20 or over	6

13. In what kind of Institution did you *complete* your *full-time* education?
    (a) Secondary Modern or Elementary — 1
    (b) Central, Higher grade or Junr. Tech. — 2
    (c) Grammar — 3
    (d) Public or Private — 4
    (e) Technical or Commercial College — 5
    (f) College of Art, Building etc. — 6
    (g) Teachers' Training College — 7
    (h) University — 8
    (i) Any other — 9
        (please name it)..................

    ....

14. What is the *highest* qualification that you have obtained?
    (a) University Degree — 1
    (b) Higher Professional Qualification — 2
        (please name it)..................
    (c) Teachers' Training Certificate — 3
    (d) Higher National Certificate — 4
    (e) Higher School Certificate/'A' level 2 or more passes — 5
    (f) Ordinary National Certificate — 6
    (g) Matric./School Cert./"O' level 3 or more passes — 7
    (h) No certificate or qualification — 8
    (i) Any other qualification — 9
        (please name it)..................
        ....

15. In addition to the class you are in now how many other adult education classes—including classes last term, one-day, weekend and summer schools—are you likely to have attended here or elsewhere during the period September 1962–August 1963?
    Insert number (   )

16. How many adult education classes—including one-day, weekend and summer schools—did you attend during the period September 1961–August 1962?
    Insert number (   )

17. Did you attend any adult education classes during the period September 1960 to August 1961?   Yes   1
                                                                                                      No   2

Present Subject Interest

18. What was your *principal* motive for taking *this* class?
    (a) General Cultural/Intellectual interest—e.g. to enrich your mind or widen your knowledge 1
    (b) Special interest in the subject 2
    (c) Social—e.g. to meet people of like mind, be with a friend 3
    (d) Service—e.g. to help you with work in a voluntary social service 4
    (e) Vocation—e.g. to help you in your job or to get a better job 5
    (f) Loyalty—e.g. to the class, the W.E.A., the Adult Education Movement . . . 6
    (g) Some other motive 7
    (h) No particular motive 8

19. What *first* brought this class to your notice?
    (a) Brochure, syllabus or circular received personally by you from the providing body . 1
    (b) A personal enquiry 2
    (c) Recommendation of a friend or acquaintance 3
    (d) Press notice or advertisement 4
    (e) Attendance at a previous class 5
    (f) Information gained from a public library 6
    (g) Information published or circulated at your place of work 7
    (h) Information received as a member of a society or association 8
    (i) Information received in any other way 9
    (j) Not sure 0

It would be appreciated if you would spare a further minute to check the accuracy of your replies. Thank you for your co-operation

In every instance, manual workers were found in small numbers despite the fact that they comprise about 70% of the nation's employed population. Furthermore, the overwhelming majority of those who did attend adult classes were skilled workers. There were minuscule numbers of semi-skilled and unskilled workers—the highest proportions were 4% and 1% respectively.

In general, the socio-economic status of students in extra-mural courses was higher than that of students in courses sponsored independently by the W.E.A. South Buckinghamshire was a particularly interesting case. Here the status of students attending tutorial classes sponsored jointly by the Oxford Delegacy and the W.E.A. was higher than everywhere else. What is more the students were predominantly married women. This may signify that in such areas as the middle-class residential suburbs around London there is not that objection to the W.E.A. on grounds of social prejudice which seems to exist in some other parts of the country. It may be, of course, that the Oxford rubric exercises a strong attraction.

As any experienced tutor would have predicted, teachers formed a significant percentage of women students. Even allowing for the omission of what may well have been a substantial number of graduate teachers who had not undertaken a period of pedagogical training, the following percentages of students who had acquired a teacher's training certificate were still high. Men are included to aid comparison.

Area	WL	OL	WO	EG	WG	OD	GH	BM	WS	CL	EI*
	%	%	%	%	%	%	%	%	%	%	%
Men	4	10	2	2	5	6	22	7	12	2	3
Married Women	14	16	17	18	9	12	15	17	14	7	2
Single Women	25	23	17	32	27	15	24	43	19	10	8

* The abbreviations stand for the following:
WL—W.E.A. Liverpool.
OL—Extra-Mural outside Liverpool (i.e. West Lancs and Cheshire).
WO—W.E.A. outside Liverpool (i.e. in West Lancs and Cheshire).
EG—Bristol University, Extra-Mural Studies, South Gloucester.
WG—W.E.A. South Gloucester.
OD—Oxford Delegacy, Extra-Mural Studies, South Bucks.
GH—Grantley Hall Residential College
BM—Burton Manor Residential College.
WS—W.E.A. Sheffield.
CL—City Literary Institute.
EI—Evening Institutes, Leeds.

A significant proportion of the women were trained nurses. Numerically, females exceeded males in all but two cases (Burton Manor and W.E.A. South-West Gloucestershire). In eight places the preponderance of females (more than 60%) was particularly striking.

Housewives were predictably numerous. It was surprising, however, to find percentage variations from place to place. If the City Literary Institute and Burton Manor be ignored as exceptional areas, a gap of 23% still remained between the Oxford figure (40%) and the figure for Liverpool W.E.A. (17%).

Retired people always represented a small percentage of student populations except for Grantley Hall (21%). Variations between providing bodies were partly accounted for by regional variations in population structures but it would also seem that some administrators devote more care than others to the needs of the retired.

On the whole there were more married than single people, particularly in extra-mural classes. Even so, considering the age structure, married people were probably under-represented, particularly married men.

Single men seemed much less likely to attend classes than married men. The following table, which excludes the small number of men in the category of Widowed/Divorced/Separated, clearly illustrates the point:

Area	WL	OL	WO	EG	WG	OD	GH	BM	WS	CL	EI
	%	%	%	%	%	%	%	%	%	%	%
Single men	33	25	22	31	20	18	24	28	31	47	27
Married men	67	75	78	69	80	82	76	72	69	53	73

The comparative figures for women are very different. It will be noted that at the City Literary Institute and the Residential Colleges single women greatly outnumbered married women. Even in the other centres the ratio was smaller than it was for men;

Area	WL	OL	WO	EG	WG	OD	GH	BM	WS	CL	EI
	%	%	%	%	%	%	%	%	%	%	%
Single women	37	48	41	25	32	34	66	59	40	80	33
Married women	63	52	59	75	68	66	34	41	60	20	67

Whereas in all centres the single men showed a tendency to appear in one of the lower age groups, the single women were relatively evenly distributed throughout the age-scale. The following table contrasts the age groups of all the single men and all the single women students.

	18–24	25–34	35–44	45–54	55–64	65 plus
	%	%	%	%	%	%
Single women	22	21	18	16	13	10
Single men	31	31	16	14	5	3

Predictably, single women were almost all confined to the 'other professional' or 'clerical worker' group:

Area	WL	OL	WO	EG	WG	OD	GH	BM	WS	CL	EI
	%	%	%	%	%	%	%	%	%	%	%
Other prof.	46	59	47	63	50	55	58	71	51	37	18
Clerical worker	38	23	34	25	20	30	22	20	29	44	43

Except in the case of Leeds, where not one of 322 women in the sample was either a widow or a divorcee, women far outnumbered men in the category of Widowed/Divorced/Separated. In this table the actual numbers are quoted:

Area	WL	OL	WO	EG	WG	OD	GH	BM	WS	CL	EI	Total
Women	9	15	33	5	5	11	21	4	29	22	9	154
Men	1	3	13	0	2	3	1	0	1	9	15	48

It is sometimes supposed that married women students belong to a higher socio-economic group than the average. This appeared to be true of some areas but not of others. The following table shows the respective percentages for the two highest socio-economic groups:

Area	WL	OL	WO	EG	WG	OD	GH	BM	WS	CL	EI
All students	48	71	52	73	47	71	57	63	50	55	31
Married women	36	73	45	71	43	83	78	69	55	9	35

A surprisingly high proportion of married students had children aged under 11. In some cases the percentage was nearly 40%. This would seem to show that having young children is no barrier to at least one parent in a family attending classes.

Even when people hold no certificate or qualification at least equivalent to the ordinary level certificate of the G.C.E. they have usually acquired some lesser qualification since leaving school. In other words, adult students in the main seem to be people who have actively gone about bettering themselves. This conclusion is reinforced by the percentages revealed in the following table based on the results of a Liverpool survey in 1961 carried out by Mr. B. W. Pashley:

Part-time Education of the students in the sample

    83% had received some kind of part-time education
    52% had attended L.E.A. evening classes
    12% had attended L.E.A. day classes
    33% had attended W.E.A. classes
    51% had attended extension classes.

The great majority (except at the City Literary Institute) who were gainfully employed went home before attending classes.

Most people did not travel very far to classes. Excluding the City Literary Institute, the great majority, even in the large towns, were within thirty minutes travelling time. Neither did it follow that people living in rural areas were prepared to travel further than those living in urban areas. On the contrary, the more rural the area the shorter the distance students seemed to travel. Excluding the City Literary Institute, quite a high proportion used their own vehicles.

The overwhelming motive for students attending classes of all kinds was general cultural/intellectual interest or special interest in the subject. Indeed, if the students attending classes specially designed for professional groups were to be removed, it would probably be found that something like 95–100% of the students had one of these two motives. It may be, of course, that many students who claimed a special interest in a subject were in part influenced by vocational considerations. In addition, special interests may have developed as a result of attending classes.

Students had heard of the existence of the classes they were attending through more or less similar channels. A personal recommendation carried weight.

The following table shows the percentage of students attending two years running and three years running, respectively:

Area	WL	OL	WO	EG	WG	OD	GH	BM	WS	CL	EI
2 years	59	55	56	66	70	77	73	61	66	70	33
3 years	48	40	44	46	44	59	50	44	56	61	24

Students in all classes: 2 years = 53%; 3 years = 45%

There was a substantial, but not remarkable, degree of continuity in attendance from year to year. W.E.A. students were no more pertinacious than extra-mural students or students at the City Literary Institute.

The degree of overlapping enrolments in all classes was calculated as follows:

For every 100 enrolments in 1961–62 there were in fact 57 students.

For every 100 enrolments in 1960–61 there were in fact 53 students.

This shows the necessity of treating global statistics with some reserve.

A comparison was drawn between students attending extra-mural classes and students attending W.E.A. classes. In respect of age and marital status there seemed to be no significant difference.

Occupationally, however, a far higher percentage of extra-mural students were in the top socio-economic group, especially if one excluded the Liverpool students. The difference in the percentages between the second socio-economic group was much less pronounced, however. Except in South Gloucester courses, where there are few openings for them, clerical workers were almost twice as numerous in W.E.A. classes. There were more manual workers in the W.E.A. classes, but except for South Gloucester courses the excess over extra-mural students was not great.

The number of extra-mural students who left school at 20 or over was higher by a noteworthy but not striking margin. At the other end of the scale, however, there was a prominent contrast, for fewer than 14% of extra-mural students had left school at 15, whereas 30% or more of the W.E.A. students had done so. Another outstanding contrast was that there were twice as many W.E.A. students who had no certificate or qualifications as there were extra-mural students.

A comparison was also drawn between students attending Leeds Evening Institutes and all other students. In several outstanding respects the students in the evening institutes at Leeds were different.

To begin with, the students were much younger—the highest number (18%) in the youngest age group and easily the smallest number (7%) in the two age groups 55–64 and 65 plus.

Oddly enough, the percentage of students in the highest socio-economic group was slightly higher than for Grantley Hall and much the same as for the W.E.A. Liverpool and the W.E.A. outside Liverpool. On the other hand, the percentage of students in the second socio-economic group was at least 10% lower than in any other area. Perhaps the most remarkable fact, however, was that the institutes attracted by far the highest percentage of shopkeepers, shop assistants and those engaged in personal service. If South Gloucester courses were excluded, the Leeds students contained substantially more workers than did the remaining groups. It is also noteworthy that the institutes held by far the least appeal for the retired. Only 1% of their students were in this category, perhaps partly because no daytime classes were available. The W.E.A. South Gloucester, with the lowest percentage of all the other groups, had four times as many retired students.

Almost half the Leeds students had left school at 15 or under; the nearest percentage among the other areas was for Sheffield—

38%. From another angle, it was seen that for every extra-mural student who had left school at 15 or under there were three in the evening institutes. At the other end of the scale the contrast was even more striking; only 12% of the Leeds students had stayed on in some form of full-time education until they were 20 or over; the nearest figure to this was for the W.E.A. students outside Liverpool—23%. Again, 67% of the Leeds students had no educational certificate or professional qualification: the nearest percentage was for the W.E.A. outside Liverpool—51%. Leeds also had easily the highest percentage of students who had completed their education in a technical college.

Far fewer students attended more than one class than in any of the other areas. Continuity of attendance was also substantially less. Almost 59% of Leeds students said that their motive for taking a class was special interest in a subject. This was easily the highest percentage of students giving such a motive.

In spite of the fact that most students in the evening institutes came from the more prosperous residential areas, their level of educational attainment was generally low. Considering that the students in evening institutes were predominantly married women it would appear reasonable to assume that the subjects offered appealed to the comparatively uneducated wives of comparatively affluent men. To confirm this speculation would require more analysis.

iv

To what extent do the characteristics of students differ according to the subjects in which they are interested? That question is often asked but has not yet received a satisfactory answer. Indeed, if any comprehensive study of the problem has been made, the results have not been published. The scope of this survey provided an opportunity to adduce some slender clues, slender because the statistical basis was too narrow to permit generalisations of much value.*

The most reliable correlation was perhaps between age and the subjects studied. Substantially the largest groups under 35 years were found in Psychology (47%), Physical Sciences (45%), Music (45%) and Recreational activities (47%). These were

* See 'Appendix Two. ii and iii' for the relevant list of subjects and statistical tables.

followed by Philosophy and Religion (36%), Archaeology and Ancient History (33%). The highest percentages of people aged over 54 were found in Sociology and General Social Studies (43%), Geography and International and Commonwealth Affairs (42%), General Political, Social and Economic History (37%) and Biological Sciences (35%). Three subjects had very little appeal for those aged over 54: Physical Sciences (6%), Recreational Activities (6%) and Psychology (9%). Retired people were apparently past caring about how their minds worked, since none of them had seen fit to enrol for a course in Psychology. The traditional adult education subjects—History, Social Studies and Current Affairs—continue to attract the more elderly. The subjects that have waxed in popularity are precisely those which are drawing in the younger people—Philosophy and Religion, Psychology and Music. Students in Local History classes are not so inclined to be elderly as is commonly supposed. On the contrary, there is a higher percentage of elderly students in General History classes. The relatively small percentage of students under 44 (40%) in Current Affairs classes may reflect declining enthusiasm for the subject. It was to be expected that Recreational Activities, popularly interpreted, would appeal to the young, but it has to be remembered that this is a compendious term also including Domestic Crafts, Paintings and Sculpture. There must be other reasons why the evening institutes have such a youthful clientele. The contrast between students in the Physical Sciences and students in the Biological Sciences is curious:

	18–34	35–54	over 54
Physical Sciences	47%	46%	6%
Biological Sciences	13%	52%	35%

Foreign Language students were not crowded towards the younger end of the scale, as might be expected. Instead, their age pattern conformed very closely with that for all classes.

Only in the case of the Physical Sciences did men outnumber women but they did so by a wide margin (3 : 1). Presumably, there is some connection between this singular fact and the youthful character of Physical Science students. A partial explanation may be that the Physical Sciences attract a significant percentage of quasi-professional and vocationally motivated students. Women outnumbered men approximately 3 : 1 in General History and the Visual Arts. For the rest, they were in a majority of 3 : 2 or more, except in the case of Archaeology and Ancient History (men—41%: women—59%) and Psychology (men—44%: women —56%). Apart from the dominant male interest in the Physical Sciences, these figures revealed no deviations from the normal female preponderance. At the same time, it is perhaps surprising that women should be so much more attracted to General History than men are. Again, it is hard to see why men should not be equally interested in the visual arts and foreign languages.

Married persons outnumbered unmarried persons except in the case of the Recreational Activity group of subjects, where the single outnumbered the married by more than 2 : 1, and Local History, where there was a narrow majority of single people. The chief deviation is again in the Physical Sciences group. This contains the highest proportion of married people (74%, nearly all of whom must be men) and no one in the Widowed/Divorced/ Separated group. A high percentage of the Widowed/Divorced/ Separated students are found in the English Language and Literature classes (14%) and the Sociology and Social Studies classes (14%).

The measurement adopted for estimating educational attainment was the age on completion of full-time education. The subject attracting the greatest number of students who had not completed their full-time education until they were 20 or over was Foreign Languages and Literature (42%). This was perhaps not unexpected for the study of foreign languages largely presupposes some primary knowledge. It was surely unexpected, however, to find Local History coming next with 41%. This, too, like the age factor, disturbs the accepted image of seemingly elderly and unexciting audiences doggedly determined to learn about local worthies and local events. All the more interesting is the fact that General History (28%) came some way behind. Archaeology and Ancient History (35%) may well interest the same sort of student as Local History.

Philosophy (37%), Psychology (34%), and the Physical Sciences (37%) all appealed to the higher educated. So did the Visual Arts (33%) and Current Affairs (30%). At the other end of the scale Recreational Activities attracted the highest percentage of students who had left school at 15. This was just as expected, but the fact that the percentage for Sociology students was 41% calls for an explanation. It may well be that it contains that group of subjects most commonly found in the traditional W.E.A. tutorial. Music had the lowest percentage of students (14% who had left school at 15 or under) but by no means the highest percentage towards the top end of the scale. In other words, it would appear that music has a particular appeal.

In the questionnaire an attempt was made to elicit information about student motivation for attending a particular class. The attempt was only partially successful since a large number of students described their reason for attending as general interest in the subject.

Except for General History and Music the appeal seems to have been overwhelmingly of an indeterminate nature. It was astonishing to find that General History had such a markedly special attraction. 74% of the students indicated a particular interest in the subject as against only 24% whose interest was general. The particular appeal of music required no explanation. At least one in three students in the following groups indicated a special interest in the subject: Biological Sciences (45%); Local History (41%); Recreational Activities (39%); Visual Arts (37%); Archaeology and Ancient History (35%). It might be expected that a predominantly male and youthful group would be categorically drawn to a subject for its own sake. Oddly enough, however, only 29% of Physical Science students indicated a special interest in the subject. It might also be expected that Foreign Languages and Literature students would reveal a high degree of special interest but again, though 7% clearly indicated a vocational motive, this was not so; 31% with a special interest in the subject was a surprisingly low percentage. The case of Psychology was also curious. Though 6% disclosed a vocational interest, only 22% declared themselves specially interested in the subject. That is hardly the assumption upon which administrators usually offer courses in Psychology. The relatively high percentage of students with a special interest in Recreational Activities was predictable.

Sociology and Social Studies had the weakest special appeal (19%). This was probably due to the fact that these subjects are most commonly studied in W.E.A. tutorial classes attended by students who, far from having a vocational motive, still frequently have a sense of social commitment and hence a strong desire to learn more about the society in which they live.

Chapter Sixteen

PARTICIPATION: UNIVERSAL AND LIFELONG?

The necessary conclusion is that adult education must not be regarded as a luxury for a few exceptional persons here and there, nor as a thing which concerns only a short span of early manhood, but that adult education is a permanent national necessity, an inseparable aspect of citizenship, and therefore should be both universal and lifelong.[1]

... it cannot be said that in the intervening 35 years adult education as an organised activity has become either universal or lifelong.[2]

... we feel that the number of people who will voluntarily seek educational opportunity will always be small.[3]

In this chapter an attempt will be made to seek provisional and imperfect answers to two outstanding statistical questions and to suggest what inferences we should draw from the present pattern of public participation in adult education. The two questions are:

(a) What percentage of the total population of England and Wales, over the age of eighteen and no longer in full-time attendance at an educational establishment, makes use of the facilities outlined in previous chapters?

(b) What sections of the population are being served by the adult education agencies or, conversely, what sections of the population do not participate in adult education?

i. *The Extent of Participation*

There is only one sure way to obtain a reliable estimate for the percentage of the population participating in adult education and that is to conduct a nation-wide sample survey. A tall order, but such a survey has been conducted in the United States and Canada and looks like becoming a regular feature of their periodic official census reports.

In 1957 the Bureau of the Census in the United States Departments of Health, Education and Welfare was allowed to include

several questions concerning adult participation in further education to a random sample of 300,000 respondents.[1] Permission to
ask these questions was given because 'the resources of the Census
Bureau were regarded as essential to a sound statistical sampling
process which would result in a scientifically determined estimate
of adult education participation in the United States'. In 1965
the results were published of a uniquely comprehensive survey of
adult students conducted on behalf of the National Opinion
Research Centre. As a result of this survey a wealth of evidence
is now available about the rate of participation by the American
public in adult education and about the characteristics of participants and non-participants.*

The Dominion Bureau of Statistics in Canada has also carried
out similar sample surveys. In addition, the Labour Force Survey,
which has two spare questions each month, was used by enumera-
tors during June 1960 to ask individuals if they had taken part in
adult education courses since the preceding September. According
to the Bureau itself the quantitative results of the latter survey,
which probably under-estimated actual participation, were not as
important as the information gained about the variety of persons,
courses and sponsors involved. The practice is now established in
Canada of conducting regular surveys and in consequence adult
educators can turn to a mass of evidence about the characteristics
of that section of the public which they serve, not to speak of the
much larger section which they do not serve.

It is hoped that consideration may be given to conducting a
nation-wide survey in the United Kingdom in conjunction with
the next decennial census. In the meantime, it should be possible
to obtain fairly accurate information by appointing a small team
of researchers to conduct a limited survey. An extra-mural department or the National Institute of Adult Education might well
undertake such a task. For the time being, however, the best one
can do is to make rough calculations based on the annual statistics
published by providing bodies.

Before making such calculations, it is important to point out
four major difficulties. The first is that since many organisations
provide educational facilities only incidentally to their main purpose, it is often impossible to know how many of their students
or members are engaged in activities which can be qualified in any

* See the summary below, pp. 331–3.

sense as educational. Take the case of the Women's Institutes. They have a total membership of about five hundred thousand but there is no means of knowing exactly how many members actively participate in their educational programmes. For the purpose of calculation it will be necessary, therefore, to compile two lists of statistics based respectively on a high and a low estimate.

The second difficulty springs from the fact that many people use more than one of the facilities provided. It is not uncommon for the same woman to belong to a Townswomen's Guild and the Soroptimists, to attend one or more extra-mural courses and to go to a week-end or a summer school or indeed both. Even if it be assumed that people never patronise more than one providing body, we still cannot be sure that they do not attend more than one course, for although some agencies are helpful and count only heads, others count only enrolments. For several years, the Department of Education and Science has wisely stipulated that local authorities should count each student once only when making returns for particular institutions, but this does not solve the problem of how to avoid counting more than once those students who attend classes in more than one institution. One can overcome the problem of multiple enrolments up to a point by grading participants according to the standing of the providing body they patronise. Thus we can obtain a fairly accurate figure for the percentage of the population attending university extra-mural courses. But when we come to deal with participants in the more informal programmes, we find ourselves groping in the dark.

The third difficulty in measuring the extent of public participation in adult education is that the student population is not static. Each year new students enrol and others withdraw. Again we can resolve the problem to some extent by estimating what the approximate annual rate of turnover appears to be; indeed it was for this purpose that two questions concerning attendance at classes in the previous year were included in the questionnaire described in the previous chapter. But if one can obtain a rough idea of the rate of turnover during very recent years, it is almost impossible, short of conducting the most elaborate survey, to ascertain what percentage of adults is likely to attend classes in the course of a whole lifetime.

The fourth and last difficulty is that annual statistics furnished by providing bodies do not always refer to the same period. Most statistics relate to the academic year, that is, roughly from 1st September in one year to 31st August in the next, whereas others relate to the calendar year. Fortunately, this difficulty can usually be overcome by careful adjustment.

The following table represents an attempt to work out a rough estimate of the situation as it was at the time of the last national census. The figures cited are taken from the reports of the providing bodies themselves but have been adjusted in so far as they were thought unreliable or were clearly inaccurate. Footnotes indicate how the calculations were reached.

The Number of Adults Participating in Non-Vocational Educational Activities by Organisations, 1961–62

	High Estimate*	Low Estimate†
1. *Evening Institutes*	767,267‡	537,450
2. *Other L.E.A. Establishments*	300,000§	200,000
3. *Education Centres*	25,969	18,172
4. *Community Associations*	362,000	36,000‖
5. *Residential Colleges¶* (long-term)	377	377
6. *Residential Colleges*** (short-term)	65,000	62,000††
7. *Responsible Bodies*	210,191	160,000
8. *H. M. Forces*	350,000	100,000§§
9. *H. M. Prisons*	15,000††	5,000
10. *Women's Institutes‖‖*	350,000	175,000
11. *Townswomen's Guilds*	144,900	72,450
12. *National Council of Women's Clubs‖‖*	80,000	40,000
13. *Industrial and Commercial Firms¶¶*	50,000	20,000
14. *The Trade Unions¶¶*	1,000	1,000
15. *The Co-operative Union*	32,000***	16,350
16. *The National Council of Labour Colleges*	78,479†††	14,000
17. *The National Adult School Union*	5,400	3,780
18. *Field Studies Council*	1,059	1,059
19. *Working Men's Clubs*	3,009	2,000
20. *Y.W.C.A.*	5,542	3,750
21. *Y.M.C.A.* (including its Residential Colleges)	8,400	5,880
22. *Rural Music Schools*	2,436	1,700
23. *British Film Institute*	100	100
24. *B.B.C., I.T.V.*	200,000	100,000‡‡‡
25. *Societies and Clubs*	500,000§§§	200,000
26. *Correspondence Courses* (Ruskin, N.C.L.C., Catholic Social Guild, Seafarers' Educational Service)	21,000	14,000
27. *Miscellaneous* (e.g. the Churches)	20,000	10,000
	3,599,129	1,800,068

In calculating the above figures no account was taken of the effect of multiple enrolments. But to do so is important, because multiple enrolments occur on a considerable scale especially in the traditional forms of adult education. At an attractive place like the City Literary Institute, for instance, there was during the session 1962–63 an average of 1·9 class enrolments per student. It has

* The high estimate represents in each instance the number of members eligible to take advantage of any educational facilities that were provided.

† Except where the figure for those attending courses is an absolute, e.g. in the case of residential colleges, I have assumed that at least 30% of the total declared did not attend more than three meetings. This percentage should probably be raised higher.

‡ The high figure for evening institute enrolments is exclusive of students in vocational classes.

§ There is no means of knowing just how many part-time students attending technical colleges, other colleges and art establishments, were in non-vocational classes.

‖ The low estimate for Community Associations assumes that only about 10% of their activities are clearly educational.

¶ In Residential Colleges (Long-Term) I have included the Co-operative Union College.

** In residential Colleges (Short-Term) I have included those which are non-grant-aided.

†† Though I obtained figures for the majority of Residential Colleges (Short-Term), I was reduced to making a rough estimate for some ten or twelve of them. This accounts for the disparity between the high and low figures.

‡‡ If regulations were strictly enforced then the high figure for H.M. Forces would be approximately correct. As it is, it is probably generous to assume that at least 100,000 men and women are attending courses in current affairs and other subjects.

§§ For H.M. Prisons the high figure includes all types of classes.

‖‖ In the case of the three large women's organisations the high figure represents the total membership less 30% for sleeping members. The low figure is based on the assumption that no more than half of the members regularly attend meetings. I have presumed that the percentage of girls under eighteen in the Women's Institutes is not significant.

¶¶ The figures for Industrial and Commercial firms and for the Trade Unions exclude vocational courses.

*** The high figure for the Co-operative Union includes the so-called informal activities; the low figure does not.

††† The high figure for the National Council of Labour Colleges includes single lectures.

‡‡‡ The figures for the B.B.C. and I.T.V. are founded on the assumption that a significant minority of people are conscientiously following some of the courses provided.

§§§ The high figure for Societies and Clubs was calculated on the assumption that the percentage of participants nationally equalled the mean percentage of participants in Wolverhampton and Liverpool respectively (see above, pp. 193–8). The low figure was based on the assumption that only two out of five members of societies regularly attend meetings.

I

also to be noted that students attending a particular class are frequently claimed by two organisations. Thus the Townswomen's Guild and the W.E.A. may run a course in collaboration and in their annual returns each shows the same members attending. In so far as the Responsible Bodies are concerned, some evidence about the frequency of multiple enrolments was extracted from the answers to the questionnaire described in chapter 15. This revealed the following facts:

For 100 enrolments in 1961–62 there were only 57 students.
For 100 enrolments in 1962–63 there were only 53 students.

The closeness of the two figures, 57 and 53, is perhaps a pointer to their accuracy.

It does not follow, of course, from this disclosure that the two totals listed above should be scaled down to 57% and 53%. For one thing, the organisations dealing with the largest numbers and providing the most informal activities are those which are least affected by multiple enrolments (on the whole, the patrons of evening institutes do not avail themselves of other facilities).* For another, the questionnaire concerned too few organisations to justify generalisations. Nevertheless, it is clear that we should regard even the low total as excessive, and when we come to the refinement of determining how many people participate in the more intensive programmes it will be necessary to allow for the factor of multiple enrolments.

Approximate Percentage of the Population of England and Wales participating in Adult Education during the year 1961–62

In 1961 the total population of England and Wales was 45,755,000. Subtracting from this total those under eighteen (12,425,000) or still in full-time education (260,275) and those who were physically incapacitated (say, 500,000) one is left with a total of approximately 32,500,000. There is no point in further eliminating those at sea, or in H.M. Forces or in H.M. Prisons, since they will be included in the educational count. This would give the percentage of the

---

* Mr Ian Hanna made this discovery in Leeds where he conducted a comprehensive survey of adult students. It also seems that the students in evening institutes seldom attend more than one course. The Principal of the Adult Institute, Wolverhampton, informed me that for 1962–63 out of 1,440 students he had only 235 or 16% of multiple enrolments.

population participating in adult education during the session 1961–62 as follows:

$$\text{High Estimate} = \frac{3,599,029}{32,500,000} = 10 \cdot 8\%$$

$$\text{Low Estimate} = \frac{1,800,068}{32,500,000} = 5 \cdot 7\%$$

Approximate Percentage of the Population Attending Classses

But so far I have been interpreting adult education in the widest sense. It may be more informative to work out percentages organisation by organisation for those actually attending classes. For this purpose I shall deliberately use the low estimates at a rate of 55% in the case of the Responsible Bodies, the Education Centres and the Short-Term Residential Colleges as a group.

Responsible Bodies	=	$160,000 = 0 \cdot 49\%$
Educational Centres	=	$18,170 = 0 \cdot 05\%$
Short-Term Residential Colleges	=	$60,000 = 0 \cdot 18\%$
Responsible Bodies	=	$\frac{55\% \text{ of } 238,170}{32,500,000}$
Short-Term Residential Colleges and Educational Centres combined	=	$\frac{125,340}{32,500,000} = 0 \cdot 41\%$

Percentage of the Population Participating in Adult Education when allowances have been made for turnover

Some people attend an adult class almost every year of their lives. Others attend from time to time. Some attend for one year and never again. But how many fall into each category no one can say.

In the questionnaire used to elicit the information presented in the previous chapter two questions (16 and 17) were inserted concerning the continuity of attendance. The two questions were: 'How many adult education classes—including one-day, week-end and Summer Schools—did you attend during the period September 1961 and August 1962?' and 'Did you attend any adult education classes during the period September 1960 to August 1961?' These results were obtained from the answers received:

Institution	1962–63 % in 1st year	1961–62 % in 2nd year	1960–61 % in 3rd year	1962–63 and 1960–61 % who had missed one year
City Literary Institute	26	10	61	3
Extra-Mural Outside Liverpool	38	15	40	8
W.E.A. Liverpool				
W.E.A. outside Liverpool	29	16	41	14
W.E.A. Sheffield	34	8	56	1
W.E.A. South Glos.	25	22	44	10
Extra-Mural South Glos.	22	22	48	8
Extra-Mural Oxford	15	19	59	7
Evening Institutes Leeds	56	10	24	11
Burton Manor	33	17	44	6
Grantley Hall	18	23	50	9

It may be helpful to tabulate several observations upon these figures:

1. With the exception of the evening institutes there is a high rate of continuity. Between 2 and 3 out of every 5 students were in their third year. This relatively high percentage may well constitute that solid core of adherents of which every adult educationist is fully aware.

2. Continuity of attendance no more characterises W.E.A. students than it does other students. The high Oxford rate is explained by the fact that most of the students were attending three-year tutorial classes.

3. The high rate at the City Literary Institute is doubtless due to its social appeal and administrative efficiency.

4. The percentage in their second year is significantly lower than the percentages in their first and third years. This may indicate that a good proportion of newcomers drop out after one year.

5. It is not surprising that the percentage of newcomers at Grantley Hall should be low, for on the whole the residential colleges draw their students from adult classes. The apparently high percentage of newcomers at Burton Manor is explained by the fact that the College provides non-vocational courses for specialist groups drawn from outside the normal adult education field.

6. It is generally accepted that evening institutes tend to have

floating populations. Hence the contrasting figures for Leeds. At the same time, it is to be expected that as the institutes lose their old-fashioned image they will begin to attract a large and faithful clientele.

7. Students return to classes after an absence of one year but not apparently in great numbers. Indeed, it could be that many of those appearing in column 4 had deliberately missed one year simply because the subject or subjects they wanted were not available. In other words, they could be regular but discriminating class-goers.

What we want to know above all, of course, is what light these figures throw on the rate of turnover. Unfortunately, they only refer to a span of three years. In order to obtain a reliable estimate of the percentage of the population likely to attend a course or courses in the span of a lifetime it would be necessary to cover a period of ten or even twenty years, and this would be virtually impossible. Apart from the immense mechanical difficulties involved, people's memories are both short and uncertain. For this reason it is worth making some tentative deductions despite the inadequacy of the period of time under review.

Evidently there is a substantial rate of turnover. If we add the percentages in columns 3 and 4, we get a total in each case, except for Leeds evening institutes, of between 50% and 65%. This suggests that there were between 35% and 50% newcomers during the last two years. It also means that of those who first joined a class in 1961–62 a certain percentage had not re-enrolled for 1962–63—at least up to the month of the questionnaire. As to the rate of turnover one might suggest a range of between 10% and 20%.

If one then takes these two extremes and assumes, say, that the average life-span from 18 is 50 years, one can make the following calculations. At the rate of 10% annual turnover there would be an eventual turnover of 500%; at the rate of 20% turnover there would be an eventual turnover of 1,000%. In turn these 'eventual turnovers' would give the following figures in terms of the percentage of the total population likely to be involved in the traditional forms of adult education. One must postulate for this purpose, of course, that the population will remain static:

(i) $5 \times 125{,}340 = 626{,}700 = 1 \cdot 9\%$ of population.
(ii) $10 \times 125{,}340 = 1{,}253{,}400 = 3 \cdot 9\%$ of population.

It would be a waste of time to try to work out similar percentages for the evening institutes and the more informal adult education agencies. But it is only fair to say that they would be many times higher. Indeed, if the attendance at the Leeds institutes is a valid example, we find an annual turnover of between 40% and 50%, and we should have to think in terms of multiplying the present evening institute population figure by at least 16. And if we were to do that, we should have to anticipate more than one in three of the eligible population attending a course at least once in a lifetime.

In the previous section it was postulated that the numbers attending classes in 1962–63 reached a peak which would not be surpassed. In truth, of course, the total population attending classes and making use of informal educational facilities is expanding all the time. A few comparative figures, chosen precisely because they have often been quoted, will illustrate this point.

In 1925 the late Harold Laski gave an estimate of the adult education population in an address to the annual conference of the British Institute of Adult Education. In 1956 Sir Ronald Adam brought Laski's estimate up to date. We shall in turn bring Sir Ronald's estimate up to date for 1962–63 and show the three estimates in adjacent columns for the sake of facilitating a comparison. For convenience we have adopted their terminology and added together some of the figures. The totals remain unaltered.

	Laski	Sir Ronald Adams	Lowe
Extension	13,000	51,000	85,000
W.E.A.	50,000	98,500	100,000
		(including tutorials)	
Adult Schools	55,799	9,000	5,000
Y.M.C.A.	89,371	—	8,400
W.I.	204,400	450,000	500,000
Evening Institutes	—	662,000	767,267
Residential Colleges	—	35,000	65,000
Townswomen's Guilds	—	150,000	207,000
TOTAL	412,570	1,455,500	1,737,667

The more detailed and comprehensive calculation shown above would make the advance up to 1962–63 even more striking.

The boom in adult education really began with the outbreak of war in 1939 and it was sustained until the session 1949–50. For a time thereafter it appeared that a recession had set in, but from the middle of the fifties progress has been rapid, particularly in the area of informal activities. Furthermore, the most recent trend seems to indicate that we have entered into a period of accelerated expansion. For instance, the numbers attending classes provided by the responsible bodies leapt by 31,000 or 17% between 1960–61 and 1961–62. The advance since 1962 has continued to be striking.

Wherever one looks, except for the Adult Schools, the figures are auspicious. As we have seen, societies have multiplied since the last war. Serious programmes on sound radio or television appeal to increasingly large numbers. Attendance at museums, concerts and art galleries is rising fast. Good books command a vast sale. There is only one cloud on the horizon but it is a big one. Nearly all this activity is being sustained by a relatively small element in the population. Adult education facilities appeal less and less to those who have had the least education.

ii. *Who Participates? Who does not Participate?*

No one supposes that students in adult education classes constitute a representative cross-section of society. At the same time, no one knows in exactly what proportions the different age groups, sexes and educational and social groups are represented. The tables in Appendix 3, which are mainly based upon the 1951 census figures rather than upon the 1961 figures, provide a clue but no more than a clue since they necessarily relate to a few limited areas.

From the tables it is possible to draw the following conclusions:

1. People in the age group 18–24 do not participate in great numbers except in evening institutes. People who are 55 or over tend not to frequent evening institutes.
2. Males are always under-represented in every institution.
3. There is no clear indication one way or the other—except at the City Literary Institute—concerning the participation of married men and women. It follows that the same would be true of single men and women.
4. It is with regard to social class and the level of education attained that we become fully aware of who does not participate. Unskilled workers are almost totally unrepresented even in the evening institutes. The partly skilled fare very much better, though it must be stressed that the great

majority of them are either shop assistants or engaged in personal service. In non-extra-mural classes skilled workers are pretty heavily under-represented by between 20% and 35%; in extra-mural classes they are, not surprisingly, under-represented by no less than 60%.

5. Those who left school at 15 or under participate in very small numbers even though they comprise between 79% and 89% of the regional populations. The percentage *not* participating in each group is as follows:

WL	WO	OL	CL	EI
67%	61%	85%	82%	42%

The value of the evening institutes in dealing with this segment of the population—in terms of numbers nationally between 25 and 26 millions—could not be illustrated more clearly.

Before attempting to draw any inferences from the foregoing estimates of adult participation in educational activities, it is important to draw attention to something which is obvious but which nevertheless needs to be stated in the present context—the fact that there are many people who occupy their leisure usefully in other ways than by attending classes or who cannot attend through force of circumstance. The following groups most readily come to mind:

1. Those people, especially the young, who give all the spare time they can afford to vocational classes and private studies; for example, thousands of people are taking correspondence courses.

2. A large number of people are fully preoccupied with causes of various kinds, e.g. the churches, the political parties and charities.

3. In spite of improved social conditions and the growing flexibility of class organisers, some people are hindered from doing what they might like to do by such obligations as having to work awkward shifts or to look after young children.

4. Other people find it necessary, or seem to find it necessary, to put in many hours of overtime in order to secure an adequate wage.

5. Some people who wish to take part in educational activities

cannot do so because no suitable facilities are available in their vicinity or because there is a shortage of public transport at the times when classes are held.

6. There are many people who are sufficiently instructed and enterprising to obtain all the intellectual stimulus they require without recourse to group or organised activities.

7. There are all those individuals, many of whom are comparatively uneducated, who are wholly engrossed in a particular hobby, e.g. gardening, pigeon fancying, stamp collecting, making or tinkering with machines, and so on.

8. Finally, there are those who spend a good part of their leisure in some game or outdoor activity which is usually done by clubs, e.g. tennis, golf, sailing and bowls.

Exactly how many people belong to these eight categories is anybody's guess, but they must constitute a substantial percentage of the population. There is, of course, a strong probability that the people in these categories are precisely those who have taken part in educational activities in the past or may well do so at some stage in the future.

iii

The statistics and percentages here quoted are by no means authoritative. It will be a long time, and it will require a good deal of thought and planning, before we can put into operation an effective system for compiling adult education statistics. But rough though they may be, the figures clearly reveal that adult education for the people of England and Wales is neither 'universal nor lifelong'. On the contrary, the overwhelming majority of the population do not participate in it at any period during their lives.

What should concern us even more than the recognition of this fact—which is hardly a new discovery—is that nearly all who do participate in adult education are already comparatively educated. It is the products of the secondary modern school by and large who are inactive.

If it could be shown that this section of the population could not profit from the continuance of its education, there might be no cause for alarm. But, in fact, every indication—from the subjective point of view of experienced tutors, who sometimes get astonishingly good results from adults with lamentably poor academic records, to the objective data at our disposal—points to the conclusion that if the right methods are used, this section can profit from continuing education. Moreover, there are many people whose formal education did not begin to draw out their latent capacities.

Everyone is aware of the thousands of students who find it difficult to secure a university place and of the tens of thousands of young children who just fail to pass 11 plus. But few are equally aware of the hundreds of thousands of men and women who left school before their minds had ever been stretched or had time to expand. The Crowther Report contained a mass of evidence that has somehow failed to attract the attention it deserves, except perhaps among adult educationists. Its most revealing data concerned the I.Q.s of recruits in the armed forces. Consider the implications of the following table:

		% leaving school at			
Ability Groups	Nos.	15 or less	16	17	18 plus
1 (highest)	681	9	33	17	41
2	1,824	65	22	6	7
3	1,014	94	4	1	1
4	1,184	98	2	Tec	Tec
5	863	98	1	—	1
6 (lowest)	374	97	3	Tec	Tec
All groups	5,940	77	12	4	7

9% of those in the highest ability group had left school at 15 or under; of the total sample this is equivalent to rather more than 1%. On first sight that looks like a minuscule number but if one can assume that the sample was a fair representation of the total occupied population, it means in effect that at least 320,000 people of the highest ability left school at the minimum leaving age. And even if we regard this as a legitimate rate of wastage, what is to be said of the fate of those in the next two ability groups who are so numerous? To suggest that all the young men in these two groups would have profited from a grammar school education up to the Ordinary G.C.E. level, let alone from a spell in a sixth form, would be foolish. Apart from any other consideration a high proportion of them were only too glad to leave school as soon as possible. The question is whether or not they deserve another opportunity. If it is thought that they do—that their dislike of school was as much a reflection upon the national system of education as upon themselves—then the public authorities should provide them with every inducement to attend classes. Meanwhile, the concern of adult educators is not only with the post-war generation who left school at 15 but with anyone however old who has never had the opportunity to measure the extent of his mental powers.

Naturally, it is increased provision of day-release facilities that is chiefly desirable not only for those in their teens but for older persons as well. But 'Further Education' alone will not produce fully developed citizens if at the same time the traditional values of 'Adult Education' are not widely diffused among the population. This means that those concerned with adult education have to bring all their energy and ingenuity to bear upon the problem of devising methods for reaching that huge proportion of the population that they have not yet managed to touch.

All this is not to recommend neglect of the better educated. They are also entitled to receive as much help as they require. But, then, it is unlikely they ever will be neglected since, unless prepared to lower standards, the universities and other bodies will continue to serve their needs. It is rather a question of providing more funds and appropriate facilities for those institutions best placed to deal with the less educated sections of the population— e.g. community associations, village colleges and evening institutes. It is also a question of deciding that adult education is a national priority, harnessing the support of school teachers and any professional group that has the power to influence public attitudes and standards, and of ensuring intimate collaboration between the schools, the youth service and adult education organisations.

iv. *Future Trends*

There may well be a ceiling for adult participation in educational activities. If so, it will be a long time before it is reached and in the meantime the scope for expansion is relatively limitless, given adequate resources and the will to expand. Should a full-scale effort be made to kindle interest among the educationally underprivileged, then almost every providing agency can anticipate an unprecedented demand for its services and a host of hitherto unknown problems.

Even if no attempt is made to attract a new clientele a steady rate of expansion for nearly all the agencies seems to be assured. These are some of the factors contributing to the rising demand:

1. The more facilities there are, the more the public asks for an increased supply.
2. Notwithstanding the cautionary lessons of recent history it now seems safe to predict that people will have more leisure time than in the past.
3. As people become better educated, so they desire more opportunities to go on learning. This signifies that university extra-mural departments in particular can expect to find their courses in demand by ever-increasing numbers, as more people go to grammar schools, stay on in sixth forms, and attend university. In a recent policy statement the Association of Tutors in Adult Education pointed out that by 1980 two million people will have completed higher education; by 2025 the number will have swelled to at least five million.
4. If the American experience is anything to go by, it also seems that there is a correlation between rising incomes and a rising interest in educational programmes.
5. The number of retired persons is steadily increasing. More significantly, the retired are more active both mentally and physically than they used to be.
6. Housewives will attend classes and take part in group activities in ever increasing numbers.
7. Recent signs indicate that the number of young people interested in adult classes is expanding fast.
8. Foreign travel which, as everyone knows, appeals to a growing percentage of the public, seems to stimulate the intellectual appetite.
9. The inauguration of the Open University in 1969, together with the growing impact of B.B.C.2 and the increasing number of specifically adult education programmes on television, seems bound to stimulate a demand for follow-up adult classes.
10. If the Responsible Bodies could be freed from their obligation to stick to strictly non-vocational provision in so far as they receive grant-aid, it is certain that they could vastly

increase the size of their programmes by meeting the insatiable demand for professional and vocational courses at all levels.

11. The trend towards the institutionalisation of adult education, which in turn reflects a growing emphasis on social factors, also seems bound to increase public demand.

12. The tendency for people to marry earlier and to have larger families fairly quickly should release for participation in educational activities many more people in precisely those two age groups, 25–34 and 35–44, which at present attend classes in the greatest numbers proportionate to the percentage of the population they represent.

13. As adult education breaks away from the tradition of concentrating upon non-vocational courses mainly in the social studies field, it will capture an increasingly large audience of people desiring professional or quasi-professional instruction, e.g. in the sciences.

v

Public participation in adult education has increased rapidly during recent years. What is more, the pace of expansion seems to be steadily quickening. All the signs indicate that for a variety of reasons the demand for the traditional types of provision will continue to increase, and that there will also be an unprecedented demand for courses aimed at certain groups such as the retired and housewives and above all those requiring instruction for professional and vocational purposes. There is, however, one serious cause for perturbation. It is that while adult education, especially in its more developed forms, appears to appeal more and more to those who are comfortably off and relatively well educated, it is not extending its appeal to the great majority of the population, namely, those who have had the least education. The question thus posed to adult educationists is whether they should apply their resources to meeting what may be described as the 'higher-level demand' or whether they should give special priority to the needs of the educationally underprivileged. It is not an easy decision to make simply because the 'higher level demand' is both apparently inexhaustible for the foreseeable future and rewarding to deal with.

One thing is certain: adult education agencies cannot hope to meet even the 'higher-level demand' adequately unless they discover more facts about the nature of the demand and experiment with new techniques, and unless there is also much closer collaboration among the providing agencies. In short, they will have to look to the need both for research and training facilities and for the co-ordination of activities at the national as well as at the local level.

REFERENCES

1. *The 1919 Report*, p. 5.
2. Extract from the Ashby Committee's Report, p. 34.
3. Extract from a W.E.A. memorandum to the Broadcasting Committee in 1950.
4. Cf. *Participation in Adult Education* (U.S. Department of Health, Education and Welfare, 1959), p. 1.
5. These figures have been extracted from the *Annual Abstract of Statistics* (H.M.S.O.) for 1961.
6. Cf. *Problems in Adult Education* (The Twenty-Third Haldane Memorial Lecture—London, 8 March 1956), Birbeck College, p. 9.

Chapter Seventeen

CO-ORDINATION IN THEORY AND PRACTICE

Uninformed critics often complain that adult education in England and Wales is thoroughly disorganised. In fact, there is some degree of co-ordination. This is mainly due to two factors: the control exercised by the central government through its Inspectorate and the L.E.A.s, and the part played by the National Institute of Adult Education.

i

The central government not only makes grants to a number of voluntary adult education organisations, it also lays certain obligations upon the local authorities besides ensuring observance of its grant regulations by means of the Inspectorate. The 1944 Education Act enjoined the local authorities to co-operate with the Responsible Bodies and empowered the formation of regional committees which should contain representatives of both; the D.E.S. still insists upon consultation as a condition of making grants.[1] Ten years later the Ashby Report (1954) made a specific proposal that the L.E.As should contribute towards the administrative costs of the Responsible Bodies and provide them with accommodation free of charge. The L.E.As are now also expected to support the activities of informal adult education agencies in so far as their resources will permit, though they are under no statutory compulsion to do so.

Between theory and practice a gap looms, however, the degree of co-operation varying greatly from place to place and from time to time. Some organisations have little regard for others and the ignorance about the rest of the field on the part of a particular organisation is often profound. The initiative taken by L.E.A.s is the vital factor simply because they conduct by far the largest programmes besides controlling most of the facilities and some of the purse-strings. Three policies are open to them: to make a conscientious attempt to co-ordinate all adult education activities in their areas and equitably to distribute whatever funds and material resources are available; to collaborate with some organisations but not with others; or to make no effort, or nearly no effort, to secure co-ordination. To estimate precisely what proportion of L.E.A.s adopt each of these policies would require painstaking inquiry, but it would seem reasonable to venture the suggestion that the majority fall into the second category with the other two categories each comprising roughly equal minorities. For convenience the relationship of the L.E.A.s with the university extramural departments, the W.E.A. and other adult education organisations, in that order, is examined before brief consideration of the policy of the Universities Council for Adult Education.

As might be expected, good relations between L.E.A.s and the universities are the norm for reasons that are fairly obvious. In the first place, the participation of the universities in adult education lends it a certain cachet. Secondly, chief education officers and the university representatives whom they meet find it easy to communicate on terms of equality. Thirdly, outside Oxford, Cambridge and London, L.E.A.s have a close interest in the activities of their local university, and indeed they usually nominate a few representatives to its governing body and its extra-mural committee. No doubt the universities also profit from the fact that the L.E.A.s do not as a rule see them as potential rivals. An extreme expression of admiration for and trust in the universities was voiced at an international seminar for adult educationists held at Bangor in 1956. On that occasion, the chief education officer for Devon declared: 'Do I want the W.E.A. to run it?—No! Do I want the university to run it?—Yes! I do! I would like ultimately the universities charged with executive responsibility for all the adult education, except the sort of evening institute classes which the local education authorities run!' Though neither practicable nor at all representative of the views of most education officials, this proposal was an indication of the prestige commonly attached to the universities in the adult education field. It is necessary to enter a small caveat because here and there university extra-mural departments attract hostility.

On the surface L.E.A.s are cordial to the W.E.A. But evidence is available of unfriendliness on the part of some authorities and sheer indifference on the part of others. For instance, whereas university extra-mural departments are usually received as welcome guests when seeking accommodation for classes, W.E.A. branches are often regarded as a nuisance. Behind this attitude lies the feeling that the W.E.A. is old-fashioned and socially irrelevant or even misguided. Some prejudice is easily explained in terms of political attitudes, for many officials as well as civic leaders unfairly stigmatise the W.E.A. as a working-class and a socialist organisation. For the rest, principals of evening institutes and many of those in charge of other local authority establishments frequently see no good reason why they should provide facilities for the W.E.A. Through ignorance of its aims they judge its work superfluous—anything the W.E.A. can do, they can do better. Since other organisations share their reservations, it is not always easy to fit the W.E.A. into a scheme of local co-ordination.

But if there is a lack of sympathy for the W.E.A., at least it is a force to be reckoned with. The same cannot be said of the other voluntary organisations, who far too often are ignored despite the valuable job they do by using their characteristically informal methods. In most communities, learned, cultural and other societies could be made far more effective, and certainly a large number of them would more consciously insert an educational element into their programmes, if they were to receive financial support and if accommodation were to be placed at their disposal. The ideal arrangement would be for L.E.A.s to deal as automatically with the requirements of informal groups as with the requirements of their evening institutes.

For their part, the universities have no ambition to rule the domain of adult education. In the 1961 Working Party Report of the Universities' Council for Adult Education, they were careful to state: 'We have no quarrel with the principle that the ultimate responsibility for securing adequate provision should rest on the local education authorities, and we do not wish to claim any monopoly or suggest any precise delimitation of sphere of action'. In their annual report for 1966–67 it was observed:

> Last year's Council's Report referred to collaboration between departments and local education authorities, but remarked that outside Scotland only Hull and Newcastle had anything significant to show in the way of joint arrangements with them. It is obvious, however, that a number of significant new developments have occurred during the past year.[3]

The report went on to catalogue no fewer than eight new examples of collaboration with the L.E.A.s. At the same time, aware that most of their work cannot be done effectively by any other body the universities have small cause to fear serious competition. They are also strengthened by the knowledge that the universities are relatively free from central government interference and that in the last resort they might be able to travel alone by drawing their funds from the University Grants Committee rather than directly from the Department of Education and Science as at present. A few extra-mural departments would hesitate to seek this refuge, however, since it would mean abandoning their key position in the adult education movement of which they are rightly solicitous.

The charge to be laid against the universities is not that of wishing to monopolise, but of paying too little attention to the efforts of others in the field. Thus at the annual professional conference organised by the D.E.S. very few university staff tutors attend, and those who do are often present as individuals rather than as representatives of particular extra-mural departments. Nor do the universities make much effort to collaborate with bodies other than the W.E.A., the residential colleges, and occasionally the evening institutes, though, of course, they work closely with the professional associations and more learned societies, since these often provide them with ready-made groups from which to form extension courses. Outside the urban centres resident staff tutors also devote much of their time to seeking out local societies and establishing good relations with them.

Even when there is a general desire for friendly relations among adult education organisations, it is still not easy to obtain effective co-operation. The main difficulty is that most of the people involved are extremely ignorant of the field as a whole. To take a few examples: university staff tutors frequently know little or nothing about the functions of the community centres; wardens of community centres are often unaware of the help they can receive from the universities or the W.E.A.; more seriously, principals of evening institutes tend to be unaware of the numerous possibilities for experiment and development that lie open to them by making use of the skills and resources of others. Before greater co-ordination can be achieved, it will be necessary to ensure that mutual understanding is widespread, for at the present time, even when there is co-operation at higher levels, friction often arises at ground level. Misunderstandings most frequently occur between the heads of local authority establishments and the Responsible

Bodies. Principals of evening institutes try to enrol as many students as possible. This is only natural, especially as their scale of payments is usually tied to the total number of names that can be counted on their registers excluding those in classes sponsored by the Responsible Bodies. In consequence, while principals may have no incentive to exert themselves on behalf of visiting groups, they sometimes have the utmost incentive to fill every available room with their own students. In many places where the only centre with educational facilities is an evening institute, this may mean that Responsible Bodies and voluntary organisations are either forced to use uncomfortable rooms or are excluded altogether.

Sometimes there is direct competition. For example, a principal may notice that in his own area, perhaps even in his own institute, an extra-mural department or W.E.A. Branch is enjoying success with a particular type of class, say, local history or art appreciation. He may then be tempted to include such a course in his own programme. In doing so, he may also realise that he will have a monopoly of the local accommodation as well as the advantage of starting his annual programme about three weeks in advance of his likely competitors. This practice is on the increase simply because, as pointed out above, the strictly vocational classes which used to dominate evening institute programmes are being gradually transferred to colleges of commerce and the like, while the evening institutes are turning their attention to non-vocational subjects and activities. It is true that very little of L.E.A. work, which is mainly recreational, coincides with that being offered by the universities or the W.E.A. True, also, that very few evening institutes can provide exactly the same courses or the same tutors as the universities, but through short-sightedness there is a danger, not perhaps to be exaggerated, that some evening institute principals will prevent the Responsible Bodies from offering certain courses while being unable to provide an adequate alternative themselves.

Fortunately, the need for a closer partnership at all levels, sponsored chiefly by the L.E.A.s and the Responsible Bodies, is appreciated by senior officials. In some areas there are regional councils with representatives from universities, L.E.A.s and voluntary bodies for the purpose of discussing common problems and helping avoid overlapping. Sometimes these groups collaborate in publishing handbooks and prospectuses and in advertising their classes. In 1965 plans were announced for the setting up of an Institute of Adult Education for the Manchester region. Her Majesty's Inspectors of Further Education are aware of the value of co-ordination and, as has been seen, they have an important advisory function. University extra-mural departments are particularly anxious to improve the existing machinery. In the words of the 1961 working party report of the U.C.A.E.: 'in some cases the relationship is already admirable, but there are far too many instances in which it is limited to provision for the representation of local authorities on extra-mural committees; the larger the authority, the less satisfactory the arrangement is'.[4] The most encouraging sign of all is that a majority of L.E.A.s now see the value of co-ordination.

The principal reforms that should be introduced may be summarised as follows:

1. Existing regional councils should be made more effective and such councils should be established in every part of the country.
2. Where local advisory committees for Adult Education do not already exist, they should be set up as soon as possible, preferably on the initiative of the appropriate L.E.A. or a group of L.E.A.s.
3. Arrangements should be made for consultations over a wider area than that of one authority. This may simply require that regional committees should appoint special adult education sub-committees.
4. At the same time there must be close liaison between R.B. representatives and individual authorities; indeed, frequent consultations between local government officers, principals of evening institutes, heads of Colleges of Further Education, and representatives of all the Responsible Bodies are essential, especially during that period of the year when annual prospectuses are being prepared.
5. Principals of evening institutes should invariably be paid on a scale that takes into account all registered students using their premises irrespective of whether they are attending classes sponsored by the Responsible Bodies.
6. A uniform policy for the payment of local authority grants to the Responsible Bodies and voluntary agencies needs to be adopted.

To introduce effective machinery for co-ordination at both the local and the national level will no doubt take time. Moreover, adult education will presumably always command more respect in some districts than in others. Nevertheless, the omens for increasing collaboration seem favourable now that senior officials in the L.E.A.s are recognising that they have a key role to play. If there is cause for despondency, it is not on account of the situation in the localities.

ii

Practitioners in the field of adult education may belong to one of four associations. The oldest of these, the Association of Tutors in Adult Education, was founded in 1918 and now has a membership of approximately 500, of whom 170 or so are full-time teachers and 250 are part-time teachers employed by university extra-mural departments and the W.E.A. The National Federation of Continuative Teachers' Association was also founded in 1918 and has a membership of approximately 1,500. It caters mainly for part-time evening institute teachers in London and Birmingham. Founded in 1960 to serve the needs of teachers of liberal studies in Colleges of Further Education, the Association for Liberal Education has a membership of approximately 300. The most recent association to be founded, in 1965, is significantly called the Association for Adult Education. This has a membership of approximately 200 and caters for teachers and organisers in adult education employed by the local authorities. In addition, there are, of course, hosts of professional workers who belong to associations whose interests impinge on the field of adult education.

Within the last few years a few practitioners in the field have struggled successfully to introduce machinery for collaboration between all professional adult educators. One positive result of their labours has been the setting up of the Adult Education Liaison Committee consisting of representatives of the four major associations along with representatives of the Community Centres Association and the wardens of short-term residential colleges. This is an important development, for in the last analysis it is among practitioners that the quest for standards and public esteem is to be pursued. Institutions may propound the most enlightened policies but in the end it is the man in front of the class who determines the quality of what is done and hitherto he has not generally known that there were such things as standards except in terms of the academic purity of his subject.

iii

Many administrators consider it futile to try to secure co-operation on a national scale. In their opinion, the adult education field is so amorphous and contains so many heterogeneous elements that it is impossible to distinguish a common purpose and to find an acceptable basis for profitable discussion and unified action; any national organisation is bound to be weak through trying to be all things to all men.

Arguments of this kind have some validity. At national conferences, for instance, it is true that speakers can only appeal to and interest particular sections of their audience, that for the sake of harmony there is a tendency to shy away from controversial topics. Yet those who ridicule the attempt to forge unity among adult education organisations overlook one cardinal point: these organisations are too disorganised at the present time to act as a national pressure group, as they must if they wish to expand. It is also vital that one association should try to comprehend adult education as a whole, and for special purposes at any rate bring every organisation within its ambit. Such is the aspiration of the National Institute of Adult Education, and if the proof of the pudding is in the eating, then by its work the N.I.A.E. has successfully demonstrated that a national association is not only necessary but can be extremely effective. Indeed, no single organisation during the last fifteen years has done anything like as much to promote the wider aims of adult education. This makes it all the more regrettable that there should be so much indifference to the nature of its work and ignorance of its achievements.

The N.I.A.E. was founded in 1949 as the result of the amalgamation of the National Foundation for Adult Education and the British Institute of Adult Education. At the outset no one really thought out what its functions were to be and no attempt was made to float it on a viable financial basis. By various shifts it now manages to raise its annual income to approximately £15,000, of which £10,000 comes from the L.E.A.s and £2,750 comes from the Department of Education and Science. Through the efforts of its secretary and in face of heavy odds it has won a good deal of support from the local authorities, support without which it could scarcely have survived. Some idea of its financial handicap may be deduced from the fact that its counterpart in Germany receives no less than £50,000 per annum to spend on its international work alone.

The constitution of the N.I.A.E. is vague. It is supposed to advise on the liberal education of adults but plainly does far more than that. In practice, the Institute appears to have ten functions:

   (i) to bring together adult educators in all branches of the movement and to give adult education a national focus;

  (ii) to convene an annual conference;

 (iii) to act as a clearing house for the gathering and dissemination of ideas and information;

 (iv) to maintain a small and low-cost library which will nevertheless offer an unusually comprehensive coverage of adult education publications;

  (v) to publish a journal for the benefit of adult educationists;

 (vi) to publish an annual Year book;

(vii) to establish and maintain close links with adult education organisations in other countries and with UNESCO;

(viii) to encourage but not to initiate experiments; to instigate enquiries;

 (ix) to nurture and assist organisations or movements which merit support—e.g. the Standing Conference on Television Viewing;

  (x) to publish meritorious monographs on important topics.

The Institute has probably been least successful in pursuing its main task of bringing adult educators together. It holds an annual conference which tends to be unwieldy and not particularly fruitful, though constructive work is manifestly done through its executive committee. At the same time, it has done much to bring coherence to the whole field. Indeed, its secretary has been largely responsible for causing a great many people to realise that adult education is concerned with much more than providing formal study courses.

As a clearing house the Institute's problem is not that it does not know what needs to be done but that it lacks the requisite resources. In so far as it can, it operates as virtually the only agency in the United Kingdom for the collection and distribution of information. A characteristic function is to publish a bi-annual list of the courses being offered by the short-term residential colleges.

Although the library of the N.I.A.E. contains relatively few volumes, it is particularly valuable in that it collects books, pamphlets, periodicals and miscellaneous items exclusively or primarily devoted to adult education. In it may be found virtually all the texts and periodicals essential to an understanding of current theory and practice. For the researcher it is indispensable. The N.I.A.E. also sponsored the publication in 1962 of an exhaustive bibliography of adult education.[5]

Adult Education, which incorporates a section of comment and short articles furnished by the Tutors' Association, is published six times a year and has a circulation of over 2,000. It does not purport to be a learned journal and dispenses with the familiar adjuncts of references and footnotes. Yet it maintains a uniformly high standard and read over a period of time will provide a full account of contemporary trends and practices in every branch of adult education. In 1966 the National Institute issued a new publication which met with instant success. This is entitled *Teaching Adults*, a publication designed mainly for the benefit of practitioners in the L.E.A. field, which had attained a circulation of over 10,500 copies by 1968.

Not the least valuable service rendered by the N.I.A.E. is its publication of an annual directory of adult education organisations in the U.K. Besides a good deal of general information this directory now contains a handlist of works on adult education published in the preceding year and research activities in progress.

The ramifications of adult education on the international plane are on the increase. The N.I.A.E. acts as Britain's main point of contact with organisations in other countries and with UNESCO.

The N.I.A.E. has neither the staff nor the resources with which to embark on its own experiments. However, it does encourage other organisations to experiment, particularly the less sophisticated ones. On its own account it has undertaken several important inquiries, the most notable being: an investigation of the relationship between liberal and technical studies; a study of education for the retired; a survey of educational facilities in museums; and a major inquiry into the staffing and accommodation problems of adult education organisations. In 1965 it was awarded a grant of £11,000 by the D.E.S. to conduct an inquiry into the adequacy of the provision for adult education in sample areas.

The N.I.A.E. encourages the foundation of new organisations but is obviously restricted in what it can achieve by lack of resources. However, it has taken under its wing the Television Viewers' Council.

The publications list of the N.I.A.E. is short but selective. It can be guaranteed that any work it publishes will serve a timely need.

The National Institute of Adult Education warrants more support. It would justify its existence if it did no more than publish *Adult Education*. As things are, it brings together most of the major adult education organisations in a single forum. Its outstanding achievement has been to extend the terms of reference of adult education.

iv

It is repeatedly said that adult education is essentially about continuous learning. But facilities for continuous learning are precisely what are most difficult to provide, partly because of purely mechanical problems, which cannot be avoided, but also because of the break which occurs between school-leaving and the age at which attendance at adult classes usually begins. Nowadays the seriousness of this break is accentuated by an unprecedented cultural gap between the generations.

Ideally, before finishing their full-time education young people should be made to perceive the social significance and personal advantage of persevering with their education throughout life. Ideally, they should progress from school to county college, from county college to youth clubs, and from youth clubs to adult classes. In practice, of course, nothing like this smooth progression takes place. When school-days are over, most people have done with education for good unless it is presented to them in the form of vocational training, and even those who attend day-continuation schools and actively participate in youth clubs and other youth associations tend not to go on with any group educational activity once they have reached their early twenties. Time and again education officials and honorary officers lament that evening classes and voluntary societies contain either very young or middle aged members. Many organisations, perturbed by the high average age of their membership, wonder how on earth they can revitalise themselves by recruiting younger members.

The problem of achieving continuity of learning is complex and there is no point in making vague proposals about what should be done. Nevertheless, it is regrettable that adult education organisations have as yet made no determined attempt to exploit the existence of a vigorous and expanding youth service, that collaboration between adult education and those employed in the youth service should be almost non-existent. Adult educators have little to do with and know little about the work of youth leaders, and youth leaders are equally ignorant of the work of adult educators. Yet both are ultimately trying to help people of whatever age to lead better lives. The solution would seem to be for senior adult educators in every part of the country to hold regular discussions with the officials and leaders in the youth service in an attempt to secure the maximum amount of co-operation. After all, if only from the narrow point of view of recruitment, they might well consider that young people are potentially the adult students of tomorrow.

Youth leaders and adult educators have reciprocal roles to play. It is the duty of the former to emphasise the importance of continuous learning to their groups and to point out the educational facilities that are available. This means that they should take the trouble to know about the present pattern of adult education activities. It means also that they should establish a close relationship with adult education organisations operating in the same districts as themselves. As for adult educators, they have to ask themselves what the problems of young people are and to what extent they can assist in coping with them. Traditional methods will hardly do. Thoughts of simply offering subjects and courses can be discarded. Instead adult educators must devise techniques that will enable them to deal with young people within the social framework of youth clubs. It is curious that in view of their generally enlightened attitudes the Department of Education and Science should refuse to allow young people under eighteen to attend adult education classes.

The most promising solution to the problem has been found by the Village Colleges, to which reference has already been made, and by the Leicestershire Community Colleges. Leicestershire now has seven community colleges and proposes to establish several more.

The feature of these colleges is that they provide, under the same roof, adult education facilities, a county library and a youth wing.

A trenchant statement about the ways in which youth leaders and adult educators can profitably work together was made at the annual general conference of the Scottish Institute of Adult Education in February 1962. The statement ran as follows:

Wherever they (youth leaders) find themselves I hope they will serve the local community by responding to the educational needs whatever they may be. I hope they will always see themselves as educators. I hope they will stimulate interests which will be beyond their own resources to meet. I am sure they then will make requests to you in adult education. Their requests may come in different form than any you have received before. They may make unnatural demands. They may call for unusual responses. They may call for an abandonment of stereotyped procedures and a breaking of bureaucratic red-tape. They may require new subjects and new people to deal with them. I am convinced, however, that when the demand comes you will meet it and I sincerely hope that in return these professional workers will be equal to any demands which you may make upon them so that jointly these two complementary aspects of our wider educational system can serve the community more effectively.[6]

It is to be hoped that the speaker was justified in concluding on such a sanguine note.[7]

V

The co-ordination of services is not simply a question of ensuring that the leading organisations work in harmony. There is also the problem of co-ordinating the activities of those organisations like the trade unions for which education is a secondary consideration, not to speak of organisations which perform an educational function without being aware of it. Co-ordination of the activities of organisations for which education is not the primary concern is hard to achieve. It requires both positive direction from the central government and the local authorities and a deliberate effort on the part of the principal adult educational organisations to establish and maintain close liaison with them. It is especially important that government ministries should create machinery for regular consultation among themselves as well as with other bodies.

vi

To sum up. Co-ordination of the planning and provision of educational services for adults demands more than friendly relations between the main providing bodies. It calls for the regular interchange of ideas and formal collaboration between the schools, the youth service, the libraries, museums and art galleries, and the professionals employed in adult education. It calls for consultation between those bodies that sponsor or finance programmes, especially government ministries. It calls for liaison between the main providing bodies and all those agencies which have education as one of their functions or which need educational services in order to operate efficiently. At the same time, it calls for intelligent differentiation of functions. Finally, the mass media have a vital role to play in publicising the facilities that are available and in stimulating people to make use of them. The twin objects of all schemes of co-ordination will be to prevent wasteful conflicts of interest and to ensure that there are as few gaps as possible in the general provision.

REFERENCES

1. Cf. *F.E.* (*Grant Regulations*) *1959*: '. . . The Ministry will require to know that there has been consultation between the Responsible Bodies and Local Education Authorities in connection with the proposed programme of classes.'
2. *Report*, p. 24.
3. p. 6.
4. *The Universities and Adult Education* (1961).
5. T. Kelly, ed., *A Select Bibliography of Adult Education in Great Britain*.
6. B. Ashley, 'The Youth Leader and Adult Education' in *Scottish Adult Education*, No. 36, p. 16.
7. For further reading consult an interesting pamphlet published by Derbyshire Education Committee: *Social Education: Report of a Study Group to consider relationships between Youth Service and other forms of Further Education* (October 1967).

Chapter Eighteen

THE NEED FOR RESEARCH

Adult Education has not been noted for meticulous attention given to self-study of its theories and practices. There are good reasons for this. A theory must exist before it can be examined, and it must exist in considerable quantity before it can be studied with precision. Adult Education, as a whole, has grown tremendously since the close of the Second World War. The persons who have nurtured this fantastic growth are not the same kinds of persons, psychologically, as those who would sit down and study it.[1]

i

Those who are professionally engaged in adult education both inside and outside the universities evince little interest in research. Some extra-mural directors do not consider it a part of their function, and there are several departments in which no member of staff has published so much as an article on adult education during recent years. Outside the universities and the N.I.A.E. virtually no research is done. A casual glance through the bibliography of adult education published in 1962[2] might at first suggest, if only because of its length, that the current output was great. A close inspection would prove to be less encouraging. A surprising number of works belong to the period before 1939, and a high proportion of the items were written by people only incidentally concerned with adult education. A few subjects receive far less attention than others; in the psychology section, for instance, only a few items appear. According to any criteria, the gaps are numerous.

During the past decade a little progress has been made thanks in particular to the efforts of the extra-mural departments of Leeds, Leicester, Manchester, Liverpool and Oxford Universities respectively, and not least, thanks to the National Institute of Adult Education under the inspiration of its energetic secretary. Mr W. E. Styler (now Professor of Adult Education, Hull University) has pointed out that whereas before the war only four books and ten articles in the bibliography mentioned above were contributed by tutors in the extra-mural field, 66 separate publications and 83 articles had been contributed by them since the last war. Though these seem imposing figures, they are less impressive when it is realised that most of the post-war publications have been contributed by the staffs of a few departments and that the total number of people employed as extra-mural staff tutors has greatly increased.

Thus we are still exploring only the fringes of the field and we have much to do if we wish to erect a solid structure of accurate knowledge. What is required is a determined assault on the major research tasks. Teams of investigators and more generous allocations of money are needed. Above all, it is important that administrators in high places should show a positive interest in research instead of the indifference they display at the present time. Nor will much progress be made so long as the overwhelming majority of adult tutors and teachers stick to their own special subjects, so long as historians concentrate upon historical problems and even sociologists seldom apply their minds to the field of adult education.

In fairness, it must be said that many adult educators question the value of research not because they wish to rationalise their own lack of interest but because the results achieved rarely seem to justify the amount of effort expended. Seeing themselves as belonging to a hard school of pragmatists, realists some might say, many senior administrators are wary if not contemptuous of theorising and hostile towards the aims of sociologists and psychologists and what they regard as the hocus-pocus of questionnaires and inquiries. Indeed, educators of adults in general have not yet perceived the relevance of the social sciences to their own work. In so far as they require information for formulating policy and designing course programmes, they prefer to rely upon their own commonsense methods. In any case, many of them consider that they are far too busy to bother with specific inquiries.

To have reservations about the value of so much of the research that has been undertaken in the educational field is perhaps reasonable. All too often researchers labour only to draw conclusions that experienced administrators could have pointed out without doing any research at all. Some research is, or may appear to be, concerned with esoteric matters having no relevance to the day to day burdens of the administrator and there is also a widespread fear that we may blindly follow the practice in the United States, where most research is thought to be conducted merely for the sake of academic promotion. In addition, many administrators believe, with some justification, that those who apply research methods to particular problems often disagree with one another about the results, that the abstract study of problems begets sterile controversies.

But when due notice has been taken of all these reservations, it is surely a form of arrogance for anyone directing an educational programme to rely exclusively upon his personal experience and his own judgment. How many cherished suppositions would withstand scientific analysis? Granted that current programmes may be good, how do we know that they could not be improved? How do we know that the methods in use are the best methods, that they are giving value for money? In the history of adult education as many surprising revelations have been uncovered as in any other field. Accepted axiomatic truths have turned out to be false sufficiently often to shake the complacency of any dispassionate administrator; several inquiries have shown, for example, that contrary to received tradition classes sponsored by the W.E.A. contained a minority of manual workers almost from their inception. It was also instructive to learn from a recent Liverpool survey that the percentage of students under the age of thirty attending extra-mural courses was as high as 28%.[3] In other words, if valid inferences are to be made, they must derive from valid evidence; if practical plans are to be drawn up, they must be based on rather more than inspired guesswork. The value of research, properly conducted, would be to distinguish those current hypotheses which are tenable from those which are not.

The conclusions reached by seasoned administrators and tutors after many years of experience are extremely valuable as a starting point for research. At the same time, collating their opinions about the limited field in which each one has been engaged will not provide an adequate body of knowledge. Though adult educators may regard subjective judgements as sufficient for their own purposes, they should not be surprised if government officials and laymen demand to see verifiable evidence. Experience shows that whenever proposals for development are put forward or criticisms levelled against official parsimony, it is difficult to fall back upon substantial supporting evidence. This is especially true when it comes to the supremely important task of presenting a case for increased financial allocations. In 1961, when a deputation of adult educators asked the Minister of Education for a larger grant, he replied that he could see no signs of a popular demand for more facilities. Even if such signs were visible, he added for good measure, it might be necessary for people to pay economic course fees out of their own pockets, since the case was not proven that the state ought to subsidise them. This response was certainly unjustified but it was to be expected. Any Minister of Education is more likely to be impressed by facts and figures than by philosophical considerations. In order to stir public servants into action strong feelings have to be reinforced by well-founded arguments. For this reason alone adult educators should recognise how vital it is to obtain more data about the nature of their work, particularly if they are dependent upon state aid.

Perhaps the most telling way of illustrating the need for intensified research is by enumerating the most urgent topics requiring attention. The first priority is to pinpoint the very topics or problems that should be isolated for detailed study. This is not a straightforward task. Because adult education has developed in an unplanned, pragmatic way, relatively few fundamental questions have been raised. Doubtless any experienced administrator could produce a list of problems that should be tackled, but something more is required than a rule of thumb. Two preliminary projects need to be undertaken. The first would necessitate inviting as many adult educationists as possible to recommend promising lines of enquiry. By sifting their suggestions one would have a basis for a systematic programme of research. The second project would involve studying the results of inquiries and depth studies carried out elsewhere, notably in the United States, the most research-minded of all countries, with a view to profiting from their experience. Why embark upon tasks already completed? And why not use the findings of other researchers as a starting point for research in Britain?

Without reference either to suggestions from adult educators in Britain or to researchers elsewhere it is not difficult to draw up a list of questions that should be answered. The first question is, are we meeting the needs of enough people? It is true that we can only speculate about the precise number of people who participate in adult education, and that if participation is interpreted in a loose sense we might be able to claim a great many. Yet it is only necessary to analyse the findings of miscellaneous inquiries about leisure-time habits to see that the greater part of the public remains untouched. If, once again, we look at the American situation, we find that a far higher percentage of the population is interested in one form or another of continuing education. Of course it can be argued with some justice that we observe higher standards than the Americans and that we are more reluctant to sacrifice quality for quantity, but even when allowances have been made for this argument the fact remains that we still neglect too large a proportion of the population.

In order to know whether we are doing enough, it is necessary to survey the needs of each community. Very little survey work has yet been attempted. In almost every locality the leading adult educators might well collaborate in carrying out a detailed study of the present position and the gaps that seem to exist. At the same time, there is a need for related surveys of community resources and how they may most efficiently be harnessed. A detailed study of the activities of a particular institution such as a short-term residential college can seem extremely boring to the non-specialist. But a series of such studies could be of immense value in enabling us to construct a detailed picture of the present scale and variety of provision. In the first instance, we should not be afraid to produce simple descriptive studies. More penetrating studies could come later.

Should we be satisfied with the quality of adult education in England and Wales? Are we even sure that we are providing the right sort of education? Is the pattern of provision created over 40 years ago still in harmony with national requirements? Most active practitioners would probably reply 'yes' to these three questions, with reservations, and maybe they would be right to do so. But it is perhaps time that we stopped taking the value of our work for granted. Allowing a profession to be the judge of its own efficiency, in the absence of controlled research, tends to assure the maintenance of the status quo. The problem of evaluation is related to the last point. So far very little attention has been paid to the need for estimating the success or failure of our work in relation to predetermined criteria, a field in which much progress has been made in the United States. More time and thought should be given

K

to the question of evaluation. Each providing body should try to estimate the size and distribution of its potential audience and then ask questions. Is it meeting the needs of this potential audience? Does its programme succeed in doing what it sets out to do? Does its programme cater sufficiently for different age, intelligence and social groups?

So far, very little attention has been paid to the study of methods in adult education, for example, the utility of group dynamics. The need here is for a number of intensive studies and enquiries. We must observe and evaluate present methods and distinguish what is best in them. Comparative studies of control groups being taught by different methods are especially needed. Arising from the study of methods is the need for the study of training requirements. This particular problem is discussed below.

We need to know more about the rate and character of the expansion that has been going on since the last war. What has been the national rate of expansion? How many more participants are there in 1969 than there were in (a) 1939 and (b) 1951? How can we account for changing fashions where subjects are concerned? How can we attempt to estimate future demands?

Before plans can be made for the future it is essential to know exactly how many people actively participate at the present time in some form of adult education. Is it a high or low percentage of the total population? Strange to say, though rough estimates are thrown out from time to time, we cannot give even an approximate answer to this question. No one has ever taken the trouble to collate all the annual statistics published by providing bodies. And it is far from easy, in any case, to draw reliable inferences from the statistics that are available, so diverse are the methods used for presenting them and so inexpertly are many of them assembled. The terminology in use is contradictory and confusing. There is the tendency for organisations to claim too much, to give maximum rather than minimum attendance figures. Even the university extra-mural departments, with their long experience and substantial resources, employ a variety of methods in compiling their annual returns. Again, although the D.E.S. deals indirectly with the great majority of adult students, its Further Education statistics contain limited information and they neither separate vocational from non-vocational registrations nor distinguish between students whose enthusiasm fails to survive the first night of attendance and the students who complete their courses. Virtually no evidence is available about either the rate of student turnover or the percentage of adults who attend more than one class. Moreover, there is a surprising amount of non-grant-aided provision that is nowhere recorded.*

It is important to learn more about the characteristics of those adults whose interests are already being served. Are they predominantly women as all the signs seem to show? At what ages are people most likely to attend classes? These are just two of the questions to which we would like to supply answers. Of course, we do not entirely lack helpful material, for the attention of many people has been drawn to this problem and a few of them have undertaken enquiries. But these enquiries have been *ad hoc*, chosen at random in areas where an inquisitive administrator or teacher has taken it upon himself to acquire information about the adults being assisted by his particular organisation.

Related to the topic of student characteristics is the question of motive. Why is it that a minority of the population seek adult education while the majority spurn it? Is it because many of them are already fully occupied with voluntary social, political and cultural activities? If we have some knowledge about the motives of those adults who do attend classes, we can only speculate about the reasons for the lack of motive of those who never come, and yet it is clearly imperative to ascertain why so many people are indifferent and why they shun any organised activity having to do with continuing education or 'culture'. Is there a vast hidden potential demand, and if so, how do we exploit it? An impressive piece of research was begun by the late John Trenaman with the aim of defining popular attitudes towards adult education. His findings, which have been brought together and prepared for publication, could be used as a point of departure for more intensive studies of public attitudes towards adult education.[4]

More evidence is required about the precise effects of extraneous factors such as geography and local government policies. Does the degree of interest shown vary from region to region? Is the percentage of attendance higher among urban than rural populations? How much hinges upon the attitudes of local authorities and universities? How important is it that classes should be held in comfortable surroundings? Given a high level of achievement in a

* These problems are discussed in detail in Chapter 16 (see above, pp. 257–8).

particular centre or area, can we single out the ingredients that go to the formation of a successful programme?

What of the structure of adult education? Precisely how many providing bodies are there in existence? Why are some so much more successful than others? Who finances them? How much co-ordination is there? Is that co-ordination effective or do we require much more of it?

By far the most substantial progress has been made in historical and institutional studies. There is still scope, however, for intensive studies of particular institutions.

Comparative studies of the aims and organisation of adult education in different counties would be especially valuable but this is an area that has scarcely been broached. In particular, it is high time we profited from the investigations and discoveries made in the United States where a great deal of attention has been paid to applied research in adult education.

Finally, there is an urgent need for studies of such practical problems as the rate and causes of student drop-out, the efficiency of publicity methods, and the methods used in student recruitment.

ii

In the United Kingdom there is an immediate need for a national research centre as well as for a number of regional research centres. The National Institute of Adult Education might well be built up into the national centre, and indeed recently recommended to the Department of Education and Science that it be empowered to establish a permanent research unit, but so far it has always been short of funds and has not commanded the unreserved support of the universities. In fact, there will always be the problem of persuading potential researchers to work anywhere but in university departments. Not only are factors of prestige and financial security involved, but universities can usually offer the best facilities. Moreover, as will be seen in the next chapter, since the need to do more research is bound up with the need to provide more professional training, it would seem that for all practical purposes universities are best fitted for the task. Whether they co-operate in forming a research centre on their own account or in furthering the claims of the National Institute of Adult Education is a matter for discussion.

There will be no point in dragooning staff tutors and other

teachers or administrators who are not interested into undertaking research in adult education; inevitably, the great majority of professionals will always be fully engrossed in their own subjects. Moreover, university extra-mural departments as presently constituted seem to be either unable or reluctant to sponsor research to any significant extent. A substantial number of special appointments will therefore be required. The problem will be where to find suitably qualified staff. None will be forthcoming unless the universities can offer security of tenure and a stipend placed high up the salary scale. At the same time, it is doubtful whether the universities or any other body will provide funds in order to pay high salaries to pure researchers. Funds might be forthcoming, however, if researchers were also called upon to help conduct a training programme. And since it would be unwise for staff to undertake research without continuing to acquire practical experience by teaching, this might well be the solution.

The Department of Extra-Mural Studies in Nottingham was first in the research field before the war but for a time abandoned its particular research function. At the present time the situation is as follows. A special department of adult education was created in Manchester in 1948 and this department besides offering a post-graduate diploma in adult education now supervises the studies of graduates who are registered for further degrees. The Leeds Extra-Mural Department was replaced by the combined Department of Adult Education and Extra-Mural Studies in 1951 and also offers facilities for research graduates. At Liverpool there is no special department but several research inquiries have been completed. In those three departments and at least a few others, it is desirable to have some members of staff, preferably with special appointments, as at Leeds, who will divide their time between research and teaching. This teaching, as recommended above and in the next chapter, might well take the form of training adult educators.

Until recently, the problem of co-ordinating research activities would have presented serious difficulties. This need no longer be the case. In 1962 the Universities Council for Adult Education appointed a research sub-committee, which could presumably see to it that there is no overlapping between departments. This sub-committee might also undertake responsibility for working out a list of research priorities.

Whichever institution finally assumes responsibility as a national research centre it should have at least four specific functions. The first would be to provide a guide to studies to supplement the recent bibliography. The second would be to act as a clearing house for staff. The third would be to maintain contact with adult education organisations overseas which are engaged in research. The fourth function would be to publish a journal of adult education. In addition, it might undertake the following duties:

(i) to ensure co-ordination and to prevent overlapping;
(ii) to publicise results as widely as possible;
(iii) to retain one copy of all research projects;
(iv) to sponsor group inquiries or projects.

REFERENCES

1. W. D. Dannenmair, 'A Brief Review of Published Research in Adult Education' in *Objectives and Methods of Research in Adult Education*.
2. T. Kelly (ed.), *A Select Bibliography of Adult Education* (N.I.A.E., 1962).
3. Cf. the unpublished M.A. thesis of B. W. Pashley (Liverpool University, 1966).
4. J. Trenaman, *Communication and Comprehension*.

Chapter Nineteen

RECRUITMENT AND TRAINING
OF ADULT EDUCATORS

Intertwined with the problem of initiating major programmes of research in adult education are the cognate problems of recruitment and training. That inter-relationship was pithily summed up in 1954 in an unpublished report by A. S. Hely, who wrote: 'The increase in the number of people engaged professionally in the field of adult education draws attention to the need for professional training while the need for such training focusses attention on adult education as a field of knowledge'.[1] Today it is necessary to add that recruitment of adult educators on the scale and with the qualities required depends upon the formation of a profession characterised by pre-service and in-service training in relation to a distinctive body of knowledge.

There are three reasons why research and training are intimately connected. First, the prime justification for research is that the results obtained from it may help to extend the knowledge and improve the techniques of the active workers in the field. Secondly, it will take time and experimentation to work out appropriate training programmes; this in itself is a task for applied research. Thirdly, in the universities—which must give a lead and where much of the training will necessarily take place—research and training will have to march hand in hand if adequate grants are to be made available, specialist departments are to be created and qualified staff appointed.

The interdependence of research and training within the universities stems from two causes. On the one hand, the public authorities will not wish to support research in adult education unless it is carried on incidentally to other functions. Indeed, L.E.A.s will always find it extremely difficult to justify making grants purely for research projects. On the other hand, the kind of person who will be required to conduct training courses will almost certainly insist upon opportunities to undertake research in those areas of adult education that specially interest him. Those who are already familiar with the field will obviously be best fitted to undertake the dual task of research and training.

The present situation and the magnitude of the problem are well documented thanks to two major inquiries conducted by the National Institute of Adult Education. To these Reports,[2] supplemented by an article by the Secretary of the N.I.A.E. that appeared in a monograph prepared by the Council for Cultural Co-operation of the Council of Europe,[3] the account that follows owes a great deal.

The new emphasis on recruitment derives from the fact that the field of adult education is expanding so fast that it requires an unprecedented influx of suitably endowed recruits. In the past, when posts were few and far between, it was possible to attract an adequate quota of recruits without creating special machinery to ensure a regular supply. Even then a job in adult education was often treated as transitional, a stepping-stone from one post to another. Now, with more adult education centres coming into operation, with the L.E.A.s steadily expanding their provision and Industrial Training Boards beginning to face up to the shortage of trainers, a casual arrangement will no longer suffice. Deliberate efforts have to be made to attract good candidates by using advanced methods of personnel selection, establishing a visible and competitive career structure, and providing both initial and refresher training courses.

Broadly speaking, three types of adult educators are required, whose functions may be summarised as follows:

(a) Administrators—those who direct programmes and determine policies. This class includes L.E.A. officials, directing staff in university extra-mural departments, secretaries of national associations and wardens of residential colleges.

(b) Organisers—those who plan and arrange particular educational activities for adults. This includes area organisers employed by L.E.A.s, resident staff tutors, tutor organisers, non-directing staff of residential colleges and so on.

(c) Teachers—Apart from the great host of part-timers employed by nearly all the adult education agencies, the full-time teachers in adult education are mainly employed in university extra-mural departments, W.E.A. districts, residential colleges and such establishments as Literary Institutes.

Three comments need to be made about this classification. First, responsibility for adult education may be combined with another job. In fact, there is already a demand, which will steadily grow, for professional workers who have a variety of skills and experience. Secondly, each of the above functions may be carried out on a part-time basis. Thirdly, it is to be assumed that there will be increasing mobility between one branch of the adult education field and another.

The first report of the N.I.A.E. published in 1962 gave a positive stimulus to recruitment, for it was quickly followed in June 1963 by the appearance of a D.E.S. circular enjoining L.E.A.s to appoint more full-time staff.[4] By 1966 the Secretary of the N.I.A.E. estimated the numbers of workers involved in adult education as follows:

Full-time

L.E.A.s	250	(Directors and organisers)
R.B.s and Residential Colleges	500	(350 teachers and 150 directors and organisers)
Others	400	
	1,150	

Part-time

L.E.A.s	50,000
R.B.s and others	8,500
	58,500

Mr Hutchinson further pointed out that the ratio of full-time to part-time staff employed by L.E.A.s was 1 to 170.[5] His figures necessarily left out many of those employed in what may be described as para-adult educational fields.

No attempt has been made to estimate the number and types of adult educators who will be required in the immediate, let alone the foreseeable, future. But it is an attempt that should be made. All that can be said in the absence of reliable forecasts from the L.E.A.s and other bodies is that two or three times the existing quota of professional adult educators could profitably be absorbed during a period of five or so years.

Very few of the full-time staff and virtually none of the part-time staff employed in adult education have had any special professional training, though many have passed through teacher training courses at various levels. Until very recently, indeed, it was the common assumption that adult educators required no training at all or at least not the kind of training that involves attendance at formally structured courses. Newcomers were expected to start with laudable motives and some relevant experience. There was also a tendency to suppose that the only way to learn about a job was to do it. The tradition, more strongly entrenched in some places than others, of relying upon the services of part-time workers did not help.

It is easy enough to understand why at any time busy administrators engrossed in the day-to-day running of programmes should be dubious about the value of training. Moreover, historically there has been much to be said against training: the post-war intake of staff tutors in extra-mural departments had usually had some relevant experience before taking up their posts; there was much work to do and little time to spare for 'the luxury' of training; outside the university extra-mural departments staff did not tend to stay long and would give but a small return for an investment in training; there were such small numbers professionally employed in the field that it seemed hardly economic to provide special courses for them; the concept of adult education remained so vague that people were hard put to define the content that ought to be taught; finally, there was a basic aversion to professionalism—as Mr F. Jessup puts it: 'It is another aspect of the view which sees voluntaryism, spontaneity, group autonomy and personal enthusiasm as the basis of true adult education, qualities which it is feared may be dulled by formal training schemes'.[6] These considerations explain why at least one extra-mural director who has been in favour of research and training for the past twenty years has nevertheless deliberately refrained from launching a training programme. He has felt especially strongly that it is unfair to encourage people to undergo training when there can be no guarantee that they will subsequently obtain suitable posts. Now, however, along with others, he faces a situation in which there are many full-time posts to be filled but few administrators, organisers and teachers with previous experience or specialist training available to fill them. What is worse, far too many people who assume they have all the skill and knowledge required in order to be an adult educator are both technically inadequate and temperamentally unsuitable; most would-be adult educators are as much in need of careful training as any other professional group. Amateurish or rule of thumb methods are no more justifiable in their case than they are for school teachers, for whom the need for training is generally taken for granted. Moreover, administrators and organisers, as well as those who teach, also need to be trained.

Specialist training for full-time adult educators is essential for five reasons. The most obvious reason is the rapid rate of expansion already mentioned. Chance alone will not ensure an adequate supply of recruits. A second obvious reason is that as the field becomes specialised so those who work in it are increasingly conscious of belonging to a profession. Qualifications deemed adequate in the past are no longer acceptable. Many more posts are being created for which rare skills and detailed knowledge are indispensable—for instance, area organisers in L.E.A. districts. Reinforcing this trend is, thirdly, the growing preoccupation with professional status of those already in the field. They would like to see stringent requirements for admission laid down. A fourth reason is that working with adults calls for different methods from those customarily demanded in other branches of education and a different relationship between teacher and taught. This truism is regularly pronounced but seldom respected in practice: for every adult educationist who has tried to learn something about how adults learn, there are probably three or four who have not. The fifth reason, which is apparently not widely appreciated, is that adult education will never secure an autonomous and primary place in the national educational system until it is seen to be manned by professional specialists who themselves discern an independent career structure. At the present time, because activities largely take place in the evenings or at weekends, to teach or arrange programmes especially for adults is commonly regarded as a makeshift and ephemeral function. The legions of part-time teachers often give an impression of being perfunctory in their approach to the job, and indeed many of them are school teachers who, wishing to augment their incomes, do not necessarily know how to deal with adults or care to find out how to do so. It has also to be admitted that some adult teaching is simply incompetent.

At the end of 1968 training facilities explicitly provided for adult educators are minimal. There are now three established full-time postgraduate courses conducted, respectively, by the Departments of Adult Education in the Universities of Manchester, Nottingham and Edinburgh. Hull University offers a part-time postgraduate diploma course. The Manchester course is for one year and unequivocally of postgraduate standard. Students are required to take three written examinations each of three hours in length on a group of subjects chosen from the following list in the light of their individual needs:

1. Adult Learning and Methods of Teaching.
2. Adult Education in Developing Societies.
3. Comparative Adult Education.
4. Management and Administration.
5. The Social Framework.
6. History and Structure of Adult Education in Britain.
7. Research and Evaluation in Adult Education.
8. Teaching and Learning Aids.
9. Planning and Organisation in Adult Education.
10. The use of Television in Adult Education.
11. The use of Sound Radio in Adult Education.
12. Lecturing to Students in Colleges of Further Education.
13. Two short courses: Lecturing Techniques.
   Discussion Techniques.

In addition, the students are obliged to write a dissertation on an approved subject and to keep a written record of their observations and practical experience. Numerous visits to adult education institutions and practical work are two special features of the course. Successful candidates are awarded a diploma in adult education.

A few universities, notably Leeds, Leicester, Manchester and Nottingham, encourage graduates to read for further degrees in adult education. Edinburgh offers an M.Sc. Social Science in Adult Education as well as facilities for Ph.D. students. Only two university institutes of education include adult education as a special subject in their postgraduate certificate or diploma courses. As a rule, teacher training colleges spare no hours in the time-table for adult education. A few establishments here and there, such as the Cambridge, Liverpool, London and Oxford Extra-Mural Departments and certain L.E.A.s, organise short-term in-service courses. For the first time the Further Education Staff College provided a residential course for full-time adult educators in

January 1968. In the same year the B.B.C. also offered a course of ten televised lectures entitled Teaching Adults. Westhill College, Birmingham, started a one year course for Community Centre Wardens in 1964. Many more organisations including some L.E.A.s attempt to meet the training needs of their staffs by arranging special day and week-end conferences, distributing notes for the guidance of tutors, and arranging occasional refresher courses; the Inner London Education Authority, for example, now organises a quite elaborate training programme for part-time teachers. As has been pointed out, the D.E.S. makes some impression on the problem by organising an annual ten-day course which draws its participants from all over the country. For the rest, organisations do nothing or depend upon hit and miss instruction in techniques on the job. In other words, whether newcomers to a particular institution are adequately inducted or not depends upon the sympathy, good sense, and willingness to sacrifice their own time of the senior staff. But even when all the various arrangements for training have been taken into account the total amount remains negligible and much of it is neither efficient nor grounded in an imaginative perception of the potentiality of adult education.

For part-time workers of all kinds the present training arrangements are sketchy in the extreme. Since the publication of the 1963 report of the N.I.A.E. there has been some improvement but the finding in that report that the number of courses organised by the L.E.A.s in 1963 was less than 50, and that of these only 11 lasted more than two or three days, gives cause for alarm. The difficulties are, of course, formidable. The great majority of those employed on a part-time basis do not see anything distinctive about adult education. The minority who do recognise the special characteristics of adult education have often neither the time nor the incentive to attend courses, even of the shortest duration. A revolutionary change of attitude is called for but will doubtless be slow in coming. In the meantime, the problem can be tackled in a practical way, as some L.E.A.s are already tackling it, by paying part-timers to attend training courses and increasing the fees of those who successfully complete them.

Plainly those who train must be careful to devise syllabuses that are strictly pragmatic. No one type of programme will suffice; neither can responsibility be placed upon one particular organisation. The need is for short as well as for long courses: sometimes it will be necessary to deal with experienced graduates; at other times it may be a question of dealing with would-be recruits who left school at fifteen or sixteen. Again, for every student available for full-time study, there will probably always be three or four who can study only in their spare time. It will also be vital to take into account the diversity of adult education and to note that the task is not simply to train and inform these people who are going to teach and administer in its more privileged branches. Provision must also be made for the voluntary worker, for the non-specialist as well as the specialist, and for the numerous workers engaged in ancillary fields. To sum up, the following courses are required:

Postgraduate degree courses.
Postgraduate diploma or certificate courses of one year's duration full-time and two or more years' duration on a part-time basis.
Short full-time courses.
Part-time courses for part-time administrators and organisers.
Part-time courses for part-time teachers.
Refresher courses of varying lengths.
Special courses of varying lengths for voluntary workers.

Mr E. Hutchinson has constructively pointed out that eight training situations may arise, viz.:

Organising, etc.

   (i) Preparatory training—full-time
  (ii) Preparatory training—part-time
 (iii) In-service training—full-time
 (iv) In-service training—part-time

Tutoring and Teaching

   (v) Preparatory training—full-time
  (vi) Preparatory training—part-time
 (vii) In-service training—full-time
(viii) In-service training—part-time

It is particularly important to distinguish the training of the full-time professional from that of part-time teachers, of whom in the L.E.A. sector alone there are between 45,000 and 50,000. For a long time to come most of the training received by the latter will be casual, incidental, and grossly inadequate. This is all the more reason why the handful of professionals must themselves be specially trained; for otherwise not only will they be ill-equipped to provide informal training for their own staff but they may well be unaware that training ought to be provided at all. The lack of concern for training, reflecting a belief that anyone can deal with adults, is currently one of the biggest criticisms to be made against the main providers of adult education.

As pointed out above, it will be necessary for every person charged with devising a training course to ensure that it is flexible. The content and length of each course will obviously depend upon a variety of factors that can only be identified in each situation. It is possible, however, to indicate the kind of knowledge and skills that should be expected of a practising adult educator:

Knowledge of the general pattern of further education as well as of adult education.

A working knowledge of the laws and regulations relating to post-school education.

Knowledge of the goals, policies and programmes of the various adult education agencies and the youth service.

Understanding of the social role of adult education.

Understanding of the factors influencing social change.

Up-to-date knowledge of the subject or agency with which the participant is concerned.

Knowledge of how adults learn and why they participate in educational activities.

A knowledge of and ability to use a variety of teaching methods.

A clear grasp of what his own institution could be at its best.

Some acquaintance with research methods, especially social survey techniques.

Some knowledge of the way adult education is perceived and organised in other countries.

Experience of doing practical work under supervision.

Experience of observing the standards achieved by other people.

Knowledge of effective publicity methods, sources of information and practical assistance.

The case for training adult educators is now receiving growing support. Partly under the influence of developments in the United States the content of existing training programmes is being amplified to advantage. Nevertheless the position remains unsatisfactory. It is essential for the D.E.S. to treat the problem more seriously by providing the greater part of the finance required for a multiplication of training programmes, by encouraging the L.E.A.s to facilitate the secondment of teachers and administrators for both short and long periods of training, and by undertaking itself or commissioning others to undertake periodic reviews of staffing and training requirements. The L.E.A.s must arrange for more in-service training courses, especially for part-timers. The D.E.S., the L.E.A.s and the universities should co-operate in appointing highly qualified training staff and in providing adequate accommodation and facilities for training courses. The universities might well assume responsibility for preparing suitable syllabi and course material for all kinds and levels of training. The N.I.A.E. might regularly publish a list of the qualities desired in a professional adult educator besides acting as a clearing house for the dissemination of information about new developments in training. Those organisations for which adult education is a secondary consideration might well arrange for the responsible officials to attend training courses. It would also help if university schools of education and the teacher training colleges would regard adult education as an appropriate subject for inclusion in all teacher training courses, and if those concerned with the training of social workers, personnel officers, industrial training officers and similar professional groups would include an adult education component in their training courses.

It is important also that training should be broadly based. Mobility is required within the adult education field so that a professional worker may fit into community development or youth work or community centre work as the occasion may arise.[7]

REFERENCES

1. Impressions of Adult Education Trends in Great Britain, p. 8.
2. 'Accommodation and Staffing' in *Adult Education*, January 1963, pp. 229–312; 'Recruitment and Training" in *Adult Education*, March 1966, pp. 319–90.
3. *Workers in Adult Education: their status, recruitment and professional training.* (Council for Cultural Co-operation, 1966), pp. 65–74.

4. Administrative Memorandum 6/63.
5. op. cit. p. 67.
6. *Workers in Adult Education: their status, recruitment and professional training*, p. 83.
7. For a comprehensive and authentic study of recruitment and training in England and Wales see the special report of the N.I.A.E. in *Adult Education*, March 1966, pp. 319–90.

Chapter Twenty

THE WAY AHEAD

In England and Wales the arrangements for the education of adults are undergoing change. Associated with an increasingly comprehensive vision of the role of 'adult education' we can distinguish several phenomena. First, there is the rationalisation of existing services, shown especially in the attention given to administrative efficiency and in the care taken to identify adult education programmes with distinctive premises such as community centres and residential colleges. Secondly, there is the emergence of a profession of adult education, springing partly from a growing tendency for employing bodies to appoint specialists and partly from the determination of adult educators themselves to insist that they command unique skills and experience. Thirdly, there is an ever-widening spread of subjects, from econometrics for managers to Japanese flower arrangement for housewives, so that it would now seem that the range of provision is relevant to all branches of life. Fourthly, there is the realisation that workers at all levels, no matter whether they are classed as wage or salary earners or as self-employed, must be prepared to go on learning if they are to be able successfully to master new techniques in their jobs and to adjust to a fluid economic and social environment. Finally, there is the proliferation of new methods of communication both on a nation-wide scale through the mass media and in the classroom through the extensive, if often misguided, use of audio-visual aids.

Alongside these phenomena we are also witnessing the expenditure of unprecedented amounts of public money on the arts and recreational amenities. The level of popular tastes in relation to the style of living has risen strikingly. People are travelling a good deal and so coming into contact with other standards of behaviour than their own and, in so far as they travel abroad, with other cultures. Television has also enormously extended the imaginative perceptions of many people so that their social expectations are much greater than they used to be.

All this change is welcome and stimulating to those who are dedicated to the education of adults. Nevertheless, it affords no guarantee that the future influence of adult education upon society will be any less marginal than it has been in the past. Such plans for development as are in existence are neither substantial nor widely known and the likelihood of most of them being implemented is remote. Moreover, anyone who sets out to describe the present condition of adult education in England and Wales and to recommend a prescription for future development is bound to be painfully aware of the many authors and members of special committees who have in the past framed admirable proposals only to see them gather dust. Yet there is today perhaps a novel reason for putting forward prescriptions. It is that the sheer number of adults currently participating in one kind of educational activity or another is now so great that the public authorities cannot afford to ignore their demands for more and better facilities if only they will present them persistently and with vigour. Pushed from behind the host of participants could do much to ensure that the existing scale of provision is steadily, if not perhaps dramatically, enlarged. And some of the pushing might well come from the emerging corps of professional adult educators, now over 1,000 in number and gaining in strength. Their first task is to draw up a list of priorities and to bend every effort to seeing that they are acted upon. What are those priorities?

The outstanding weakness of adult education in England and Wales continues to be its uninspiring reputation. The public at large still tends to perceive it in terms of stereotypes such as the class provision or what they may wrongly suppose to be the class provision of the W.E.A. To many of the educated it appears déclassé and disorganised. How can its reputation be enhanced?

An infusion of enthusiasm is clearly the first answer. The enjoyment of and confidence in the worth of their jobs which almost all adult educators feel must be communicated to outsiders. The image of both organisers and teachers as somehow engaged in a second-best sector of the education profession, in a fringe activity not truly homogeneous with the practice of education as a whole, must be dispelled. A sense of solidarity within the ranks of adult educators, like that which sustained the pioneers of 'the movement' in the first two decades of this century, is an obvious requisite. A readiness to recognise and respond to new developments is equally important. Although the methods and programmes of the providing bodies have recently shown striking improvement, the thinking of adult educators is still too often circumscribed. Many have yet to see their function as much more than devising academic courses or recreational facilities for those who can be bothered to take advantage of them. They are still far from hammering home to the public the message that continuing education ought to be an integral part of the business of living.

Everyone directly concerned with the education of adults must abandon the narrow definition once and for all. 'The field is as broad as the range of human interests and human needs.'[1] Many people want little encouragement to complete their secondary, tertiary and, in some cases still, their primary education. Very well, then, let us encourage them. Vocational educational services remain inadequate. Let us extend those services. Not thousands but millions of people now earnestly want to extract more purposeful satisfaction out of their leisure-time pursuits. Let us assist them to do so, and not mind that it may mean revolutionising time-honoured ways of financing and organising services. There would seem no grounds for fearing that such changes will detract from the continuing importance of liberal studies: on the contrary, as the field broadens so it appears that the demand for Responsible Body classes increases.

Upon the existence of a buoyant, united and broadly based profession of adult educators, having certain clearly defined aims, depends also the capacity to exert political leverage. The profession needs to bring pressure to bear upon borough and county councillors, local government officials, and ministers of the Crown, and what is first required of the policy-makers is not in doubt: a statement in unequivocal terms of how much the education of adults is worth in hard cash. Out of the aggregate expenditure on all forms of education is its value 1% or 3% or 10%—or only the fraction of 1% currently at its disposal? Pleas for support should no longer be based upon abstract declarations of principle but upon practical arguments. It must be impressed upon the public authorities that visible results can be obtained for a relatively small outlay. (A recent computation by the National Association of Public School Boards in Adult Education in the United States revealed that educational facilities for every adult in that country could be provided for an outlay of 3% of the national expenditure on schools.) The D.E.S. should be urged immediately to appoint a Minister of State for Adult Education or Post-School Education and to establish a special section to supervise all aspects of the education of adults and to make frequent earmarked grants to qualified agencies for research and experimentation.

As for the L.E.A.s, their national contribution would at least be trebled if all spent as much *per capita* as the upper quartile of them are already doing. An annual ranking list, giving details of expenditure and published by the D.E.S., might well act as a spur to defaulters.

Though money spent on community education is a sound social investment, a shortage of funds besets nearly all the agencies described in the present survey. Even so, it is not axiomatic that grants from the public purse should alone defray costs. There is a strong case to be made for a large increase in the current scale of fees. In keeping with a tradition largely confined to Britain facilities are usually offered at virtually no cost to the consumers. By contrast, in North America providing bodies usually expect students to bear all or at least the greater part of the financial burden even when their programmes have no vocational value. The effect of this is that the fee for a course of lectures may well be twenty times as high as that for a course of similar length in England and Wales. An increase could be introduced here by stages and without detriment to such social groups as old age pensioners, for whom the nominal fee could be retained. Indeed for some sections of society services might well be offered entirely free of charge—those attending literacy classes, for example.

In order to justify higher expenditure, the providing bodies themselves will, at the same time, have to see their way to adopting more *dynamic policies*. At the present time programmes still tend to select the students rather than the other way round. Adult educators should try to predict trends in public interests and to anticipate changing social and economic needs. This means that they cannot rely upon periodic re-vamping of old programmes but must deliberately seek people out and persuade them that the experience of taking part in an organised educational venture could lead to a sense of personal fulfilment and maybe to an easing of some of their particular problems. To stimulate participants into moving from what is commonly a passive role into a positively active role requires a shift in the balance of subjects usually offered. There should be stress upon parental and family problems, pre-retirement courses, consumer affairs and, in general, upon classes and activities designed to isolate and analyse personal and community wants.

Contemporary society faces such problems as urban renewal, rural depopulation, traffic safety, racial conflict, violence, misery in old age and loneliness. It should be the responsibility of adult educators to study the social problems of their respective communities and to devise courses and projects which will help people to cope with them. This entails persuading key personnel in the community like school teachers and voluntary social workers that there exists an interlocking relationship between education and social change, that only through an understanding of its nature can societies assimilate change. Perhaps the most important function adult educators can perform is to plan courses and projects about the characteristics and effects of social change and cajole community leaders into attending them.

So far we have been concerned with ends. In turning to the question of means we tread on firmer ground. A big expansion in the volume of provision is obviously dependent upon the rationalisation and expansion of resources. The essential requirements may be summarised as follows:

1. Increased co-ordination and more effective administrative control. Pending the expected reduction in due course of the existing number of L.E.A.s it is desirable to set up regional adult education councils which should contain representatives of all the various agencies concerned either directly or indirectly with the education of adults, including the Youth and Community service, physical recreation, museums, libraries and so on. The path to closer co-ordination would be greatly eased if the confusing terminology currently in use could be rationalised, so that, for instance, a single term might replace the ambiguity of 'tutor', 'teacher', 'lecturer' and 'instructor'.

2. More accommodation for the exclusive or primary use of adult education. In the planning of all new educational buildings consideration should be given to the potential needs of adults. All those who are responsible for designing new buildings or renovating old ones should be furnished with a list of requisites for adult education facilities. L.E.A.s should establish and support more independent centres. The

N.I.A.E. could perhaps add to its many services frequent reports on the ingenious use of existing buildings.

3. More equipment. By and large adults are taught by word of mouth. Most of them would profit from exposure to some of the many techniques now used in other branches of education. Some also want access to laboratory facilities, at present almost always denied to them. In schools where evening classes are held the audio-visual equipment is commonly locked away at 4 p.m., yet adults as well as children may learn more easily if helped by teaching aids. An important function of Regional Councils might well be to supply and maintain audio-visual aids. In courses other than those run by university extra-mural departments students would be encouraged if they could more easily obtain recommended books.

4. More professionally trained full-time adult educators. Instead of 1,000 professionals the field could usefully employ 3,000. Even the smallest L.E.A. ought to have a small staff of specialists. For most of these specialists training will necessarily be restricted to in-service courses of limited duration but a minority should be directed to full-time university courses.

5. More efficient part-time teachers and administrators. This is again a matter of providing appropriate training courses in abundance and rewarding those who attend with higher fees. The field would be guaranteed a regular flow of recruits if all university schools of education and teacher training colleges would include in their curricula at least an optional course in the aims and methods of adult education.

6. More efficient methods. The methods in current use tend to be inflexible. The timing of activities should reflect the reality of people's daily lives; facilities should be offered in the mornings and in the afternoons as well as in the evenings, and throughout the year. Those who plan programmes must know something about the principles of learning so that the most appropriate method or combination of methods is adopted in each learning situation. A preoccupation with the assessment of programmes is essential, especially with the value of activities to the community as distinct from the individual. The prejudice against the measurement of students' progress, which does not necessarily imply a resort

to written examinations, must be dispelled. So must suspicion of correspondence courses and such schemes as the Open University. There are many ways of reaching adults and all should be tried until found wanting.

7. More knowledge based on national and local operational research projects. To further this development the D.E.S. and the L.E.A.s should insist that providing bodies carry out penetrating studies of the effectiveness of their programmes as a condition of qualifying for grant-aid. They should also allocate ample funds for research. As for providing bodies, they must become research-minded and realise that to devote a proportion of their resources to gathering and interpreting data will often pay economic as well as educational dividends.

8. More knowledge and experience of the practice of adult education in other countries. From comparative studies there is much to be learned. It is not simply a question of looking to North America or Scandinavia, but of examining the achievements of adult education in Russia and Eastern Europe and noting the original approaches of many adult educators in the developing countries.

Whatever reforms are introduced it must remain a golden rule not to sacrifice diversity for the sake of uniformity. Thus while it is imperative that the D.E.S., the L.E.A.s, the universities, and the Further Education institutions should play a bigger part in the education of adults, they should not do so at the expense of the voluntary associations. Rather they must stimulate the voluntary associations to more intensive effort and persuade those organisations for which education is a secondary or marginal concern to give it more concrete support.

Sooner or later the education of adults will come to be treated as an essential part of the State system of education, if only because governments will become aware of its bearing upon their plans for national development and its usefulness in dealing with social problems and in fostering community development. Beyond primary, secondary and tertiary education there will then be the fourth level of adult education. In order to bring that day forward, however, it will be necessary to accelerate the historical process of moving away from the traditional concentration upon education for non-vocational ends towards the notion that throughout their lives adults should continue to learn according to their personal needs and capacities and the needs of the community and nation. The appearance of Industrial Training Boards, The National Extension College and, very shortly, the Open University, is a propitious augury.

From the beginning of 1967 the National Institute of Adult Education started to press for a national inquiry into the current aims and provision of adult education. At first, the government of the day appeared reluctant to respond, presumably because its intractable economic problems precluded risking any new financial commitments, especially in view of its obligation generously to support the Open University. Late in 1968, however, it was officially accepted that an enquiry would be undertaken as from 1 April 1969. The time is clearly ripe for the kind of fundamental, nation-wide investigation conducted by the 1919 Committee. It is to be hoped, however, that the '1969 Committee' will perceive education as a life-long necessity and insist, unlike its predecessor, upon examining *all* aspects of the education of adults. If it fails to do so, then its starting date will prove to have been aptly chosen.

REFERENCES

1. McMahon, Coates and Knox, 'The Position of Adult Education in the United States' in *Adult Leadership*, Vol. 15, No. 9, March 1967.

Appendices

1. Adult Education in Wales.

2. Characteristics of Adult Students:
   (i)   Comparative Tables
   (ii) Coding for Subject Choices.
   (iii) Students and the Choice of Subjects.
   (iv) Continuity of Attendance.

3. Levels of Participation in Particular Areas.

4. Summary of Findings: Johnstone and Rivera, *Volunteers for Learning*.

ADULT EDUCATION IN WALES

At the beginning of the last war it was possible for a working party of Welsh adult educationists to observe: 'A survey of the historical development and geographical distribution of Adult Education in Wales leads to the conclusion that in this, as in so many other respects, the cultural life of the Principality differs considerably from that of England.'[1] Though the more rural regions of Wales are still not anglicised, particularly in the geographical centre and in Merionethshire and Caernarvonshire, it is questionable whether the Welsh way of life still continues to be as sharply dissimilar from that of England as some patriots would like to suppose. Sometimes it seems that the chief mark of distinction is simply the negative feeling of Welshmen that they are not English. Moreover, within Wales itself, there are important contrasts: whereas the area around Cardiff is industrialised and displays nearly all the characteristics of any urban culture, South-West Wales, the Central region and the north are, in varying degrees, rural in outlook. Nevertheless, when it comes to Welsh attitudes towards education and the way it is organised, it is proper to distinguish a few national characteristics.

The Welsh value education, maybe for good economic reasons. Adults want it for themselves almost as much as they want it for their children. The desire for continuous learning is deeply rooted and associated with a tradition of voluntary endeavour. Sunday school classes have always been aimed at adults and both cultural festivals and literary debating societies have flourished for a long time. As a consequence, public participation in various forms of education is very much greater and the habit of community co-operation is very much stronger than in England. This becomes clear if one looks at the kind of activity that may be found throughout the Principality.

The two activities especially characteristic of Wales may be summarised as follows:

(i) *Festivals*. First, there is the Eisteddfod movement. Every community of any size holds its annual eisteddfod and some communities annually hold several eisteddfods. Though much of the material presented is parochial and undeniably amateurish, these festivals nevertheless encourage individual effort and help to conserve the traditional culture.

(ii) *Choirs and Vocal Groups.* Then there are the famous choirs and vocal groups. Repertoires tend to be limited and critics often deplore the lack of any real musical understanding. Yet how many choirs there remain and what *joie de vivre* they inspire in performers and audiences alike.

Especially remarkable in Wales is the attention given to religious education. On all sides people lament that chapel life is not what it used to be—congregations have rapidly dwindled and the decline shows no sign of coming to a halt. Nevertheless, the chapels still exercise a great deal of influence and though their horizons may be narrow, they are always concerned to induce hard thought and personal commitment. No preacher is worthy of his hire who cannot hold forth for at least half an hour and preferably much longer. What is more, he is expected to use his text not as an excuse for retailing pious platitudes but as a peg upon which to hang a wide-ranging survey of contemporary problems. If it is true that many sermons are tendentious, stuffed with prejudices and over-simplified judgments, the weekly sermon nevertheless teaches people how to listen and gets them accustomed to appreciating the architecture of a spoken essay. It is not surprising that the public lecture should still be popular in Wales. Furthermore, the chapels still hold their weekly services, over which laymen frequently preside and which usually assume the form of discussion groups.

The pull of traditional societies is strong in Wales. One may take note of the old literary and debating societies and of the Cymm-Reigyddion and CymmRodorion. This attachment to tradition denotes a passionate desire to preserve a distinctive Welsh culture. In adult classes, Welsh language and literature still occupy an important place. Many classes are conducted in Welsh and it is extremely difficult for someone to obtain an appointment as a teacher in adult education unless he is bilingual.

Finally, the people of Wales identify themselves far more closely with the State system of education than do the people of England. The affairs and policies of the University Colleges are deemed to be matters of public concern. An adult educational centre in South Wales sees itself as having a cultural and missionary function within the whole community. The sense of identification is reciprocated by the providing bodies. Thus, long ago one of the first functions of University College, Bangor, was to provide agricultural education for farmers in the rural districts. The broad American concept of university extension as a public service is to some extent accepted.

Apart from the above distinctive features, adult education is organised on much the same lines as it is in England. There are a few minor differences. The L.E.A.s are less active than in England. The evening institutes seem to have made less progress. But the general run of organisations found in England are also usually found in Wales. The Women's Institutes are relatively far more powerful than the Townswomen's Guilds. Perhaps another mark of distinction is the tighter organisation of the general provision.

Those who have worked in the adult education field for a long time feel that social attitudes in Wales have changed irrevocably for the worse. They argue that as rural depopulation increases and as more and more people own motor cars and sit night after night with their eyes glued to the television set, habits are being standardised. This pessimistic view may have validity. Yet, to the outsider at any rate, adult education in Wales still seems a healthy plant. The old traditions remain strongly entrenched as can be seen from the relative resilience of the tutorial class and the continued desire for sustained study.

REFERENCES

1. *Survey of Adult Education in Wales* (University Extension Board—University of Wales, 1940), p. 87.

THE CHARACTERISTICS OF ADULT STUDENTS

i

Comparative Tables

(a) *Age groups*

	18–24	25–34	35–44	45–54	55–64	65 plus
W.E.A. Sheffield	10%	20%	19%	22%	20%	10%
W.E.A. Liverpool	15%	27%	13%	19%	16%	9%
W.E.A. outside Liverpool	5%	16%	20%	22%	25%	11%
W.E.A. South Gloucester	3%	21%	32%	25%	12%	8%
E.M. South Gloucester	10%	24%	25%	25%	12%	4%
E.M. outside Liverpool	7%	21%	24%	26%	14%	9%
E. M. Oxford	6%	21%	31%	25%	10%	7%
City Literary Institute	12%	21%	22%	23%	13%	8%
Burton Manor	12%	20%	24%	24%	15%	6%
Grantley Hall	11%	16%	13%	16%	26%	17%
Leeds Evening Institutes	18%	25%	28%	23%	5%	2%

(b) *Sex and Marital Status*

	Males	Females	Single	Married	Widowed etc.	Children under 11
W.E.A. Sheffield	38%	61%	33%	58%	9%	22%
W.E.A. Liverpool	36%	64%	49%	46%	5%	15%
W.E.A. outside Liverpool	38%	62%	30%	60%	10%	20%
W.E.A. South Gloucester	51%	49%	23%	67%	9%	29%
E.M. South Gloucester	44%	56%	25%	71%	4%	36%
E.M. outside Liverpool	43%	57%	33%	62%	5%	23%
E.M. Oxford	33%	67%	26%	68%	6%	37%
City Literary Institute	32%	68%	63%	28%	9%	6%
Burton Manor	54%	46%	45%	52%	3%	20%
Grantley Hall	27%	73%	43%	45%	12%	9%
Leeds Evening Institutes	30%	70%	27%	69%	3%	31%

(c) Age upon completion of Full-Time Education

	15 and under	16 yrs.	17 yrs.	18 yrs.	19 yrs.	20 or over
W.E.A. Sheffield	38%	19%	7%	6%	3%	28%
W.E.A. Liverpool	28%	23%	13%	7%	1%	28%
W.E.A. outside Liverpool	34%	24%	10%	6%	3%	23%
W.E.A. South Gloucester	30%	18%	14%	6%	3%	30%
E.M. South Gloucester	14%	22%	13%	8%	6%	38%
E.M. outside Liverpool	13%	19%	12%	9%	4%	42%
E.M. Oxford	13%	20%	16%	12%	4%	36%
City Literary Institute	14%	17%	16%	13%	7%	34%
Burton Manor	22%	13%	10%	9%	6%	41%
Grantley Hall	21%	20%	9%	9%	6%	31%
Leeds Evening Institutes	47%	25%	10%	5%	2%	12%

(d) Highest Qualification Obtained

	University Degree	Higher Prof. Qualification	Teachers' Training Cert.	Higher Nat.Cert. Higher Sch.Cert.	Ord.Nat. Cert. and Matric.	No cert. or qualification
W.E.A. Sheffield	15%	2%	14%	4%	18%	47%
W.E.A. Liverpool	12%	4%	15%	7%	21%	41%
W.E.A. outside Liverpool	9%	5%	12%	4%	18%	51%
W.E.A. South Gloucester	18%	4%	11%	4%	16%	47%
E.M. South Gloucester	17%	9%	14%	11%	27%	22%
E.M. outside Liverpool	22%	7%	17%	9%	17%	28%
E.M. Oxford	19%	12%	11%	9%	27%	23%
City Literary Institute	26%	6%	7%	12%	22%	28%
Burton Manor	19%	5%	20%	5%	14%	38%
Grantley Hall	13%	3%	21%	2%	20%	40%
Leeds Evening Institutes	4%	4%	4%	2%	19%	67%

(e) Occupational Groups*

	Higher Administra- tive, etc.	Other Administra- tive, etc.	Clerical Workers	Shopkeepers Shop Assistants and Personal Service	Foremen and skilled workers	Semi-skilled and unskilled workers
W.E.A. Sheffield	14%	36%	19%	7%	14%	4%
W.E.A. Liverpool	11%	37%	24%	8%	13%	1%
W.E.A. outside Liverpool	14%	38%	21%	12%	13%	2%
W.E.A. South Gloucester	15%	32%	11%	7%	26%	0%
E.M. South Gloucester	40%	33%	10%	4%	8%	1%
E.M. outside Liverpool	20%	51%	10%	3%	9%	0%
E.M. Oxford	30%	41%	10%	4%	6%	2%
City Literary Institute	19%	36%	32%	3%	8%	1%
Burton Manor	19%	44%	13%	3%	14%	3%
Grantley Hall	11%	46%	15%	9%	11%	2%
Leeds Evening Institutes	11%	20%	20%	16%	21%	5%

* In most cases a small proportion of respondents were unclassifiable.

ii.

Survey of Students in Adult Education Courses—Feb. 1963
Coding for Subjects—Question 1

1. Archaeology and Ancient History
2. Local History
3. (i) General Political, Social and Economic History
   (ii) Other Historical Subjects
4. (i) Geography
   (ii) International and Commonwealth Affairs
5. Political Science, Government and Law*
6. Economics and Economic Problems*
7. Industrial Organisation and Industrial Relations*
8. Sociology and General Studies
9. Philosophy and Religion
10. Psychology
11. Physical Sciences:
    (i) Physics
    (ii) Astronomy
    (iii) Geology
    (iv) Maths
    (v) Other
12. Biological Sciences:
    (i) Botany
    (ii) Zoology
    (iii) Other
13. English Language and Literature (Public Speaking and Elocution)
14. Foreign Languages, Literature and Culture
    Welsh Language, Literature and Culture
15. Ancient Languages, Literature and Culture*
16. Music
17. Visual Arts
18. General Schemes

* Not included in section on subjects and student characteristics because insufficient students were taking courses.

L

iii.

Tables Illustrating Relevance of Student Characteristics to the Choice of Subjects

(a) *Age*

	18–24	25–34	35–44	45–54	55–64	64 plus
Archaeology and Ancient History	11%	22%	24%	24%	13%	7%
Local History	7%	18%	23%	23%	17%	12%
General Political, Social and Economic History	7%	17%	14%	24%	18%	19%
Geography and International Affairs	7%	16%	17%	19%	24%	18%
Sociology and General Social Studies	7%	15%	23%	12%	31%	12%
Philosophy and Religion	8%	28%	18%	17%	17%	12%
Psychology	13%	32%	23%	21%	11%	0%
Physical Sciences	14%	33%	27%	19%	5%	1%
Biological Sciences	2%	11%	19%	33%	24%	11%
English Language and Literature	5%	19%	25%	26%	15%	10%
Foreign Languages and Literature (inc. Welsh)	19%	13%	27%	24%	18%	9%
Music	18%	27%	23%	18%	9%	5%
Visual Arts	7%	17%	20%	29%	19%	7%
Recreational Activities	20%	27%	25%	22%	4%	2%

(b) Sex and Marital Status

	Male	Female	Single	Married	Widowed, Divorced, Separated
Archaeology and Ancient History	41%	59%	35%	59%	6%
Local History	36%	64%	47%	45%	8%
General Political, Social and Economic History	27%	73%	34%	59%	8%
Geography and International Affairs	36%	64%	40%	53%	7%
Sociology and General Social Studies	36%	64%	26%	62%	12%
Philosophy and Religion	39%	61%	39%	55%	6%
Psychology	44%	56%	37%	57%	6%
Physical Sciences	76%	24%	26%	74%	0%
Biological Sciences	40%	60%	32%	59%	9%
English Language and Literature	31%	69%	34%	52%	14%
Foreign Languages and Literature (inc. Welsh)	32%	68%	45%	45%	10%
Music	38%	62%	33%	62%	5%
Visual Arts	27%	73%	38%	52%	10%
Recreational Activities	30%	70%	66%	31%	3%

(c) Age on Completion of Full-Time Education

	Under 15 yrs.	16 yrs.	17 yrs.	18 yrs.	19 yrs.	Over 20 yrs.
Archaeology and Ancient History	21%	16%	11%	12%	5%	35%
Local History	18%	8%	24%	6%	3%	41%
General Political, Social and Economic History	29%	20%	11%	10%	2%	28%
Geography and International Affairs	28%	19%	11%	10%	3%	30%
Sociology and General Social Studies	41%	14%	11%	5%	7%	22%
Philosophy and Religion	25%	13%	9%	10%	6%	37%
Psychology	25%	20%	12%	6%	3%	34%
Physical Sciences	21%	14%	12%	11%	5%	37%
Biological Sciences	37%	25%	8%	7%	3%	30%
English Language and Literature	21%	23%	14%	7%	4%	31%
Foreign Languages and Literature (inc. Welsh)	16%	15%	11%	10%	6%	42%
Music	14%	23%	19%	10%	4%	29%
Visual Arts	22%	22%	10%	8%	4%	33%
Recreational Activities	46%	23%	11%	5%	1%	14%

L*

(d) *Motivation*

	a	b	c	d	e	f	g	h
Archaeology and Ancient History	53%	35%	4%	0%	0%	1%	2%	1%
Local History	51%	41%	3%	0%	2%	0%	0%	0%
General Political, Social and Economic History	24%	73%	0%	0%	0%	0%	2%	0%
Geography and International Affairs	64%	32%	1%	0%	1%	1%	1%	0%
Sociology and General Social Studies	65%	10%	5%	2%	4%	3%	2%	0%
Philosophy and Religion	58%	32%	1%	3%	1%	1%	1%	2%
Psychology	65%	22%	3%	2%	6%	0%	2%	0%
Physical Sciences	61%	29%	0%	0%	7%	0%	2%	0%
Biological Sciences	47%	45%	0%	0%	3%	2%	1%	0%
English Language and Literature	60%	26%	2%	3%	3%	3%	2%	1%
Foreign Language and Literature (inc. Welsh)	58%	31%	2%	1%	7%	0%	0%	1%
Music	38%	57%	2%	1%	1%	1%	0%	0%
Visual Arts	56%	37%	1%	0%	2%	1%	3%	0%
Recreational Activities	40%	39%	9%	2%	3%	0%	3%	3%

a General Cultural/Intellectual interest—e.g. to enrich your mind or widen your knowledge.
b Special interest in the subject.
c Social—e.g. to meet people of like mind, be with a friend.
d Service—e.g. to help you with work in a voluntary social service.
e Vocation—e.g. to help you in your job or to get a better job.
f Loyalty—e.g. to the class, the W.E.A., the Adult Education Movement.
g Some other motive.
h No particular motive.

iv.

Continuity

Percentage of Students Attending Two Years Running

	2 years	3 years
Extra-Mural, Lancs. and Cheshire	55	40
W.E.A. Lancs. and Cheshire	56	44
W.E.A. City of Liverpool	59	48
W.E.A. City of Sheffield	66	56
W.E.A. South Gloucester	66	44
Extra-Mural South Gloucester	70	48
Extra-Mural Oxford	77	59
City Literary Institute	70	61
Leeds Evening Institutes	33	24
Burton Manor	61	44
Grantley Hall	73	50

Students in *all* classes:

2 years = 53 %   3 years = 45 %

The Rate of Overlap

For every 100 enrolments in 1961–62 there were in fact 57 students
For every 100 enrolments in 1960–61 there were in fact 53 students

Appendix Three

LEVELS OF PARTICIPATION IN PARTICULAR AREAS

A. *Comparison between the Student sample in Extra-Mural and W.E.A. classes in West Lancashire and Cheshire and the Adult Population of Lancashire and Cheshire.*

(i)	Age	1951 census	Extra-Mural Sample	W.E.A. Sample
	18–24	11%	7%	5%
	25–34	19%	21%	16%
	35–44	21%	24%	20%
	45–54	19%	26%	22%
	55–64	15%	14%	25%
	65 plus	14%	9%	11%

The youngest groups are under-represented. The over-65's are slightly under-represented. The W.E.A. sample is overweighted in the 55–64 group.

(ii)	Sex	Census (20 plus)	E.M. (18 plus)	W.E.A. (18 plus)
	Males	46%	43%	37%
	Females	54%	57%	62%

As expected males are under-represented and females are over-represented.

(iii)	Marital Status	Census (20 plus)	E.M. (18 plus)	W.E.A. (18 plus)
	Married	70%	62%	60%

Married people are under-represented. These blanket figures are not very informative, however. If possible, it would be more interesting to take into account two factors: age and the extent to which having young children to care for discourage attendance of classes.

(iv) Social Class (using 5 classifications)

(a)		Census	E.M. (6% unclassifiable)	W.E.A. (7% unclassifiable)
	i. Professional	3%	20%	14%
	ii. Intermediate	14%	54%	38%
	iii. Skilled	53%	19%	33%
	iv. Partly Skilled	15%	1%	7%
	v. Unskilled	16%	0%	1%

(b)

	Census	E.M.	W.E.A.
Partly Skilled and Unskilled	31%	1%	8%

(v.) Age on Completing Full-Time Education

	Census	E.M.	W.E.A.
15 and under	88%	13%	34%
16	7%	19%	24%
17–19	3%	25%	19%
20 and over	2%	42%	24%

No comment!

B. *Comparison between the Student Sample in W.E.A. Classes and the Adult Population of Merseyside*

(i)

Age	Census	Sample
18–24	18%	15%
25–34	23%	27%
35–44	20%	13%
45–54	18%	19%
55–64	12%	16%
65 plus	9%	9%

There is a refreshing degree of conformity here, though as with the classes outside Liverpool there is under-representation of the 35–44 group and over-representation of the 55–64 group. It is encouraging that the retired should be so well represented.

(ii)

Sex	Census (20 plus)	Sample (18 plus)
Males	46%	36%
Females	54%	64%

These figures are as expected.

(iii)

Marital Status	Census	Sample
All married	61%	66%
Married men	66%	67%
Married women	57%	63%

(iv)

Social Class	Census			Sample (including 6% unclassifiable)		
i. Professional	3%			11%		
ii. Intermediate	12%			40%		
iii. Skilled	51%	} 85%	} 34%	37%	} 44%	}7%
iv. Partly Skilled	12%			7%		
v. Unskilled	22%			0%		

The under-representation of the 'educationally under-privileged' could scarcely be more pronounced than in category v.

(v) *Age on Completing Full-Time Education*

	Census	Sample
15 and under	86%	28%
16	8%	23%
17–19	4%	21%
20 and over	2%	28%

C. *Comparison between the sample from the City Literary Institute and the Adult Population of Greater London*

This comparison had to be made on the assumption that the catchment area of the City Literary Institute is Greater London. In fact, of course, the Institute attracts a large proportion of people who work and live in or near the centre of the city.

(i) *Age*

	Census	Sample
18–24	17%	12%
25–34	24%	21%
35–44	19%	23%
45–54	17%	23%
55–64	13%	13%
65 plus	10%	8%

There is a slight under-representation of the young, probably because many of those who would be interested in the Institute's courses are already full-time students, and over-representation of the age group 35–54.

(ii) *Sex*

	Census (*20 plus*)	Sample (*18 plus*)
Males	46%	32%
Females	54%	68%

Males are distinctly under-represented.

(iii) *Marital Status*

	Census	Sample
All married	64%	27%
Married men	70%	53%
Married women	60%	20%

The discrepancies look striking but are explained, of course, by the fact that a high proportion of those who work in London are single men and women.

(iv) *Social Class*

	Census	Sample (including 2% unclassifiable)
(i) Professional	5%	19%
(ii) Intermediate	16%	36%
(iii) Skilled	55%⎫	39%⎫
(iv) Partly Skilled	11%⎬ 79%⎫ 24%	9%⎬ 48%⎫ 9%
(v) Unskilled	13%⎭	0%⎭

(v) *Age upon Completing Full-Time Education*

	Census	Sample
15 and under	79%	14%
16	11%⎫	17%⎫
17–19	7%⎬ 21%⎫ 10%	36%⎬ 87%⎫70%
20 and over	3%⎭	34%⎭

D. *Comparison between the sample of Students in Leeds Evening Institutes and the Adult Population of Leeds*

(i) *Age*

	Census	Sample
18–24	10%⎫	18%⎫
25–34	19%⎬ 50%	25%⎬ 70%
35–44	21%⎭	27%⎭
45–54	19%	23%
55–64	14%⎫ 27%	5%⎫ 7%
65 plus	13%⎭	2%⎭

(ii) *Sex*

	Census	Sample
Males	44%	30%
Females	56%	70%

(iii) *Marital Status*

	Census	Sample
All married	71%	70%
Married men	80%	73%
Married women	51%	67%

Married women are substantially over-represented.

(iv) *Social Class*

	Census (males only)	Sample (includes 7% unclassifiable)
(i) Professional	3%	11%
(ii) Intermediate	14%	24%
(iii) Skilled	58%	40%
(iv) Partly Skilled	13%	17%
(v) Unskilled	14%	1%

(v) *Age on Completing Full-Time Education*

	Census	Sample
15 and under	78%	47%
16	6%	25%
17–19	3%	16%
20 and over	2%	12%

Appendix Four

SUMMARY OF FINDINGS: JOHNSTONE AND RIVERA, *VOLUNTEERS FOR LEARNING*

In the United States, in 1963, the results were published of a large survey of adult students carried out in 1961-2 under the auspices of the National Opinion Research Centre by J.W.C. Johnstone and R.J. Rivera (*Volunteers for Learning*, Chicago, 1965). An adult was defined as over 21 and either married or head of a household. An activity was deemed educational if its main purpose was to enable an individual to learn or acquire knowledge, information or a skill and if it was organised around some form of instruction involving a teacher and student relationship.

By administering a survey to a random sample of 12,000 householders and by interviewing in depth two smaller samples of adults who, respectively, had participated and had not participated in an educational activity at some point in their lives, the authors sought to obtain hard information about the educational habits of the adult population of the United States. They also undertook case studies in four medium-sized cities and interviewed a random sample of young people aged between 17 and 24 in order to elicit data about and to ascertain the impact of their post-school educational experiences.

The major findings of this uniquely comprehensive and scholarly survey were as follows:

  (i) The scale of participation for the year under survey is illustrated by the following table:

Student Status	Per Cent	Estimated No.
Full-time students	2·3	2,650,000
Part-time students	15·0	17,160,000
Independent Study	7·8	8,960,000

  (ii) Probably half the adult population in the United States participates in an educational activity at one time or another.

 (iii) The majority of students enrol in the first instance with a vocational motive or a desire to master a practical skill. Young people, especially, almost always enrol for a vocational reason, whereas older people are more likely to attend a course out of interest in a subject for its own sake. Significantly, only 3 per cent of the sample were interested in public affairs.

(iv) The methods of study differed markedly from those used in the formal system of education. Ignoring self-education, the authors noted that more than half the educational activities took place outside the classroom setting. Study by correspondence, through private institutions, on-the-job training, group discussions and public lectures accounted for 45 per cent of the recorded activity. Surprisingly, fewer than 300,000 people had followed a course of instruction on television.

(v) Adults mainly frequented such institutions as the churches, the armed forces and government agencies, for which education was not a primary function.

(vi) Four outstanding characteristics distinguished the samples from the population at large:

(*a*) More than half the participants were under 40; four out of five were under 50.

(*b*) *Education.* The average participant had received more formal education than the average adult in the total population. Thus, during the year of the survey only 4 per cent of the participants had no schooling as against 47 per cent who had received more than sixteen years of education.

(*c*) *Occupation and Income.* Occupation and income were influential factors though not to the same degree as the amount of formal education. Plainly participation in adult education is primarily a middle- and upper middle-class phenomenon.

(*d*) The rural areas and small towns were under-represented, the main concentration of activity being in the suburbs and outlying areas of the large cities.

(vii) Apart from these four distinguishing characteristics the characteristics of the samples conformed with those of the population at large. Men and women participated in more or less equal numbers; the religious sects were evenly represented; Negroes and Whites of similar educational background were equally likely to participate.

Two key statements from the report are worth special notice. The first has planning implications for the future: 'The typical adult student today is young, urban, and fairly well educated and this is exactly the type of person who will be around in greatly increased numbers in the very near future.' In other words, the potential audience for adult education seems destined to increase more rapidly than the population as a whole.

The second statement has a painfully familiar ring to adult educators in England and Wales:

The paradox is that the segment of the population which may realise the greatest increment of free time in an age of automation is, on the one hand, the least well prepared to handle it and on the other, the least likely to turn to continuing education to develop and expand its spare-time interests. And it is this, perhaps, that constitutes the most critical challenge to the adult educators of the future.

In the United States as in England and Wales the great gap between the educational haves and have-nots will inexorably widen unless revolutionary methods are adopted to narrow it.

SELECT BIBLIOGRAPHY

A Note on Sources

To trace the principal available sources for a study of adult education in England and Wales is easy enough. An excellent general bibliography first appeared in 1952 and was republished in greatly expanded form in 1962 (T. Kelly [ed.], *A Select Bibliography of Adult Education*). Annually the National Institute of Adult Education publishes a bibliography of the previous year's work and details of research in progress, meticulously edited by Mr C. D. Legge. Since 1965 the ERIC Clearing House at the University of Syracuse has also regularly been circulating handlists of unpublished materials and published works relating to Britain as well as to the rest of the world. Indeed, the chief problem now is how to identify the essential works and to avoid wasting time on irrelevant or out-dated material.

Besides reading works expressly concerned with adult education it has also steadily become more important to track down relevant works in the related disciplines of psychology and sociology, economic and social history and in the wider field of education itself. For example, though few sociologists have trained their sights on the problems or phenomena of adult education as such, a significant portion of what they write is nonetheless relevant; certainly, today adult educationists cannot afford to ignore the findings and methods of researchers in the social sciences and must keep abreast of current trends within them.

It is no less essential to look beyond England and Wales to the research output of adult educationists in the world at large, especially in the United States, the Commonwealth and Europe. Undoubtedly it would also be rewarding to examine the publications of researchers and observers in Soviet Russia and Eastern Europe. Neither is it sufficient to be acquainted with published works alone for much valuable material has not appeared in print, especially in the United States. It would be inadvisable, for instance, to launch an inquiry into the motivation of summer school students without first consulting the results of similar enquiries now lying idle in the records of a number of extension divisions in the United States.

The enlarged bibliography published in 1962 listed no fewer than 1,152 substantive items and to grade them in terms of their relative significance would be both arbitrary and misleading. At the same time, there is a select number of seminal works which every researcher in this field ought to consult and which has helped to form the ideas of many adult educationists. For this reason the following select bibliography is divided into two parts: (*a*) key works; (*b*) other works consulted.

KEY WORKS

Since the *1919 Report* no general account of adult education in England and Wales has been published, though R. Peers' *Adult Education: a Comparative Study* dealt comprehensively with the traditional segment of the field. More recently, A. J. Peters' *British Further Education* provided a painstakingly thorough survey of *further education* as defined in the official regulations. Experienced adult educationists might argue against the choice of one or two items in the following list of key works, but they would probably acknowledge the importance of most of them.

Harrison, J. F. C., *Learning and Living, 1790–1960* (London, 1961).

Kelly, T., *A History of Adult Education in Great Britain* (Liverpool, 1962).

Livingstone, R., *The Future in Education* (Cambridge, 1941).

Ministry of Education, Pamphlet No. 8. *Further Education: the Scope and Content of its Opportunities under the Education Act, 1944* (London, 1947).

Ministry of Reconstruction (Adult Education Committee), *Final Report* (London, 1919).

Oxford and Working Class Education—Report of a Joint Committee of University and Working-Class Representatives on the Relation of the University to the Higher Education of Workpeople (2nd edn. rept., 1951).

Parry, R. St. John (ed.), *Cambridge Essays on Adult Education* (Cambridge, 1920).

Peers, R., *Adult Education: a Comparative Study* (London, 1958).

Peters, A. J., *British Further Education* (London, 1967).

Raybould, S. G. (ed.), *Trends in English Adult Education* (London, 1959).

Trenaman, J. M., *Communication and Comprehension* (London, 1967).

Waller, R. D., Introduction to *A Design for Democracy* (abridged version of the *1919 Report*: London, 1956).

OTHER WORKS CONSULTED

A. *Bibliographies*

Kelly, T. (ed.), *A Select Bibliography of Adult Education in Great Britain* (1963).

Legge, C. D. (ed.), 'Guide to Studies in Adult Education' (Annually 1962—current) in *The Year Book of the National Institute of Adult Education.*

Peters, A. J., *A Guide to the Study of British Further Education.*

Published Sources on the Contemporary System. National Federation for Educational Research in England and Wales: *Occasional Paper No. 15* (Slough, 1966).

B. *Periodicals*

Indispensable for the student of adult education is:

Journal of Adult Education. Bi-annually. Vols. I–IV, 1926–34 (British Institute of Adult Education).

Continued as

Adult Education. Quarterly. Vols. VII–XXXIII, 1934–60; bi-monthly, Vol. XXXIV—current (B.I.A.E. until 1949, then N.I.A.E.).

BACIE Journal. Bi-monthly. Vols. I–X, 1947–56; Quarterly, Vol. XV—current. (British Association for Commercial and Industrial Education.)

Industrial Training Journal. Monthly, 1966—current.

New Society. Weekly.

Plebs. Monthly, 1909—current.

Rewley House Papers. Annually. 1927–1967 (irregular: Oxford University: Extra-Mural Delegacy).

Times Educational Supplement. Weekly (1910—current).

Tutors' Bulletin. Nos. 1–105, 1922–56 (Association of Tutors in Adult Education).

The Vocational Aspect of Secondary and Further Education. Bi-annually 1948–current.

C. *Books, Pamphlets and Unpublished Works*

Adam, Sir R., *Problems in Adult Education* (London, 1956).

Albemarle Report, Ministry of Education. The Youth Service in England and Wales (1960).

Allan, D. A., *Museums and Education* (1949).

Allaway, A. J., *The Educational Centres Movement: a Comprehensive Survey* (London, 1961).

—— *Adult Education in England: a brief history* (Duplicated, Leicester, 1951).

Anon, *The Story of Ruskin College* (Oxford, 1955).

Ashby, E., *The Pathology of Adult Education* (Belfast, 1955).

Ashby Report, Ministry of Education. Organisation and Finance of Adult Education (London, 1954).

Ashley, B., 'The Youth Leader and Adult Education' in *Scottish Adult Education*, No. 36, pp. 13–16.

Banks, F., *Teach Them to Live* (London, 1958).

Belson, W. A., *Television and the Family* (London, 1959).

Blumler, J., The Effects of Long-Term Residential Adult Education in

Post-War Britain with particular reference to Ruskin College, Oxford. (Unpubd., Univ. College, Oxford, 1962).

Board of Education—Adult Education Committee, Paper No. 11, *Adult Education and the Local Education Authority* (London, 1933).

—— Welsh Department, Memorandum No. 5, *Report on Adult Education in Wales* (1936).

Bratchell, D. F., *The Aims and Organisation of Further Education* (London, 1968).

Brew, J. M., *Informal Education* (London, 1946).

British Broadcasting Corporation, *New Ventures in Broadcasting: a Study in Adult Education* (London, 1928).

—— *The People's Activities* (1936).

Cauter, T., and Downham, J. S., *The Communication of Ideas: a study of contemporary influences on urban life* (London, 1954).

Cawson, F. H., *The Education of the Adult* (London, 1951).

Champness, E., *Adult Schools: a Study in Pioneering* (Wallington, 1941).

Cherrington, P., 'Management Education in Britain' in *Adult Education*, Vol. XXXIII, No. 1, May 1965, pp. 21–6.

Clegg, H. A., and Adams, R., *Trade Union Education* (London, 1959).

Cleugh, M. F., *Educating Older People* (London, 1962).

Cotgrove, S. F., *Technical Education and Social Change* (London, 1958).

Council for Cultural Co-operation, *Workers in Adult Education: their status, recruitment and professional training* (Strasbourg, 1966).

Crowther Report—Ministry of Education—15 to 18 (2 vols., 1959–60).

Dannenmair, W. D., 'A Brief Review of Published Research in Adult Education' in *Objectives and Methods of Research in Adult Education.*

Dent, H. C., *Part-time Education in Great Britain: an Historical Outline* (London, 1949).

Derbyshire Education Committee, *Social Education: Report of a Study Group to consider relationships between the Youth Service and other forms of Further Education* (Derby, 1967).

Draper, W. H., *University Extension: a survey of fifty years, 1873–1923* (Cambridge, 1923).

Dudley, R. D., *A Survey of New Developments, 1945–55* (Birmingham, 1956).

Educational Centres Association, *Annual Reports.*

—— *The Centre Idea* (London, 1967).

Edwards, H. J., *The Evening Institute* (London, 1961).

Elsdon, K. T., *Centres for Adult Education* (London, 1963).

Floud, J. E., Halsey, A. H., and Martin, F. M., *Social Class and Educational Opportunity* (London, 1956).

Gould, J. D., *The Recruitment of Adult Students* (Leicester, 1959).

Green, E., *Adult Education: Why this Apathy?* (London, 1953).

Greenwood, A., *The Education of the Citizen* (London, 1920).

Groombridge, B. (ed.), *Liberal Education in a Technical Age* (London, 1955).

—— 'New Objectives for Adult Education' in *Adult Education*, vol. XXX, 1957–58, pp. 197–215.

—— *Education and Retirement* (London, 1960).

—— *Report on the Co-operative Auxiliaries* (Manchester, 1960).

—— *The Future of the Auxiliaries: A Postscript* (Loughborough, 1962).

—— *Adult Education and Television* (London, 1966).

Hanna, I., 'Adult Education Students' in *Rewley House Papers*, 1965–66, p. 14–43.

Harris, W. J., 'Education by Post' in *Adult Education*, Vol. XXXIX, No. 5, pp. 269–73, p. 277.

Harrison, J. F. C., *A History of the Working Men's College 1854–1954* (London, 1954).

Heaven, S., 'Intra-Mural Education' in *Adult Education*, vol. XXV, No. 3, Sept. 1962, pp. 115–19.

Hely, A. S., *Impressions of Adult Education Trends in Great Britain* (unpubd., 1953).

Heron, A., *Preparation for Retirement: Solving New Problems* (London, 1961).

Hodgen, M. T., *Workers' Education in England and the United States* (London, 1925).

Hoggart, R., *The Uses of Literacy* (London, 1957).

Hope, R., *Spare Time at Sea* (London, 1954).

Horrabin, J. F., and W., *Working-Class Education* (London, 1924).

Hudson, J. W., *The History of Adult Education* (London, 1851).

Hunter, G., *Residential Colleges; some new developments in British Adult Education* (N.Y., 1952).

Hutchinson, E. (ed.), 'Accommodation and Staffing for Adult Education' in *Adult Education*, Vol. XXXV, No. 5, January 1963, pp. 229–312.

—— 'Recruitment and Training' in *ibid.*, March 1966, pp. 319–90.

Jackson, B., *National Extension College 1967, Four Years' Work, and the Future* (Cambridge, 1967).

Jenkins, D. W. T., *Adult Education in Wales* (Cardiff, 1966).

Jenkins, I., *History of the Women's Institutes of England and Wales* (Oxford, 1953).

Jessup, F. W., 'The Changing Pattern of Adult Education' in *Rewley House Papers*, 1965–66, pp. 44–55.

Jolliffe, H., *Public Library Extension Activities* (London, 1962).

Kelly, T., *Outside the Walls: Sixty Years of University Extension at Manchester, 1886–1946* (Manchester, 1950).
—— *George Birkbeck, Pioneer of Adult Education* (Liverpool, 1957).
—— *Adult Education in Liverpool: a Narrative of Two Hundred Years* (Liverpool, 1960).
Kent Education Committee, *Adult Education in Kent* (Maidstone, 1955).
Klare, H., *Anatomy of Prisons* (London, 1960).
Legge, C. D., 'Facts and Figures in Further Education—the Place of the Responsible Bodies' in *Adult Education*, vol. XXVI, pp. 269–. 75, 1953–5.
—— 'Training Adult Educators in the United Kingdom' in *Convergences*, Vol. i, No. i, March 1968, pp. 55–9.
Levitt, J., 'Adult Education in Working Men's Clubs' in *Adult Education*, vol. XXVIII, 1955–56, pp. 260–72.
Maclean, R., *Television in Education* (London, 1968).
McMahon, Coates and Knox, 'The Position of Adult Education in the United States' in *Adult Leadership*, Vol. 15, No. 9, March 1967.
Malone, E. W. F., 'W.E.A., a New Phase' in *Adult Education*, vol. XXXIII, 1960–61, pp. 78–82, 116–21.
Mansbridge, A., *An Adventure in Working-Class Education: being the story of the Workers' Educational Association, 1907–15* (London, 1920).
Manvell, R., *Film* (London, 3rd edn., 1950).
Marks, H. E. S., *Community Associations and Adult Education* (London, 1949).
Marshall, R. L., *Co-operative Education* (Manchester, 1948).
Martin, G. C., *The Adult School Movement: its Origin and Development* (1924).
Maurice, J. F. D., *Learning and Working* (London and Cambridge, 1855).
Mayfield, G. E. T., 'The University of Hull Department of Adult Education' in *U.C.A.E. Report 1959–60*.
Millar, J. P. M., 'Forty Years of Independent Working-Class Education' in *Adult Education*, Vol. XXI, 1948–49, pp. 210–15.
Ministry of Education, *Annual Reports and Statistics*.
—— Pamphlet No. 28, *Evening Institutes* (London, 1956).
—— *Community Centres* (1946).
Morris, H., *The Village College: a Memorandum* (Cambridge, 1924).
Morris, Mary, *Voluntary Organisations and Social Progress* (London, 1955).
National Adult School Union (annually), *Adult School Year Book and Directory* (1901—current).

National Co-operative Education Association, *Annual Reports*.
National Council of Social Service, *Voluntary Social Services: Handbook and Directory* (London, 5th edn., 1960).
National Council of Y.M.C.A.s, *Annual Reports*.
National Federation of Women's Institutes, *Annual Reports*.
National Foundation for Adult Education, *Adult Education in the Development Plans of L.E.A.s* (1948).
National Institute of Adult Education, *Museums and Adult Education* (1956).
—— *Annual Directory* (1961–current).
—— *Social Aspects of Further Education: a Survey of Local Education Authority Action* (1952).
National Society, *The Church and Adult Education* (London, 1944).
National Union of Students, *Adult Education* (1966).
National Union of Townswomen's Guilds, *Annual Reports*.
Nettleton, J. A., and Moore, D. J., *School and Community: Adult Centres in Cumberland Schools*, (London, 1967).
Nuffield College, *Industry and Education* (1943).
Pahl, R. E., *Adult Education in a Free Society* (London, 1962).
Pashley, B. W., *University Extension Reconsidered* (Leicester, 1968).
Paterson, R. W. K., 'Values in Adult Education' in *Rewley House Papers*, Vol. IV, no. iii, 1964–65, pp. 36–52.
Peers, R. (ed.), *Adult Education in Practice* (London, 1934).
Perraton, H., 'Why Use Television' in *Adult Education*, Vol. XXXIX, No. 5, January 1967., pp. 267–8.
Peters, R. S., *Authority, Responsibility and Education* (London, 1919).
Pilkington Report—Postmaster General—Report of the Committee on Broadcasting, 1960 (London, 1962).
Poole, H. E., *Perspectives for Countrymen*, (1942).
Prime Minister, *A Policy for the Arts: the First Steps* (1965).
Prison Department, *Annual Reports*.
Pritchard, E. P., *University Extra-Mural Libraries* (London, 1961).
Raybould, S. G., 'Adult Education in Transition' in *Political Quarterly*, Vol. XXVIII, 1957, pp. 243–53.
—— *The English Universities and Adult Education* (London, 1951).
—— *University Extra-Mural Education in England, 1945–62: A Study in Finance and Policy* (London, 1964).
Rees, A. D., 'Adult Education in Wales' in *U.C.A.E. Report, 1956–57*.
Richards, D., *Offspring of the Vic: a History of Morley College* (London, 1958).
Robbins Committee, *Higher Education* (London, 1963).
Robinson, J. (ed.), *Educational Television and Radio in Britain: Present Provision and Future Possibilities* (1966).

Rouse, R. C., *An Introduction to the History of Adult Education* (London, 1933).

Rowntree, B. S., and Lavers, G. R., *English Life and Leisure* (London, 1951).

Rural Music Schools' Association, *Annual Reports*. From 1935.

Scupham, J., *Broadcasting and the Community* (London, 1967).

Seafarers' Education Service, *Annual Reports*.

Shearman, H. C., *Adult Education for Democracy* (London, 1944).

Smith, H. P., *Adult Education and Society Series* (Oxford, 1959–66).

Speak, L., Residential Adult Education in Great Britain (unpublished M.A. thesis, Leeds, 1949).

Standing Conference on Television Viewing, *Pilkington and After* (London, 1963).

Stead, H. G., *The Education of a Community* (London, 1942).

Stern, H. H., *Parent Education: an International Survey* (Hamburg, 1960).

Stocks, M. D., *The Workers' Educational Association: the first fifty years* (London, 1953).

Stone, W. G., *Local Authorities and Adult Education: report prepared for the Rome Congress, September 26–October 1, 1955* (The Hague, 1955).

Styler, W., *Who Were the Students?* (London, 1960).

—— and Waller, R. D., *Tutors and their Training* (London, 1954).

Tawney, R. H., 'An Experiment in Democratic Education' in *Political Quarterly*, May 1914, pp. 62–84.

Thornton, A. H., and Bayliss, F. J., *Adult Education and the Industrial Community* (London, 1965).

Trades Union Congress, *Annual Reports*. From 1873.

Trenaman, J., and McQuail, D., *Television and the Political Image: a Study of the Impact of Television on the 1959 General Election* (London, 1961).

Turner, H. A., 'The N.C.L.C., the W.E.A., and the Unions' in *Plebs*, Vol. XLIII, pp. 271–6 and Vol. XLIV, pp. 16–20, 1951, 1952.

Tylecote, M., *The Future of Adult Education* (London, 1960).

Universities Extra-Mural Consultative Committee, *Reports* 1924–1944–45.
Continued as
Universities Council for Adult Education, *Reports*, 1944–45–current.

—— *The Universities and Adult Education* (1961).

University of Oxford Delegacy for Extra-Mural Studies, *Workers' Education* (Oxford, 1965).

University of Wales Extension Board, *Survey of Adult Education in Wales* (Cardiff, 1940).

Venables, P. F. R., *Technical Education: its Aims, Organisation and Future Development* (London, 1955).

Waller, R. D., Wilson, A., and Ruddock, R., *After Work: Leisure and Learning in Two Towns* (London, 1959).

Waller, R. D., *Learning to Live* (London, 1946).

Wavell, Lord, *Minerva's Owl or Education in the Army* (London, 1948).

Wellens, J., *Education and Training in Industry* (Manchester, 1955).

White, A. C. T., *The Story of Army Education 1643–1963* (London, 1963).

Whitehead, A. N., *The Aims of Education* (3rd edn., London, 1950).

Williams, R., *Culture and Society 1780–1950* (London, 1958).

Williams, W. E., and Heath, A. E., *Learn and Live* (London, 1936).

Williams, W. E. (ed.) *Adult Education in Great Britain and the United States of America* (London, 1938).

——— *The Auxiliaries of Adult Education: a Brief Survey of those Movements which are contributing in the more Informal and Incidental Ways to the Education of Adults in England* (London, 1934).

Wiltshire, H. C., 'Towards Co-operation—RB and LEA' in *Adult Education*, Vol. XXXVI, No. 4, November, 1963, pp. 184–92.

Workers' Educational Association, *Aspects of Adult Education—A Report* (London, 1960).

——— *Trade Union Education* (London, 1953).

——— *Workers' Education in Great Britain* (2nd edn., 1945).

——— *Working Party on Structure, Organisation and Staffing* (1966).

——— *Action and Advance—the WEA on the March* (1968).

Working Men's Club and Institute Union, *Annual Reports* (from 1862).

Yeaxlee, B. A., *Lifelong Education* (London, 1929).

——— *An Educated Nation* (Oxford, 1920).

Yorkshire Council for Further Education, *Further Education and the Countryside* (Leeds, 1950).

Young Women's Christian Association of Great Britain, *Annual Reports*.

FOREIGN WORKS

Among foreign works the following were found particularly useful:

Blakeley, R. J., *Adult Education in a Free Society* (Toronto, 1958).

Brunner, E. de S. *et al.*, *An Overview of Adult Education Research* (Chicago, 1959).

Grattan, C. H., *In Quest of Knowledge: a Historical Perspective on Adult Education* (New York, 1955).

Hely, A. S. M., *New Trends in Adult Education: from Elsinore to Montreal* (Paris, 1962).

Houle, C. O., *The Inquiring Mind* (University of Wisconsin Press, 1961).

Jensen, G., Liveright, A. A., and Hallenbeck, W., *Adult Education:*

Outlines of an Emerging Field of University Study (Adult Education Association, U.S.A., 1964).

Johnstone, J. W. C., and Rivera, R. J., *Volunteers for Learning* (Chicago, 1965).

Kidd, R. J., *How Adults Learn* (New York, 1960).

Knowles, M. S. (ed.), *Handbook of Adult Education in the United States* (Adult Education Association, U.S.A., 1960).

—— *Informal Adult Education* (New York, 1950).

Lindemann, E. C., *The Meaning of Adult Education* (Montreal, 1961).

Liveright, A. A., and Haygood, N. (eds.), *The Exeter Papers* (Boston, 1968).

Mead, Margaret, 'Thinking Ahead—Why is Education Obsolete' in *Harvard Business Review*, November 1938, Vol. 36, No. 6.

Thorndike, E. L., *et al.*, *Adult Learning* (London, 1918).

UNESCO, *Report on International Seminar on the Role of Museums Education* (Paris, 1954).

U.S. Dept. of Health, Education and Welfare, *Participation in Adult Education* (Washington, 1959).

Verner, C., and Booth, A., *Adult Education* (Washington, 1964).

Wechsler, D., *The Measurement and Appraisal of Adult Intelligence* (4th edn., Baltimore, 1958).

INDEX